ZAINABU'S
African
Cookbook
with Food Stories

Zainabu Kpaka Kallon

CITADEL PRESS
Ke...
ww...

I dedicate this book to my children Abass Bona and Tarfoi Sayea; to
Saata Mawoni, Masah Tawai, and Tarfoi Sayea Kpaka; to the rest of
my family, and to the daughters of Africa everywhere.

CITADEL PRESS BOOKS are published by

Kensington Publishing Corp.
850 Third Avenue
New York, NY 10022

Copyright © 2004 Zainabu Kpaka Kallon

All Kensington titles, imprints, and distributed lines are available at special quantity discounts for bulk purchases for sales promotions, premiums, fund-raising,
educational, or institutional use. Special book excerpts or customized printings
can also be created to fit specific needs. For details, write or phone the office of the
Kensington special sales manager: Kensington Publishing Corp., 850 Third Avenue,
New York, NY 10022, attn: Special Sales Department; phone 1-800-221-2647.

CITADEL PRESS and the Citadel logo are Reg. U.S. Pat. & TM Off.

Designed by Leonard Telesca

First printing: January 2004

10 9 8 7 6 5 4 3 2

Printed in the United States of America

Library of Congress Control Number: 2003106187

ISBN 0-8065-2549-5

Contents

PART III: SNACKS, SWEETS, AND DRINKS

Introduction

I was privileged to invite a lawyer and his family to our home for an African dinner. He thanked me and asked, "What do Africans eat?" I replied, "You'll have to come and find out!"

I have talked with many Americans about Africa. The one question I have heard the most—second only to questions about African animals—is, "What foods do Africans eat?" An honest answer to that question is that the African people eat the same foods other human beings eat: foods high in carbohydrates such as rice, potatoes, and cassava; high-protein foods such as meat, fish, and chicken; fresh fruits such as mangoes, pineapples, and bananas; vegetables such as okra, spinach, and beans; nuts and oils such as palm oil, groundnut (peanut) oil, and sesame oil; dairy products; and herbs and spices. Africans have the same physiological needs others have.

The difference, however, lies in the art and method of cooking. Africans are so knowledgeable about food combinations and food preparation that they do not need to use recipes; they are natural cooks. One reason could be that the girls start taking cooking lessons from mothers and grandmothers at an early age. Another reason could be that culinary art ability is in the blood, so to speak; just like music and dancing, literature and storytelling, and sports are all part of the African heritage. In other words, Africans can't help but freely express themselves in these and many other areas.

How much do you know about African foods and African cooking? This book, *Zainabu's African Cookbook with Food Stories*, is an attempt to show ways our people put foods together to come up with great results every time. We hope that the book will answer most, if not all, of your food questions and that you will have a great time cooking the African way.

THE AFRICAN COOK AND HER STYLE

The African woman has always cooked by putting together a little of this and a little of that. Using her creative skills, experience, and what I call "an extra sense," she always measured only with her eyes and hands, and she knew just how much of an ingredient she needed to use in any given dish. (I say *she* because cooking was and still is traditionally done, for the most part, by the women.)

Traditional African meals consist of fewer meats, more whole grains and beans, and lots of fresh fruits and vegetables. In other words, the African diet is just what the doctor now orders for the American population and for people around the world. This book should help the cook who is only now learning this new, exciting, and healthy way of cooking and eating—the African way.

One can learn much about any group of people by examining their eating habits. A common saying is "We are what we eat." By looking at African foods and the ways of cooking them, one may even discover new and interesting things about a group of people whose home is the second largest continent in the world.

MEAL TIME

Meal time is very important in any African home. It is the one time during the day when everything stops, and all family members sit down and enjoy one another. They share food from a common bowl as they share their lives and events of the day. Each family member is made to feel important, loved, wanted, and needed.

THE NEED FOR AN AFRICAN COOKBOOK

There has always been a great need to write down family recipes, handed down by word of mouth and by observation for many generations. This is true in my own family and in many families across Africa. It is a privilege to write down recipes that great African women have used in their kitchens for years.

Some old African recipes have been updated. That is why the book suggests "salt to taste." Many recipes caution the cook to use herbs and spices "to taste" so that one is at liberty to use the amount of seasoning desired. There is nothing bland about most African cooking. One should only use as much of the herbs and spices as one desires, however. In the end, you and your family will eat what you cook.

THE AMERICAN AND OTHER COOKS

We want American cooks to have no difficulties getting the ingredients and to have fun following the recipes. This book is not meant to collect dust on the kitchen shelf. When a recipe calls for ingredients that are not readily available, local substitutes are used to enhance the dish in taste and appearance, and to make it more nutritious. What is the point of a recipe if the ingredients are not available?

Banana akarah is a good example. The recipe calls for African rice flour. Because it is not possible to get the flour in America, whole wheat flour and white flour are used in the recipe. The result is a better-tasting and better-looking *akarah*. Whole wheat flour is also more nutritious than rice flour, which is an added bonus. There are many such recipes in the book.

FOOD STORIES

This cookbook contains many food stories. This is to highlight names of dishes and to help you gain more insight into the African culture. It is also for the sheer joy of telling stories, a very old African tradition.

One memory of my grandmother has to do with listening to stories she told as we watched the moon and the bright stars at night. I can almost feel fresh ocean breezes from the Atlantic gently blowing across our small village, Liiyah, bringing the smell of fish, ripe breadfruit, and mangoes. Most of all, I can again hear Grandmother's happy, soft voice, telling us stories. There is no doubt in my mind that Liiyah Village was, for me, one of the most desirable places on earth. Today that village lies buried at the bottom of the Atlantic Ocean. The memories of Grandmother, the stories she told us, and our village lie buried forever in my heart. We want to continue the African tradition of storytelling and happy memory building.

WHERE ARE THE RECIPES FROM?

Often more than one country is home for the same recipe, except for the use of a different herb, spice, or oil. When such is the case, all countries are mentioned. In other words, several countries can be home for one and the same dish.

Acknowledgments

I want to thank Jim Harvey for all his work and support. Mr. and Mrs. Akpo-Esambe, Jeanne Bergad, Ann Perbohner, and Karen Thomas, my editor. I especially thank Jane Stevens Mbayo, Olive Weaver, Elaine M. Gasser, and Wavelene Babbitt, my teachers in English and Home Economics.

PART I

MEAT AND FISH

Beef

Some West African tribes believe that true happiness is raising family and cattle. This is the only life they sincerely enjoy living. "The African Midwife's Story" takes place in the northern region of Sierra Leone, West Africa. This is where the Fula, Limba, Madingo, Susu, and the Timne tribes live. Here they raise their families and here they raise cattle. The story shows how families and cattle are the common threads used to weave and hold together the way of life of these tribes as people.

The African Midwife's Story

Tator arrived the previous year to replace another midwife. It was difficult to come but even more difficult to leave. The high level of infant mortality and the significant death rate among child-bearing women plagued that part of Sierra Leone; she came to help.

She visited women as they bought and sold food at the open markets. She talked with them while they did the laundry at the riverside. She held the children and played with them. She even made simple sundresses for the very young babies. Tator visited each home in every village many times over. The result was always the same. The women listened politely when she talked with them, but they refused to have anything to do with her.

"Becoming a midwife is something a woman learns only by becoming a mother, over and over again," they repeated.

3

"She is very young and does not have children. She is not even married. So how can she help us deliver our babies?" they asked one another.

Again Tator talked to the village chiefs. She begged them to ask mothers and expectant mothers to come to the maternity and well-baby clinics. "Women bear our children; but who helps them to deliver the babies is their choice. Men only go along with what they are told about the matter" was the usual reply.

One day she again went to talk with one of the chiefs. This time he was more friendly than usual. "I feel that you want to help our women. I wish I could do something that will enable you to do so." He was quiet for what seemed a long time, then he spoke. "It is a man's job to acquire cattle. These animals are part of our way of life. When a baby is born, a cow is killed to celebrate. In the presence of God, family, and friends, the baby is given a name, making the child an important member of the community and the tribe. A calf is killed to mark the time of maturity in a young person's life. At the time of marriage," he went on, "the young man and his family would give to the family of the bride a cow, part of the dowry, making the marriage legal." He somberly reflected. "When a man dies, a bull is killed to remember the dead."

There was again a long silence. When he spoke, he looked directly at her.

"There is a valuable cow not too far from here. This animal went into labor two days ago, and she has still not yet delivered."

At this time someone announced the arrival of an important visitor. The chief stood up. Turning to her, Chief Almame Dura said good-bye and went to meet the visitor. Tator was almost angry as she left. "He did not finish what he started to say! Why did Chief Dura talk about cows instead of people? What was he trying to say?" The more she thought about the visit, the more questions she had.

That afternoon she learned that another young lady died earlier in the day. The woman was in labor for two days. This was the third time since her arrival that a young pregnant woman had died in the region; and she had been there not quite two months. Again the message came loud and clear. "For now, you need to stay and help."

Tator lay awake, wondering what to do next. She finally fell asleep. When she awoke, it was already dark. She looked outside. The people were returning home from the last prayer for the day. The only regular event at Kalaba was the Moslem prayer time. Nothing interrupted that, not even the tragic death of a young woman and her unborn baby. So the small clock on the table was correct. She had slept for four hours.

Tator made a cup of lemongrass tea. The aroma filled the little house. She stirred in some honey. The cup of tea was halfway to her lips when she set it down on the table with a frown, spilling some of the tea on the small table. She could not believe what went through her mind. Finally she took a sip, but she set the cup down again. "It is my turn to pray," she said aloud.

When Tator prayed, it was more like arguing with God than it was praying. "How can I help a cow deliver?" she angrily asked. "I am not a veterinarian. The first and only time I saw a cow deliver was when I was a little girl, not quite seven years old. And what is this that I have to help an animal deliver in order to earn this community's trust?" She drank some tea while her mind drifted.

When she stood up, her knees hurt; she had knelt in prayer for so long. She drank more tea, now very cold. It tasted sweet, almost as sweet as spending time with God. She ran through the door, saying, "Human or animal, babies travel the same route—the birth canal." She ran back to the house, got the delivering kit she had forgotten, and ran out again. While still running she heard herself say aloud, "Human or animal, babies travel the same route—the birth canal." She felt reassured hearing herself say those words. Moreover, the words sounded like she meant what she said, and that she knew what she was talking about.

When Tator arrived, the animal was alone, groaning with pain. She thought it strange that she was alone. With the aid of the bright moonlight she examined the cow. Gently rubbing her back, she said to the animal, "We must do this together, for your sake and mine. God, please help us!"

She became alive, energetic, and confident. She and the cow went to work. Two hours later Tator reached for a blanket to wrap the baby. Then she remembered that this was a different kind of baby; not the human kind that she was used to delivering. She tossed the blanket away and started to laugh. After laughing uncontrollably for several minutes, she realized that she was not alone. From among the tall elephant grass people were laughing just as hard.

Early the next morning Tator was quietly awakened by singing voices. A few minutes later a young man was banging at her door. "My wife is having a baby," he told her. "If you can help a cow deliver, I know you can help my wife deliver my baby." Together they ran toward the clinic.

Cattle is a status symbol among many African tribes. A large herd may represent much wealth. Meat-eating African tribes, such as those who live in the northern part of Sierra Leone, the Samburu tribe in East Africa, and many more, raise cattle for the meat, milk, wool, and their monetary value.

AFRICAN CONCEPT OF MEAT AND VEGETABLE DISHES

When Africans cook fresh vegetables, they add a small portion of meat, only enough to season the vegetables. It is interesting that medical doctors and nutritionists now tell us that we should use small portions of meat and other animal protein, the way Africans have always done. This way of using meat is a new concept, even foreign to the American way of thinking. The American public is used to thinking of meat as the main dish, usually served in large portions. As you know, it always takes time to make changes. It takes an even longer time to change eating habits. That is because people learn to eat from their parents very early. What we learn we use as reference material for life.

Zainabu's African Cookbook with Food Stories should be helpful. The dishes are what the doctor has ordered, namely, less meats and oils, more whole grains and beans, and lots of fresh fruits and vegetables. The women are used to gathering fresh vegetables from the garden just before they cook them. When fresh vegetables are cooked with wonderful herbs and spices, very little meat for seasoning is needed to help bring out the great natural taste.

Beef is used in the dishes in this section. We hope you enjoy cooking and eating them.

Njolabehteh (Sweet Potato Leaves) with Beef

This dish is from West African countries. The name may not be the same in each country.

Helpful Hints:

a. It is your choice to use an expensive or less expensive cut of beef. The women often use more than one kind of meat (beef or chicken) in one dish.
b. Wash potato leaves well. Drain and chop. Do not chop leaves of any kind before washing them.
c. Sweet potato leaves can be found in African or Asian food stores. If you cannot find them in your area, fresh chopped spinach or fresh or frozen chopped broccoli may be used as a substitute.
d. Serve with boiled rice.

½ pound beef (or amount desired), cut up
4 pieces of chicken
1 large onion, chopped

¼ pound white mushrooms cleaned and sliced
1 large tomato, chopped
3 tablespoons tomato paste

fresh palm oil or groundnut
(peanut) oil, amount desired
fresh ginger, finely chopped
and to taste
fresh hot pepper, chopped
and to taste
salt to taste

1½ pounds young, sweet
potato leaves or fresh broccoli
(washed, drained, and
chopped
½ pound fresh shrimp, shelled
and deveined
4 green onions, chopped

1. Put oil in a heated skillet and lightly brown meat and chicken. Add white onion and ginger and cook until onion is tender.

2. Stir in rest of ingredients except potato leaves, shrimp, and green onions. Stirring occasionally, cover and cook until meat is almost tender.

3. Increase heat to medium-high and stir in remaining ingredients. Continue to cook, for 8-10 minutes, stirring now and then until leaves are done, but still bright green. Avoid cooking greens longer than 10-12 minutes. Remove from heat and serve hot.

Did You Know?

Did you know that sweet potato leaves are among the most popular vegetables in West Africa? There are several varieties of this green, leafy vegetable. *Wehganya,* meaning "hardly any leftover," is the most popular as well as the tastiest. Another well-known variety is not popular for taste as much as it is for its medicinal value. The broad, dark, mildly bitter leaves are crushed and used in the treatment of chicken pox and mumps. When I got mumps *(kpokpo kplokplo),* Grandmother mixed it with white clay *(hojeh),* and she gently rubbed it on my jaws and around my ears. She applied the same mixture on the skin to treat chicken pox.

Hondii (Spinach) with Beef and Mushrooms

ᘒᘓ

This popular dish is prepared in most countries in Africa. There are different varieties of the vegetable, each delicious.

Helpful Hints:

a. Fresh spinach must be washed and drained before it is chopped. If it is frozen, thaw it before cooking.
b. Use any cut of beef desired. When a less expensive cut is used, cook it in water until tender before using it in the dish.
c. Serve with boiled rice.

½ pound of beef or amount desired, cut up
1 pound kpohwoh (portabella) mushrooms, chopped
3 tablespoons tomato paste
fresh palm oil or oil of choice, amount desired
fresh hot peppers, chopped and to taste

1 large onion, chopped
ground cumin to taste
fresh ginger, finely chopped and to taste
salt to taste
2 pounds hondii (fresh spinach), chopped

1. Add oil to heated skillet that is over medium heat. Stir in all ingredients except spinach. Cover and cook until meat is almost done and most of liquid is gone.
2. Add spinach and mix with a wooden spoon. Cook only until spinach is wilted and bright green (6–10 minutes). Remove from heat and serve.

Hondii (Spinach) with Beef, Curry, and Beans

This is a simple and delicious dish often made in East, South, and West Africa.

Helpful Hints:

a. It is important that the fresh spinach used is well drained. After washing, it may be wrapped in a clean dish towel and chopped just before cooking.
b. Unlike groundnut (peanut) oil, sesame oil does not take heat too well. Avoid high heat when cooking with it.
c. Serve with boiled rice.

2 pounds fresh spinach, chopped
sesame oil, amount desired
½ pound good cut of beef or
   amount desired, cut up
fresh hot peppers, chopped
   and to taste
curry powder to taste

1 bunch green onions, chopped
salt to taste
1 cup fresh or frozen broad (lima)
   beans (cook according to pack-
   age directions and drain)
¼ cup roasted and ground
   sesame seeds for garnishing

1. Add oil, meat, and peppers to skillet that is over medium heat. Cook until meat is almost done.

2. Add rest of ingredients except ground sesame and beans. With a wooden spoon, mix and cook until spinach is done. (It takes very little time to cook it.)

3. Add beans and heat through. Remove from heat and put in a serving dish. Garnish with ground sesame and serve.

Tohluga (Porcelain) Ginger Kenema Fry

The African people enjoy eating this delicious and nutritious green vegetable. Although it is not planted, it usually shows up, often in abundance, in soil that has been loosened or prepared to plant other crops. Porcelain can be bought in organic foodstores or grown along with vegetables in backyard gardens. Fresh spinach can also be used.

Helpful Hints:

a. Soak *tohluga* in cold water, then wash, drain, and chop.
b. Serve with boiled rice.

groundnut (peanut) oil, amount
   desired
½ pound cooked beef, cut up
2 pounds tohluga (porcelain),
   chopped
1 bunch green onions, chopped

grated fresh ginger to taste
fresh peppers, chopped and to
   taste
salt to taste
chopped roasted groundnuts
   (peanuts) for garnishing

1. Put oil in a heated skillet that is over medium heat. Add all ingredients except groundnuts.

2. Increase to high heat. Using two wooden spoons, mix and fry until vegetables are done. (It takes just a few minutes.)

3. Remove from heat and put in a serving dish, garnish with groundnuts (peanuts), and serve.

Variation:

Use curry powder to taste instead of ginger and rest of above ingredients.

Tohluga (Porcelain) Salad

sesame oil, amount desired
⅓ cup fresh lemon juice or to
* taste*
salt to taste
sugar to taste
1 pound tohluga (porcelain),
* washed, drained, and*
* chopped*
1 cup fresh spinach, chopped
⅓ cup roasted sesame seeds

cooked beef, chopped or sliced
5 green onions, chopped
2 large tomatoes, cut up
* in chunks*
fresh ginger, chopped and
* to taste*
1 sweet pepper, chopped
fresh hot peppers, chopped and
* to taste*

1. Mix well liquids, salt, and sugar.
2. Put rest of ingredients in a bowl, add liquid mixture, and toss.
3. Put in a serving dish and serve at room temperature.

Beef with Gbuhen and Mushrooms

This dish is prepared in most countries in West Africa using local names, herbs, and spices.

Helpful Hints:

a. *Gbuhen* looks like asparagus and has a slightly bitter taste. This vegetable grows wild in the African tropical rain forest. Because it is not readily available, asparagus is used in this dish.
b. An inexpensive cut of beef will be used in this dish, but a more expensive cut may also be used.
c. Serve with boiled rice.

fresh palm oil or groundnut (peanut) oil, amount desired
½ pound cubed stew beef, or amount desired
⅓ pound pearl onions
½ pound kpohwoh (portabella) mushrooms, cleaned and chopped
1 sweet bell pepper, chopped
2 large tomatoes, chopped
3 tablespoons tomato paste
fresh hot peppers, chopped and to taste

fresh ginger, chopped and to taste
salt to taste
2 pounds fresh asparagus, washed (break off tough ends, chop ⅓ inch in length)
3 green onions, chopped
*1 cup **poponda** (fresh basil), chopped*
chopped parsley for garnishing

1. Add oil to skillet that is over medium heat and lightly brown meat. Stir in pearl onions and cook until onions are tender.

2. Add rest of ingredients except asparagus, green onions, *poponda* (fresh basil), and parsley. Cover and cook until meat is about three-quarters done, stirring occasionally and adding more water as needed.

3. Stir in asparagus, cover and cook until tender. Add green onions and *poponda,* and cook a few more minutes. Put in a serving dish, garnish with parsley, and serve.

Beef with Butternut Squash

This dish is prepared in Central, East, and West African countries. Chicken or fish may also be used if so desired.

Helpful Hint:

Serve with boiled rice.

1 medium butternut squash
½ pound boneless beef of choice
　or amount desired, cut up
1 white onion, chopped
2 cloves garlic, crushed
1 large tomato, chopped
3 tablespoons tomato paste
grated peel of 1 lime
fresh hot peppers, chopped
　and to taste

groundnut (peanut) oil or fresh
palm oil, amount desired
Spicy Groundnuts (Peanuts) for
　garnishing (recipe follows)
salt to taste
⅔ cup cooked green peas for
　garnishing (cook only until
　bright green)
3 green onions, chopped

1. Peel and wash squash. Cut it in half lengthwise. Remove seeds and fibers with a spoon. Cut each half into two equal portions lengthwise. Cut all four pieces into equal chunks or slices.

2. Lightly brown meat in oil. Stir in white onions and cook until onions are tender. Stir in rest of ingredients except butternut squash, green peas, and green onions.

3. Cover and cook, stirring occasionally; continue to cook until meat is almost tender. (Add some water if needed.)

4. Stir in squash and green onions, and mix. Without again mixing (so that squash is not mashed), cover and cook until squash is fork tender.

5. Arrange squash and meat at the center of a serving platter. Put cooked rice around squash. Garnish with green peas and spicy groundnuts (peanuts) in that order, and serve.

Spicy Groundnuts (Peanuts)

Spicy groundnuts (peanuts) are used for garnishing or served as *hamu hamu* (snack).

Helpful Hint:

Use as much groundnuts (peanuts) as you want. Make your meal as spicy as you would like it to be.

toasted groundnuts (peanuts), amount desired
grated fresh ginger to taste
powdered hot pepper to taste

groundnut (peanut) oil (just enough oil to coat nuts)
salt to taste
sugar to taste

1. Add all of the ingredients except sugar into a skillet that is over medium heat.
2. Using a wooden spoon, mix until nuts are heated and well coated with oil and spices. Stir in sugar and mix a few more minutes. Remove from heat, cool, and serve.

Variation:

Spicy Coconut: Remove coconut from shell; see "How to Break and Remove Coconut from Shell" (p. 238). Peel away the dark outer skin and cut coconut into thin strips. Cook like spicy groundnuts (peanuts). Watch closely because coconut burns easily.

Note: You may use other kinds of nuts instead of groundnuts (peanuts).

Beef with Kiwi and Curry

You probably know that Africans enjoy cooking meats with fruits, creating wonderful results. Kiwi-like fruits may grow wild in the

African rain forest. Try this and other meat and fruit dishes in this book. Discover how delicious they are.

Helpful Hints:

a. Make Spicy Groundnuts (Peanuts) in advance to serve with this dish.

b. Serve with cooked rice that is garnished with sliced fresh kiwi.

groundnut (peanut) oil, amount desired
1 medium white onion, thinly sliced
1 medium red sweet bell pepper, thinly sliced lengthwise
1 large tomato; seeds removed and chopped
3 white mushrooms, thinly sliced
2 cloves garlic, crushed
grated peel of 1 lime
3 green onions, chopped into ½-inch-length pieces
juice of same lime
grated fresh ginger to taste
5 kiwi fruits, each peeled and sliced across
salt to taste
1 pound good cut of meat, thinly sliced
curry powder to taste
fresh hot pepper, chopped and to taste
sliced fresh kiwi for garnishing
Spicy Groundnuts (Peanuts) (p. 14)

1. Add to heated skillet: 2 tablespoons of oil, white onions, sweet peppers, tomatoes, and mushrooms; also add about a half portion each of garlic, lime peel, green onions, lime juice, and ginger. Mix and cook for about 5 minutes.

2. Add kiwi and salt. With 2 wooden spoons gently toss and cook only until mixture is heated through (1–2 minutes). Remove from skillet, arrange all on a serving platter, and keep warm.

3. To same skillet add some oil and stir in rest of ingredients except kiwi and Spicy Groundnuts (Peanuts). Increase heat to medium high and cook, mixing often, until meat is done as you like it. Then season with salt to taste.

4. Remove skillet from heat and arrange meat over kiwi. Garnish with sliced fresh kiwi and Spicy Groundnuts (Peanuts), and serve with rice.

Mango Ehbeh

Any *ehbeh* dish has two main characteristics: It is a meal in itself, and there is always plenty for all. *Ehbeh* usually consists of vegetables and fruits cooked in meat, chicken, or fish sauce. During my growing years, mango *ehbeh* was my favorite. I enjoyed licking the sweet sauce from the mango seed until it was clean. I then washed and dried the seed. I would comb the long, hairlike fibers. From it I learned to braid.

This dish is prepared in many countries in Africa using local names, fruits, and vegetables.

Helpful Hints:

a. For the corn to be creamy, it must be cooked before it is crushed.
b. You are encouraged to use local fruits, vegetables, herbs, and spices to make this dish your very own. Cook the quantity you want.
c. Cut *kpogii* (taro), cassava, and white and sweet potatoes into chunks of equal thickness so they all cook at the same rate.

½ pound beef or amount desired, cut up
1 large white onion, chopped
salt to taste
fresh ginger, finely chopped and to taste
6 cups water or meat broth
2 cups whole kernel corn, cooked; 1 cup crushed (may also use canned creamed corn)
⅓ cup groundnut (peanut) butter (optional)
1 white potato, peeled and cut into equal-sized chunks
1 sweet potato, peeled and cut into chunks of the same size

1 medium kpogii (taro), peeled and cut into chunks of the same size
1 green banana, peeled and cut into ½-inch slices
1 medium ripe plantain, peeled and cut into ½-inch slices
4 chunks of breadfruit (optional)
1 sweet pepper, chopped
2 large tomatoes, chopped
fresh hot peppers, chopped and to taste
green and ripe mangoes, as many as possible, peeled

1. Put meat, onion, salt, ginger, and about 6 cups water or meat broth in a large saucepan. Cook on medium heat, stirring occasionally. Continue to cook until meat is almost done.

2. Stir in rest of ingredients except ripe mangoes. Cover and cook until *kpogii* (taro) is almost done.

3. With a wooden spoon gently stir in ripe mangoes and more liquid as needed. Cook on medium high until *kpogii* (taro) is done. Remove from heat and serve to your family and friends; there is enough for all.

Ground Beef with Okra and Spinach

This dish is prepared in many African countries.

Helpful Hints:

a. The longer you cook okra, the less slimy and less bright green it becomes.
b. Serve with boiled rice.

groundnut (peanut) oil or fresh palm oil, amount desired or about ¼ cup
½ pound lean ground meat or amount desired
1 large white onion, chopped
2 cups sliced fresh mushrooms
fresh ginger, chopped and to taste
1 pound fresh okra, washed (remove ends and cut into ⅓-inch slices)
1 large tomato, chopped

3 tablespoons tomato paste
2 cloves garlic, crushed
fresh hot pepper, chopped and to taste
salt to taste
2 cups fresh or frozen lima beans (cook according to package directions and drain)
1 pound fresh spinach, washed, drained, and chopped
3 green onions, chopped

1. Add oil, meat, white onions, mushrooms, and ginger to a preheated skillet over medium heat. Mix and cook until onions are tender.

2. Stir in rest of ingredients except beans, spinach, and green onions. Stirring often, cover and cook for about 9 minutes or until okra is almost done.

3. Add rest of ingredients and mix. Cook only until spinach is wilted or done the way you like it. Serve with boiled rice.

THE HISTORY OF COOKING MEAT BELOW THE GROUND

History tells us that Africans have cooked meat this way for as long as they have hunted animals for food. After killing an animal and preparing it for cooking, Africans dug a shallow hole in the ground that was large enough to hold the meat and edible roots they gathered. Then they generously lined the hole with large banana leaves. They placed the meat in the hole and laid more leaves in place before covering it with soil.

After the food was covered with soil, a large fire was built above ground, over the meat. The high heat cooked the meat below. It is understandable that the cooking started as early as possible, and the fire was kept burning for most of the day. Nothing was hurried. At the end of a hard day's work, they had a feast fit for a king. The meat always turned out tender, juicy, and delicious. No wonder some African tribes still employ this method of cooking and believe it is worth all the waiting.

Chicken

The Adventures of Brightfeathers and Softfeathers

One pleasant morning, Brightfeathers mistakenly took a wrong turn. He flew out of the only home he had known all his life, a rich farm in the Becongoh Valley. When he realized what had happened, he said, "This is my day for adventure, and I must take advantage of it. I am going to see what the world is like on the other side of this beautiful valley."

As luck would have it, he immediately saw another chicken feeding nearby. Unlike Brightfeathers, the other chicken was dressed in soft, dark feathers, which made him blend in well with his surroundings.

"I am Brightfeathers; so glad to meet you. It is very different out here! What's your name?"

Coming closer, Softfeathers said, "I agree your name is most fitting." Looking around, Softfeathers then continued, "Where on earth are you from? Don't you know that no one wears bright colors in these parts of the forest? It is a sure way of inviting trouble. Here we do not look for trouble! Heaven knows it always comes looking for us." Moving even closer he whispered, "My name is Softfeathers. If you intend to live around here, I suggest that you do something about your attire fast—or I will not be seen within ten miles of you."

Happy for the possibility of getting a new friend, Brightfeathers said, "For you, my first friend, I'll do whatever you say."

Again looking around, Softfeathers said, "That's a wise thing to do, because your life just might depend on it."

Brightfeathers told Softfeathers about life in the village. He talked about Mr. Koniwa, the farmer, and what a good provider he was. He also talked about the beautiful farm, with a nice home, and more food than any chicken could possibly eat. At some point Softfeathers had just about all he wanted to hear. Again he turned around. As he was about to talk, Brightfeathers interrupted. "Do you have to look around all the time?"

Softfeathers' reply was firm but kind. "I do not want to hurt your feelings, my friend. But are you out of your mind? Why will you, or anyone for that matter, walk away from all you say you have? Why have you come to a lawless place like this? The only law we know is 'Catch before you are caught.'" Softfeathers added, "Now to answer your question, I look around all the time because I don't want to become someone's next meal. You better start doing the same soon, if you want to stay alive."

Spreading his wings and standing on one foot, Softfeathers said, "I was just thinking. You are the only chicken I have ever met from the valley. To be honest, I would not have left if I had a home like yours. Why did you come?"

Looking around for the first time, and pleased that he remembered to do so, Brightfeathers replied, "Leaving the farm was by accident. I made a wrong turn and found myself on this side of the farm. Then I decided to come and see what this other side of the valley is all about."

As he looked around Softfeathers said, "I was right! You know, the first time I saw you, I had a feeling that underneath those bright feathers was a wise chicken. One has to be intelligent and caring to want to know what life is like on the other side of anything. Knowing how others live can help bring better understanding. What a great world it would be if we were not chasing or being chased all the time. I would rather make friends with those I meet than hurt them or run away."

Brightfeathers agreed. "I have heard Farmer Tokowa say more than once, 'The world would be a much nicer place for all, if everyone was a little kinder and less intimidating.' He was talking about people, of course."

Again Softfeathers looked around and said, "I am glad that you agree with me. That is why I am going to ask you for a favor."

Surprised, Brightfeathers asked, "What kind of a favor?"

Clearing his throat, Softfeathers said, "I have always wanted to see the other side of the valley; I mean, to see how the rich live. How do you feel about you and me exchanging identities? You stay here and become me, feathers and all. I will pretend to be you and will live in your home for a few days. I promise it will be an experience we will never forget. What do you say?"

Soon arrangements were made. Each taught the other how to live in his new home. After asking and answering many questions, it was time for each to go his separate way. The new Softfeathers looked in all directions and disappeared into the woods ahead. A fox looking for a much-needed meal showed up even before he settled in his new home.

"Are you sick? You are slow tonight! Better watch it, or you'll be history!" A friend of Softfeathers called out to the New Softfeathers as he flew by to get away from the old fox. New Softfeathers was a little scared but glad that others thought him to be their old friend.

New Brightfeathers, on the other hand, made a few wrong turns but soon found himself on the rich side of the fence, on the Tokowa Farm. The land was rich, beautiful, and so different from what he called home, he could not believe his eyes. He hardly got to his new home when it was feeding time. He ate so fast and so much, he almost became sick. "You must be very hungry today. Did you eat at noon?" Whitefeathers, another chicken, asked in amazement, as she watched Brightfeathers almost choking on his food. He said very little, too busy eating this grain or that feed, all delicious and new to him. After eating much all day, he was tired and more than ready to retire that evening.

The New Brightfeathers joined a group of no more than

four dozen chickens as they settled in a small house for the night. A little boy said, "Uncle Salia has arrived. Let's hurry and shut the doors!" He and his friend ran out and slammed the door behind them. The New Brightfeathers went to sleep, thinking that was the last he would see or hear from the two boys that night. He could not have been more wrong.

The New Brightfeathers was fast asleep, having the dream of his life. The next thing he knew, two strong hands pulled him away from the wall. The young man picked him up with both hands and felt his legs and thighs twice. He held him under the wings and moved him up and down several times, as if trying to determine his weight. The New Brightfeathers became very dizzy because of the movement; then he started feeling sick.

Finally the young man said to his friend, "Too bad! This chicken is large, but it has skinny legs and thighs. Mother wants one with plump legs and thighs. She says the meat is more tender and tastier."

The New Brightfeathers' heart stopped for a moment. The boy finally let him down, and he soon walked away with a chicken a few feet away. At that moment, the New Brightfeathers could not have been happier for spending so much time running in the forest. The lifelong exercise had made his legs and thighs lean, strong, and tough. He never saw that poor chicken brought back.

Far into the night the New Brightfeathers heard much merriment. It must have been quite a celebration. He did not sleep the rest of the night. How could anyone sleep after such a near-death experience? It was dangerous like the forest; but there he could run or fly away. Here he was locked in a room and had no way out. There was absolutely nothing he could do to escape.

In the morning he could not wait to leave. When no one was looking, the New Brightfeathers took off and did not even wait for breakfast. He wanted to be out of sight and out of mind for good. By now he was more familiar with the lay of the land. Running across the border, he did not stop until he saw the real Brightfeathers.

"Am I glad to see you!" he called out, running into his friend's embrace.

"How did it go?" Brightfeathers asked.

After they came face to face, they did not say much. Yet they said all they needed to say as they looked at each other. Each chicken, now a bit wiser than before, returned the other's feathers. When they put them on, they never felt better. Brightfeathers was more than glad to be in his own outerwear and was ready to go back to his own home. He and Softfeathers soon said good-bye and went their separate ways.

When Brightfeathers saw his old friends again, it all came back to him. Through the experience he had learned some lessons about life that he will never forget. He discovered that things are not always what they seem to be. Although the farm was rich and beautiful, it had its unique problems, like any other place. He also learned to enjoy what he had, especially family and friends, because they really count. He'd known that before, but now he truly believed it. Everyone learned a lesson; to appreciate who we are, what we have.

Chicken is very popular in Africa and around the world. It is good and delicious hot or cold; it is reasonable in price, yet highly nutritious; it is high in protein, low in cholesterol, and low in fat. (When it is cooked skinless. The skin may hold as much as 80 percent of its fat.)

Chicken is easy to cook, and there are almost countless ways to prepare it. Serve it often to family and friends. They will enjoy it every time.

Chicken in Groundnut Poponda Sauce

This is a popular dish among natives and non-natives alike. It is prepared in most countries in Africa, and each country may use local herbs and spices.

Helpful Hints:

There are many kinds of basil in many parts of Africa. Now, one can buy African basil in special African or Asian food stores.

a. *Poponda* is an African herb. The only thing close to its incredible aroma is fresh basil, which will be used in this dish.
b. Remember that groundnut (peanut) butter also has some oil; use as little oil as possible when you sauté chicken.
c. The dish is at its best when it is freshly made.
d. Use less peanut butter for thinner sauce and more for thicker sauce.
e. The dish is served with boiled rice, cooked green bananas, boiled plantain, or cassava. I have also served it with plain noodles and spaghetti.

2–3 pound broiler or frying chicken, cut up	⅓ to ½ cup groundnut (peanut) butter (mixed with 2 cups water)
salt to taste	
groundnut (peanut) oil, amount desired	fresh hot peppers, chopped and to taste
1 large white onion, chopped	1 large sweet bell pepper, chopped
grated fresh ginger to taste	
2 large tomatoes, chopped	4 green onions, chopped
3 tablespoons tomato paste	fresh poponda (basil), chopped and to taste
2 cloves garlic, crushed	
4 white mushrooms, sliced	roasted peanuts for garnishing (optional)
	chopped parsley for garnishing

1. Remove excess fat and skin from chicken as desired. Wash chicken and cut into small portions. Season with salt.

2. Add ⅓ cup oil to skillet that is over medium heat, sauté chicken until light brown.

3. Stir in white onions and ginger; cook until onions are tender. Add all of the ingredients except green onions, roasted nuts, *poponda* (basil), sweet peppers, and parsley.

4. Mix, cover, and cook over medium heat. Stirring occasionally, cook until chicken is almost done, about 45 minutes. Stir in peppers and continue to cook until chicken is done.

5. Gently stir in green onions and basil, and cook a few more minutes.

6. Remove from heat and put in a serving dish. Garnish with roasted peanuts and parsley in that order. Serve hot with boiled rice.

Calorie Reducing Tip: To add fewer calories, do not brown chicken and onions.

Semabu Lane Kobo Kobo Curry Chicken

This great dish is prepared in East, West, and South African countries. Serve it with pride to your special people.

Helpful Hints:

a. To keep it from turning dark, peel and cut up *kobo kobo* (eggplant) just before cooking it.
b. Serve dish with boiled rice.
c. Make Spicy Coconut (p. 14) in advance to serve with dish.

3-pound broiler or frying chicken, cut up
salt to taste
¼ cup groundnut (peanut) oil, or amount desired
1 large onion, chopped

2 whole cloves
2 large tomatoes, chopped
3 tablespoons tomato paste
1 large sweet bell pepper, chopped
curry powder to taste

2 cups coconut milk; use store bought or see How to Make Coconut Milk (p. 239)
fresh ginger, chopped and to taste
fresh hot peppers, chopped and to taste
1 medium kobo kobo (eggplant) peeled and cut into chunks
4 green onions, chopped
chopped fresh parsley for garnishing
Spicy Coconuts (p. 14)

1. Remove excess fat and skin from chicken as desired. Wash chicken, cut chicken into small portions; do not remove bones. Add salt, and mix.
2. Add oil to heated skillet and lightly brown chicken. Remove excess oil or add more oil (1 tablespoon) to skillet as desired. Coconut has its own oil. Add white onion and cook until onion is tender.
3. Stir in rest of ingredients except green onions, *kobo kobo* (eggplant), parsley, and spicy coconuts.
4. With cover in place, bring to a boil over medium heat. (Take care that pot does not boil over.)
5. Gently mixing occasionally, cook until chicken is almost done. Stir in *kobo kobo* and green onions. Cook only until *kobo kobo* is done and sauce is reduced to desired amount. Put in a serving dish, garnish with parsley, and serve with spicy coconuts.

Cabbage Mango Chicken

This special dish is prepared in many countries in Africa. It is low in cholesterol and calories, and it tastes great.

Helpful Hints:

a. Use both green and ripe mangoes; the green mango adds a sour taste to the dish while the ripe one gives it the sweet flavor that makes the dish so special.
b. This dish is usually served with cooked green bananas, plantains, or boiled rice.

2½-pound broiler or frying
  chicken, cut up
salt to taste
1 small green cabbage,
  shredded
⅓ pound pearl onions
2 large tomatoes, cut into
  chunks
1 sweet bell pepper, chopped
1 cup shredded fresh coconut
2 cups coconut milk; use store
  bought or see How to Make
  Coconut Milk (p. 239)

fresh ginger, chopped and to taste
grated peel of 1 lime
fresh hot peppers, chopped and
  to taste
2 large mangoes, 1 ripe and firm,
  1 green (peel each mango, cut
  meat in chunks, and discard
  seeds)
3 green onions, chopped
1 cup chopped cooked carrots for
  garnishing

1. Remove excess chicken fat and skin if desired, wash, and put chicken and salt in a heavy cooking pot and mix well.

2. Add rest of ingredients except mangoes, carrots, and green onions. Stirring occasionally, cook on medium heat until chicken is almost done.

3. Gently stir in mangoes and green onions, and cook until chicken is done. Put in a serving dish, garnish with carrots, and serve while it is hot.

Odofoh Chicken

This dish is prepared in East, South, and West African countries, using local names. It is luscious and fun to make.

Helpful Hints:

a. Even though the recipe calls for tropical fruits, use local ones to make this dish your own. Fruits must be firm and not overripe.
b. To get the desired flavor, sesame seeds must be roasted before they are ground. (Unroasted seeds have an undesirable, bitter taste.)
c. Serve dish with African Rice Balls (p. 152).

2 pounds boneless chicken breast
   or amount desired
¼ cup roasted sesame seeds
salt to taste
grated fresh ginger to taste
sesame oil to taste (use little;
   sesame paste also has some oil)
1 red and 1 green sweet bell
   pepper (cut into 1-inch by
   1-inch portions)
4 white mushrooms, sliced
grated peel of 1 lime
1 large tomato, seeds removed
   and chopped

2 tablespoons tomato paste
1 cup or more orange juice
2 chunks each of the following
   fruits: ripe, firm banana;
   green mango; ripe mango;
   pineapple; and kiwi
½ cup roasted sesame seeds,
   crushed into paste
4 green onions, chopped into
   ½-inch portions
fresh hot peppers, chopped and
   to taste
honey to taste (1-2 tablespoons)
chopped parsley for garnishing

1. Cut chicken into bite-size pieces. In a bowl, combine chicken, unground sesame seeds, salt, and ginger.

2. Add oil and chicken to a heated skillet that is over medium heat. Stir and cook until chicken is just done. Remove from skillet and return to the bowl. Set aside.

3. Add a little more oil to same skillet if so desired. Stir in sweet and hot peppers, mushrooms, lime peel, chopped tomatoes, and tomato paste. Mix and cook only until sweet peppers are done without overcooking them.

4. Return chicken to skillet, mix and cook only until chicken is heated through.

5. On a serving platter arrange chicken, peppers, etc., but keep as much sauce in skillet as possible. Add orange juice and fruit chunks except kiwi to skillet. Cook only until fruits are just done. Remove from heat and arrange fruit chunks over and around chicken. Also garnish chicken arrangement with kiwi. The fruits are ripe but firm-ready to be eaten. They only need to be heated thoroughly.

6. Return skillet to heat and stir in sesame paste, some orange juice and green onions. If sauce is too thick or more sauce is needed, stir in some orange juice and boil 1 or 2 minutes.

7. Remove from heat and spoon sauce over chicken and fruit. Garnish with parsley and serve.

Note: This dish is dedicated to the fond memory of Betty Odofoh Dakiyai.

Kpakayehma Ohleleh Shrimp Chicken

This is a special West African bean sauce that keeps chicken and meats very moist and tasty.

Helpful Hint:

This dish is served with boiled rice.

1 medium chicken
salt to taste
peanut oil or oil of choice,
  amount desired
⅓ cup or more ohleleh beans;
  see How to Make Ohleleh
  Beans (p. 30)
2 cups or more coconut milk; use
  store bought coconut milk or
  see How to Make Coconut
  Milk (p. 239)
2 large tomatoes, chopped
3 tablespoons tomato paste

1 large onion, chopped
ground cumin to taste (optional)
2 cloves garlic, crushed
fresh hot peppers, chopped and
  to taste
½ pound fresh shrimp, cleaned,
  deveined, and chopped
4 green onions, chopped
½ cup cooked red beans for
  garnishing
chopped fresh parsley for
  garnishing

1. Remove excess chicken fat and skin as desired. Wash, cut up, add salt, and mix well.

2. Add oil to heated skillet, lightly brown chicken, drain, and set it aside.

3. Add more oil to skillet or remove some as desired.

4. Using a wooden spoon, mix and cook *ohleleh* beans in oil until beans separate.

5. Stir in coconut milk and bring to a boil. If sauce is too thick, stir in more coconut milk or water and bring it to desired consistency.

6. Add chicken to bean mixture, and rest of ingredients except green onions, shrimp, red beans, and parsley.

7. Cover and cook on reduced heat, stirring occasionally, until chicken is done. Stir in shrimp and green onions, and cook a few more minutes.

8. Remove from heat and put chicken and sauce in a serving dish. Garnish with beans and parsley in that order and serve hot.

How to Make Ohleleh Beans

Helpful Hint:

Although other beans may be used, black-eyed peas are most often used.

> **1 cup black-eyed peas or amount   cold water**
>   **desired**

1. Wash peas and remove dirt and sand. Put peas in a bowl, cover with cold water, and soak for about 5 hours.
2. Take a handful of peas and rub between both hands. Repeat until skin is removed. When all peas are done, add more cold water.
3. The skins will float and the peas will fall to the bottom of the bowl. Remove and discard skins.
4. Drain peas and puree in a blender or in a food processor with as little water as needed. (In Africa the peas are ground between two stones or in a mortar with a pestle.) Use ¼ cup of water at a time and blend each time. If more water is needed, peas will not blend. Repeat until peas are pureed to the consistency of fine cottage cheese.
5. The crushed peas are called *ohleleh* beans because the beans are used to make a dish called *ohleleh* in Sierra Leone, *moi moi* in Nigeria, etc. The same crushed beans are used to make a special sauce in which one cooks chicken, fish, or other meats. Other beans, fresh or dry, can also be made into *ohleleh* beans and used in many other dishes. The skin must be removed before beans are crushed.

Kobo Kobo Lamb Chicken

The name is one of many used to refer to gardeneggs or eggplant, and there are several varieties. The male *kobo kobo* is more desirable for cooking because the seeds are fewer and less developed. The female fruit usually holds many more hard and matured seeds. They are both low in calories, and many Africans enjoy eating this creamy and delicious vegetable. Press first with tips of fingers. Female fruit feels hard while male fruit feels less hard because of less seeds.

Helpful Hints:

a. If possible, use young and male fruit in dish.
b. To keep eggplant from turning dark, peel and cut it up just before cooking.
c. Serve dish with boiled rice.

2½–3 pound broiler or frying chicken, cut up
salt to taste
¼ cup fresh palm oil or groundnut (peanut) oil, amount desired
½ pound boneless lamb, cut up
1 large white onion, chopped
2 large fresh tomatoes, chopped
5 white mushrooms, sliced
1 medium kobo kobo (eggplant) peeled and cubed
3 tablespoons tomato paste

1 cup cooked fresh lima beans (cook according to package directions and drain)
fresh ginger, finely chopped and to taste
2 cloves garlic, crushed
fresh hot peppers, chopped and to taste
⅓ pound fresh spinach, washed, drained, and chopped
4 green onions, chopped

1. Remove excess chicken fat and skin if desired. Wash, and season with salt. Lightly brown chicken in oil, then remove from skillet, drain, and set aside.

2. In same skillet lightly brown lamb, drain, and set it aside. Adjust oil (¼–⅓ cup or desired amount). Stir in white onion and cook on medium heat until onion becomes transparent.

3. Add lamb, chicken, tomatoes, and mushrooms, and mix. Stirring occasionally, cover and cook until chicken and lamb are almost done.

4. Stir in rest of ingredients except spinach and green onions. Without again mixing it, cook only until *kobo kobo* is done. Gently stir in spinach and green onions. Cook 8 minutes and serve hot.

Jongor's Nonoh-Coconatii Curry Chicken

Nonoh is one kind of African-made yogurt. There is nothing quite like chicken cooked in coconut milk, curry, and this kind of yogurt. It is so simple and delicious. Make this dish—you'll see how good it is.

Helpful Hints:

a. Use plain yogurt instead of *nonoh,* which is not readily available.
b. Serve dish with cooked rice, cassava, plantain, or bread of choice.

2-pound broiler or frying chicken, cut up
1 large white onion, chopped
salt to taste
fresh hot peppers, chopped and to taste
fresh ginger, finely chopped and to taste
2 cups coconut milk; use store bought or see How to Make Coconut Milk (p. 239)

½ cup shredded fresh coconut
curry powder to taste
1 sweet bell pepper, chopped
1 large tomato, seeds removed and chopped
1 cup nonoh (plain yogurt)
3 green onions, chopped
chopped mint leaves for garnishing

1. Remove excess chicken fat and skin as needed, wash chicken, and cut it up into desired portions.

2. Put chicken, white onion, salt, hot pepper, ginger, and coconut milk in a cooking pot. Mix, cover, and bring to a boil.

3. Stir in rest of ingredients except yogurt, green onions, and chopped mint leaves. Cook, stirring occasionally, until chicken is done.

4. Remove chicken from sauce, arrange it in a serving dish, and keep it warm.

5. If sauce is more than you want, boil it on medium high until sauce is reduced to about ⅔ its original volume. Then stir in yogurt and green onions, and bring it to a very gentle boil on low heat. Spoon sauce over chicken, garnish with chopped mint leaves, and serve hot.

Lasa Chicken

If you like tender, juicy chicken with wonderful aromatic herbs and spices, you'll enjoy lasa chicken. This great dish is made in many countries in Africa. Enjoy it.

Helpful Hints:

a. This chicken dish is just as good when cooked in the oven as it is when cooked on top of the stove. (In Africa it is most often cooked over three fire stones.)
b. Serve dish with boiled rice, boiled green bananas, or cooked ripe plantains.

3-pound broiler or frying chicken, cut up
salt to taste
1 large onion, chopped
fresh ginger, finely chopped and to taste
2 whole cloves
⅓ teaspoon ground cinnamon or to taste
freshly ground black pepper to taste
2 cloves garlic, crushed
grated peel of 1 lime
juice of same lime

fresh hot peppers, chopped and to taste
1 sweet bell pepper, chopped
3 large fresh tomatoes, chopped
1 kpohwoh (portabella) mushroom, chopped
3 white mushrooms, sliced
ground cumin to taste
honey to taste (optional)
4 green onions, chopped
⅔ cup chopped parsley
chopped fresh poponda (basil) for garnishing

1. Remove excess chicken fat and skin as desired. Wash chicken, cut it up, and season with salt.
2. Put in a cooking pot all ingredients except green onions, parsley, and fresh *poponda* (basil). With lid in place bring mixture to a boil over low heat.
3. Stirring occasionally, continue to cook until chicken is done. Gently stir in green onions and parsley, and remove from heat.
4. Put chicken in a serving dish, garnish with fresh chopped *poponda* (basil), and serve hot.

Sayama Chicken

෬෨

This dish is prepared in West and South African countries. It is colorful and elegantly delicious.

Helpful Hints:

a. Deboned chicken thighs will be used in this dish. Other parts of the chicken may be used as long as bones are removed.
b. Stuff each thigh loosely so that the beans and rice will have room to expand during the cooking process.
c. You may need to use gloves when stuffing because hot peppers can irritate the skin.
d. Put chicken bones in a pot, cover with water, and cook for about 15 minutes. Use broth to cook dish as needed.
e. Serve with boiled rice.

⅔ cup half-cooked rice
½ cup ohleleh beans; see How to
    Make Ohleleh Beans (p. 30)
½ pound ground chicken
fresh ginger, finely chopped
    and to taste
curry powder to taste
salt to taste
fresh hot peppers, chopped
    and to taste
2 cloves garlic, crushed
8 chicken thighs or number
    desired (debone and leave
    skin intact; wash and season
    with salt)

groundnut (peanut) oil or fresh
    palm oil, amount desired
1 white onion, chopped
2 tablespoons or more ohleleh
    beans (for sauce)
3 large fresh tomatoes, chopped
3 mushrooms, sliced
1 green sweet bell pepper,
    chopped
10 tender gbuhen (asparagus
    spears), cleaned (each
    chopped 1-inch long)
green onions to taste, chopped,
    and for garnishing

1. In a mixing bowl, combine rice, ½ cup *ohleleh* beans, and ground chicken. To taste add ginger, curry powder, salt, and a portion each of green onions, chopped hot peppers, and garlic.

2. Use mixture to stuff each thigh. Pull skin in place and secure with 1 or 2 wooden toothpicks.

3. Add ½ cup oil to a skillet and brown chicken on all sides. Remove chicken from oil, drain, and set chicken aside.

4. Stir and cook white onions in skillet until they are transparent. Remove onions from skillet and set it aside. Your amount of oil should be about ⅓ cup.

5. Stir in 2 tablespoons plus *ohleleh* beans. Mix and cook until beans separate. Stir in ⅔ cup to 1 cup water (may use more if needed) and bring sauce to a desirable consistency. (You want thin sauce.)

6. Add chicken and rest of ingredients, except *gbuhen* (asparagus). Mix, cover, and cook. Stirring occasionally, continue to cook until chicken is about half done.

7. Stir in asparagus and cook on low until chicken and asparagus are done. Remove wooden toothpicks and put chicken and sauce in a serving dish. Garnish with chopped green onions and serve.

Talia Mandeh Plantain Chicken

This dish is served on many small African farms and in villages.

Helpful Hints:

a. Use ripe plantain that is firm.
b. Serve with boiled rice.

2½-pound broiler or frying
   chicken, cut up
salt to taste
2 tablespoons sesame oil, or
   amount desired
1 large ripe plantain, peeled and
   chopped
1 large white onion, chopped
⅓ cup roasted and ground mandeh (sesame) seeds mixed with
   ⅔ cup of water

3 large tomatoes, chopped
1 green sweet bell pepper,
   chopped
fresh hot peppers, chopped and
   to taste
grated peel of 1 lime
juice of same lime
fresh ginger, finely chopped and
   to taste
4 green onions, chopped
parsley, chopped for garnishing

1. Remove excess chicken fat and skin as desired. Wash and place in cooking pot and season with salt.
2. Put oil, plantain, and white onions in another skillet. Stir and cook for about 13 minutes.
3. Add mixture to chicken. Also add rest of ingredients except green onions and parsley. Cover and bring to a boil.
4. Cook, stirring occasionally, until chicken is done. Stir in green onions and remove from heat. Put in a serving dish, garnish with parsley, and serve hot.

Mamokoh Chicken Balls in Mushroom Sauce

Mother often made these very special African chicken balls in which she would use ground chicken, groundnut (peanut) butter, herbs, and spices. She then cooked the balls in ground mushroom *poponda* (basil) sauce. They are so delectable, you have to eat them to know what I am talking about.

This is a West African dish. Please use local mushrooms, herbs, and spices to make it your own.

Helpful Hints:

a. Make *Mamokoh Chicken Balls* in advance.
b. Do not soak mushrooms unless dry because mushrooms can absorb much liquid.
c. Serve with boiled rice.

2 pounds white mushrooms or mushrooms of choice
3 tablespoons tomato paste
2 large fresh tomatoes, chopped
1 large white onion, chopped
fresh ginger, finely chopped and to taste
fresh hot peppers, chopped and to taste
groundnut (peanut) oil, ⅓ spoon or amount desired
salt to taste
Mamokoh Chicken Balls (see p. 342)
4 green onions, chopped
grated peel of 1 lemon
1 cup poponda or fresh basil, chopped
black beans, cooked as desired, for garnishing (cook according to package directions)

1. Clean and coarsely grind mushrooms. To heated skillet add all ingredients except chicken balls, green onions, lemon peel, black beans, and *poponda* (fresh basil).

2. Stir and cook until about half the liquid is gone.

3. Gently stir in rest of ingredients except beans and continue to cook until most of liquid is gone. Remove from heat and put in a serving dish, garnish with beans, and serve with rice.

Yehmassah's Mango Chicken

This luscious and colorful mango chicken dish is made in East, West, and South African countries.

Helpful Hint:

Serve with boiled rice.

*3-pound broiler or frying
   chicken, cut up
ground cinnamon to taste
grated fresh ginger to taste
ground hot pepper to taste
salt to taste
grated peel of 1 lime
groundnut (peanut) oil, ¼ cup
   or amount desired
1 large onion, thinly sliced
1 red, 1 green sweet bell
   peppers, sliced lengthwise.*

*juice of same lime
3 large, almost ripe mangoes
   (peel each and cut meat away
   in large chunks)
honey to taste
salt to taste
roasted and ground sesame seeds
   for garnishing
chopped fresh parsley for
   garnishing
4 white mushrooms, sliced or
   chopped*

1. Remove excess chicken fat and skin as desired, wash, and cut in small portions. Place chicken in a bowl and add the next 5 ingredients to taste, mix, and set aside.

2. Add oil to heated skillet over medium heat and lightly brown chicken on all sides. Remove from oil, drain, and set aside.

3. Adjust amount of oil in skillet so that there is left about ¼ cup or as desired. Add white onions, sweet peppers, and mushrooms.

Cook on medium heat until onions are tender. Remove from skillet and set aside.

4. Return chicken to skillet and top it with onion-pepper mixture. Cover and cook on medium heat until chicken is done. Arrange on a serving platter only the chicken but keep broth in skillet and reheat.

5. Stir in remaining ingredients except sesame and parsley. Cover and cook only until mangoes are heated through and still firm.

7. Garnish chicken with mangoes, sesame, and parsley in that order and serve hot.

Mamba Pumpkin Leaf Chicken

This Central, East, and West African chicken dish is moist, delicious, and very easy to make.

Helpful Hint:

Serve with boiled rice or cooked green bananas.

*3-pound broiler or frying
   chicken, cut up*
⅓ pound pearl onions
salt to taste
2 large tomatoes, chopped
*2 cups coconut milk; use store
   bought or see How to Make
   Coconut Milk, (p. 239)*
1 sweet bell pepper, chopped
*fresh ginger, chopped and
   to taste*

2 cloves garlic, crushed
*fresh hot peppers, chopped and
   to taste*
*½ pound chopped young pump-
   kin leaves or fresh spinach*
4 green onions, chopped
*½ cup shredded fresh coconut
   for garnishing*

1. Remove excess chicken fat and skin as desired, wash, and cut it up.

2. Put chicken, pearl onions, and salt in cooking pot. Cover, bring to a boil, and cook for about 5 minutes.

3. Stir in rest of ingredients except pumpkin leaves, shredded coconuts, and green onions. Cover and cook on low heat, stirring occasionally. Continue to cook until chicken is done.

4. Gently stir in pumpkin leaves and green onions. Boil a few more minutes and put in a serving dish. Garnish with shredded coconut and serve hot.

Mango Sauce Spicy Chicken Wings

These succulent, spicy chicken wings are made in most countries in Africa and often use local herbs and spices. Also, other chicken parts are often used instead of wings.

Helpful Hints:

a. Make in advance Spicy Groundnuts (Peanuts) (see p. 14) and Vaama Green Mango Sauce (see p. 40).
b. Make wings only as spicy hot as you like them.
c. Serve with bread of choice and Spicy Groundnuts (Peanuts).

3 pounds chicken wings
salt to taste
ground hot pepper to taste
Vaama Green Mango Sauce
(recipe follows)
ground semengii (cinnamon)
to taste

grated fresh ginger to taste
grated peel of 1 lime
juice of same lime
ground cumin to taste
1 bunch green onions, chopped
honey to taste
chopped parsley for garnishing

1. Wash wings, tuck in wing ends, and mix with salt and pepper. Put wings in skillet and bring to a boil on medium low heat.

2. Add rest of ingredients except parsley. Cook, stirring occasionally, until wings are done.

3. Arrange wings on a serving platter; garnish with parsley and serve with Spicy Groundnuts (Peanuts) and bread of choice.

Vaama Green Mango Sauce

Helpful Hints:

a. Green mango is hard and tart. When cooked, it becomes soft and creamy.
b. Mango is very high in fiber.

4 large green mangoes   *honey and/or sugar to taste*
¼ cup water

1. Peel each mango and remove meat from seed. Place meat of mango in a pot with water and bring to a boil on low heat. Cook, covered, over reduced heat until soft.
2. Mash and run mango through a fine strainer to remove fibers. Stir in honey and/or sugar to taste.

BONDOH—GUMBONDOH—GUMBO—OKRA

Bondoh is the Mende word for okra. A special Mende okra dish is called *gumbondoh.* When I found out that Americans down South have an okra dish called gumbo, I could not help but want to know the connection, if any, between the Mendes' *gumbondoh* and the American gumbo.

You may know that okra originally came from Africa. You may also know that when Africans came to America a long time ago, some Mendes were among them. Any Mende-speaking person most certainly has in his or her vocabulary the word *bondoh,* because *bondoh* is part of the Mendes' way of life. It is found in each and every garden and rice farm in Mende land. I know of no Mende person who does not like to eat *bondoh.*

There are long and short *bondoh* and more in between. It comes in green, yellow, red, and other colors. The Mendes cook fresh and dry *bondoh.* They crush it into powder when it is dry and cook it into thick sauce. They fry it, stuff and fry it, and steam or boil it. They cook *bondoh* whole, chopped, or crushed. They cook and crush it, then cook it again. Mendes cook *bondoh* with fish, chicken, seafood, lamb, goat meat, and much more. It is cooked with beans, corn, and a multitude of leafy vegetables. It is served with rice, plantain, banana, cassava, breadfruit, and much more.

For inspiration a Mende person would say to his friend, "Why don't you go ahead and do what you want to do? To carry out your plan is like planting *bondoh* seeds. If there is no fruit, you can always eat the leaves." The Mendes also eat okra leaves, and they are delicious. In African society, most things eventually lead to, and end with, music. The Mendes even have *bondoh* songs.

There is a very high probability that long ago Africans in America used *gumbondoh* in their vocabulary because the Mendes among them used it in Africa. When the younger generations began to do things the American way, such as use the short form of words and names, the word *gumbo* may have gradually replaced *gumbondoh*. Today *gumbo* has a place in the American vocabulary.

Chicken and Shrimp Gumbondoh

This dish is from Sierra Leone, West Africa. The Mendes enjoy cooking it on the farms and in the small villages. People in other West African countries cook some dishes similar to it. They may also use their own local herbs and spices.

Helpful Hints:

a. The main ingredients that give the name *gumbondoh* to the dish are sesame paste, whole fresh okra, broad beans, mushrooms, and cherry tomatoes. The farmer's wife gathers all these ingredients from her farm just before she cooks them. The meat of choice (more than one kind may be used), peppers, etc. are then added.
b. Serve with boiled rice.

2½-pound broiler or frying chicken, cut up
salt to taste
1½ pounds whole okra
½ pound mushrooms of choice, cleaned and chopped

1 pound cherry tomatoes, crushed
1 sweet bell pepper, chopped
fresh ginger, finely chopped and to taste

*fresh hot peppers, chopped
  and to taste*
*¾ cup sesame seeds, roasted
  and ground into smooth
  paste*

1½ cups fresh broad lima beans
*½ pound fresh medium shrimp,
  cleaned and deveined*
1 bunch of green onions, chopped

1. Remove excess chicken fat and skin as desired. Wash, add salt, mix, and set aside. After washing cut chicken, there is enough water with the chicken that you can bring the chicken to a boil on medium or low heat without adding water.

2. Wash each okra and remove both ends. Make 3 shallow cuts on the diagonal at different locations and set aside.

3. Put chicken in pot with water and bring to a boil. Stir in all ingredients except beans, sesame paste, shrimp, okra, and green onions. Cover and cook until chicken is about half done.

4. Mix sesame paste with ½ cup water. Add mixture and rest of ingredients to chicken except shrimp and green onions. Mix, cover, and cook until chicken and beans are done.

5. Gently stir in shrimp and green onions. Cook only a few more minutes (5–7 minutes); do not overcook; and serve with rice.

Nikilii Bondoh Chicken
(Peanut Okra Chicken)

All ingredients from Chicken and Shrimp Gumbondoh (see pp. 41–42)

*⅓ cup groundnut (peanut)
  butter instead of sesame
  paste*

*chopped roasted peanuts for
  garnishing*

1. Follow instructions for Chicken and Shrimp Gumbondoh.

2. Put in a serving dish, garnish with chopped nuts, and serve with boiled rice.

The Bondoh Story

My hand resting on the bag, I asked the second time, "How much did you say this bag of okra is?" Jimmy, the produce clerk, looked at me with angry eyes. "I am busy!" he said. "Can't you read? It is one dollar!" Talking to the younger man who was arranging apples alongside him, he said, "Them foreigners come to this country and don't know nothing. I don't believe she don't know how to read one dollar!" He opened a large box of bananas and began to display them. I heard him the first time, but I could not believe what I'd heard. I looked at the price again to make sure I heard right. The large brown paper bag was almost full of okra. They were not fresh, but they were not at their worst. Several times in the past I bought okra at the same super-market for more than one dollar per pound, and they were not much better looking than those in the bag.

As I looked at the okra more closely, my friend, Jimmy, turned around and saw me examining the bag's contents again. "You think them okra is not cheap enough for you? This is America. People don't want produce that is not fresh. Them okra is dry," he said. "If you want it, take it for fifty cents or leave it." As he spoke, he changed the price from one dollar to 50 cents on the bag.

I immediately put the bag in my empty grocery cart and wheeled it to the closest check-out counter. Just one other person stood ahead of me in line. When my turn came, Jenny (that's what her name tag read) looked into the bag. "Jimmy," she called to my friend while she continued to chew gum, "are we giving stuff away today, or are we still in the money-making business around here? I am ready to call my kids to help me take home as many bags of grocery as possible. Why is a large bag, almost full of okra, only fifty cents?"

Coming closer, Jimmy said, "Them okra is dry and no-body wants it. She is doing us a favor to pay fifty cents for it.

For the past two days I tried to sell it for one dollar. Them people don't want it. I am ready to throw it out."

Mumbling to herself, Jenny said, "If you say so."

"Nobody wants dry okra, but this somebody does," I said under my breath. Smiling, I gave Jenny a dollar and added, "I am doing you a favor. Don't forget that."

Smiling back, she replied, "I have seen you here before. The next time you come to buy okra, I'll remind you of the price." Before Jenny gave me my change, I was walking through the door. "Say, you, okra lady, here's your change," she called and ran toward me. "Don't cheat yourself. What are you going to do with a bag of dry okra anyway? Feed it to the — ?"

Before she finished talking, a rough, scratchy male voice filled the air. "Jenny!" the voice boomed over the store intercom. "Come back here! Can't you see that customers are waiting for you?" Jenny hurriedly gave me the 50 cents and ran back to her register.

When I finally got a seat on the bus, I put the bag of okra on my lap. I saw the folded food list still in my left hand. After I read it, I put it in my wallet and moved to my right to make room for an elderly lady who was about to sit down. I had gone to the store to buy some chicken, rice, tomatoes, oranges, mushrooms, and peanuts. I did not get any of them. There was no need to think about that now. I had had a long, busy day and I was tired. I was not about to go back to that store tonight, even if my life depended on it.

I got off the bus at my stop and started walking home. Today had been unusually warm, something rare in Milwaukee. Walking under the big oak trees, I enjoyed the cool breeze. I saw several squirrels running among the lower tree branches. They were showing off their long bushy tails. I often fed them peanuts, but tonight I had nothing to give them. I walked up the steps to the apartment.

Mrs. S. was watching a game show. B., my friend from Ghana, was still at school. The three-bedroom apartment was small, but B. and I were gone most of the time, either at school or at work. Mrs. S. got the apartment from the landlord. Then she rented the rooms to us. She rented only to students and said, "Students are gone most of the time." She had said that it was not easy for her to call us by our African names, so she called each person by her first initial. We only agreed to it if we also called her Mrs. S. At first it felt a little odd to call her just by her initial. If she had tried a little harder, I am sure she would have learned to call us by name. You would think that one would try to call by name the people with whom one shared a dwelling. But we got used to that American way of life as well. Soon my friend and I were also calling each other by the first initial and thinking nothing of it.

Mrs. S. was a nice lady, and we all tried to get along well. The refrigerator was a little too small for three people. The freezer section was so small, after the ice trays were in place, there was hardly room for food. B. and I usually got groceries twice a week on our way home from school. That was one reason why dry okra made a lot of sense to me when I was at the store. After I dried them, I was going to crush them into powder and put them in a jar. Then I would cook them whenever I wanted. The more important reason, however, was that I liked dry okra. Back home in my village, my grandmother often cooked it with some fish and fresh palm oil.

The following morning I got up half an hour earlier. I listened to the weather forecast while I got ready for school. In Milwaukee there was not much need to listen to the forecast. People knew the weather as well as they knew their own names because it changed so very little. One just had to remember "Lots of snow and more snowstorms." That just about covered it, except for those rare days like today when the sun surprised everyone, including itself. But when sunshine was forecast, you could depend on it, or the weatherman would be in big trouble with too many people. That was why he did not forecast sunshine unless he was as sure about it as death itself. So when I heard, "Plenty of sunshine again all day," I knew I could depend on it like yesterday.

I laid a large piece of cardboard on one step of the fire escape just below my small bedroom window. I covered it with

an old sheet, then spread the okra on the cloth. I was pleas-
antly surprised that there was much more okra in the bag
than I had expected. The sun was already coming out as I ran
to catch the bus. When I got to Tetonia, I saw the rear end of
my bus. I had to run two more blocks in order to catch another bus that was going to the university. This was going to
be a long day for me, classes all day and a late biology lab. By
the time I got home, it would be almost midnight. The okra
would sun-dry all day with no one to bother it.

My day finally over, I got on the last Tetonia bus for the
night. I was going to have time for only a quick shower before I got into bed. Then I remembered that something was
waiting for me on the step of the fire escape below my window. I almost felt like a child about to open a gift package.
My keys were in my hand even before the bus got to my stop.

When I opened the door, Mrs. S. called out, "Is that you,
Z.?" What was going on? Mrs. S. was never up this late on
weekdays. She went to bed early and left for work early
every day except Sundays, and during the winter months,
when the Kings were in Florida. She had met Judge King,
then a young judge, because of an unfortunate circumstance.
Judge King had promised young Mrs. S. leniency if she
"cleaned up her act." She did clean up her act, better than
anyone had imagined. She also cleaned the Kings' home, raised
their two children, and put delicious meals on their table
daily. She had worked for the Kings for over 40 years. Her
large, beautiful brown eyes sparkled in the light. Her voice
was like an excited child's as she said, "You will never guess
what happened today!" She came toward me as fast as her
arthritic knees would allow her. "The Kings gave you one
million dollars," I said, "in appreciation for a lifetime of hard
work. From today on, my room is rent free because you no
longer need the money."

"Wishful thinking. Guess again," came B's voice as she
stood at her bedroom door.

"I have lived in Milwaukee most of my life," Mrs. S. went
on, "but I was never on TV until now. It took dry okra and
squirrels to put me on Channel Twelve today!"

I heard myself say, "Okra! What okra?" I dropped my books, opened my bedroom door, and turned on the light. Looking down at the fire escape, I saw that the okra was gone. Not one pod was on the old sheet, which still lay on the cardboard. "Who took in my okra?" I asked, having a strange feeling that no one did.

"The squirrels ate your okra," B. said, and she began to laugh really hard.

"The squirrels? What do you mean, 'The squirrels ate my okra'?" I asked and turned to Mrs. S., who was also laughing, but not as hard.

She said, "When I got home this afternoon, Channel Twelve and many people were here because someone had called. They were taking pictures of lots and lots of squirrels eating your okra. They also took pictures of me and asked questions about the apartment. I watched the eleven P.M. news and saw myself on TV for the first time! I also saw lots of squirrels eating your okra. It was so funny!" She began to laugh all over again.

"And Jenny wanted to know what I was going to do with dry okra," I sighed. "I hope she saw the answer on Channel Twelve tonight."

"Who is Jenny?" Mrs. S. asked.

"Just someone I know," I replied and walked away.

"Only in America!" B. said between laughs.

"Only in America," I echoed as I walked into my room.

Chicken and Crawfish in Dry Okra Sauce

A common way Africans preserve food is the sun-dried method, thanks to the tropical sun. Foods such as okra, tomatoes, peppers, and beans can dry in the hot sun in a short time, cost free.

This delicious and easy-to-cook okra dish is prepared in East, Central, and West Africa.

Helpful Hints:

a. You may also use other drying methods. Crush sun-dried okra into powder or cook it whole. When cooked whole, dry okra is crunchy, an added dimension to the dish.
b. Serve with boiled rice.

fresh palm oil or groundnut (peanut) oil, amount desired
1 chicken, washed and cut into small pieces
1 large onion, chopped
grated fresh ginger to taste
warm chicken broth or water
⅓ cup ground dry okra
1 cup chopped fresh okra

4 white mushrooms, chopped
2 large tomatoes, chopped
3 tablespoons tomato paste
fresh hot peppers, chopped and to taste
ground black pepper to taste
salt to taste
½ pound crawfish, cleaned
4 green onions, chopped

1. Add oil, chicken, white onion, and ginger to heated skillet that is over medium heat. Cook and mix until onions are tender.

2. Stir in about 2 cups warm broth or water and the rest of ingredients except crawfish and green onions. Stirring often, cook until chicken is done and sauce is about the consistency of spaghetti sauce. (You may add more water as needed.)

3. Stir in rest of ingredients and cook a few more minutes. Serve with rice.

Ngeh Ngeh Sambeh Chicken

This sauce is made in Central, East, and West African countries and may be known by different names in different countries.

Helpful Hints:

a. The leafy vegetable used in Africa is slimy and bright green. Because it is not readily available, okra and spinach will be used (fresh or frozen).
b. Serve with boiled rice.

1 pound okra (wash and remove only top ends)
1 pound fresh or frozen spinach, washed and chopped (thaw if frozen)
a pinch of lube (baking soda), use no more
fresh palm oil or vegetable oil, amount desired
2½-pound broiler or frying chicken, cut up into small portions and washed after removing excess fat if so desired

1 white onion, chopped
2 cloves garlic, crushed
2 large tomatoes, chopped
3 tablespoons tomato paste
fresh hot peppers, chopped and to taste
salt to taste
4 green onions, chopped

1. Put okra and about ⅓ cup water in a cooking pot. Cook only until okra is almost tender but still bright green.
2. Mix spinach and *lube* (baking soda) well, add it to okra, and mix. Cover and cook only until spinach has become wilted and bright green.
3. Remove from heat and put in a mixing bowl. While still warm, use a wooden spoon and mix okra and spinach until it forms a sauce, as smooth as possible.
4. Add oil to skillet and lightly brown chicken. Stir in white onion, cover, and cook for 3 minutes.
5. Stir in rest of ingredients except spinach-okra sauce and green onions.
6. Stirring occasionally, cover and cook until chicken is done.
7. Now gently stir in rest of ingredients and cook for a few minutes. Serve hot with rice.

Lagba Lagba Ginger Chicken

Most countries in Africa prepare this dish or one similar to it and may use local herbs and spices.

Helpful Hints:

a. Please use fresh lemon juice.
b. *Lagba lagba* means "sour." This dish is spicy, tart, and sweet. Make it only as sour and sweet as you like it.
c. Serve with rice, roasted breadfruit, or bread of choice.

2½–3 pound broiler or frying chicken, cut up
groundnut (peanut) oil, amount desired
1 white onion, chopped
¼ pound fresh ginger or amount desired (scrape skin off, cut into very thin slices)
juice of 1 lemon
grated peel of same lemon
honey to taste
fresh hot peppers, chopped and to taste

3 whole cloves
2 cups coconut milk; use store bought or see How to Make Coconut Milk (p. 239)
1 red and 1 green sweet pepper, cut into equal-size chunks
salt to taste
6 slices fresh or canned pineapple
1 small bunch green onions, chopped
mint leaves, chopped for garnishing

1. Remove excess chicken fat and skin as desired. Wash, cut up, and season with salt.

2. Add oil to heated skillet and brown chicken. Remove chicken from skillet, drain, and set aside. Adjust oil to the amount you want. Stir in white onion and cook for 2 minutes.

3. Return chicken to skillet and stir in rest of ingredients except sweet peppers, pineapples, green onions, and chopped mint.

4. With cover in place and mixing occasionally, cook until chicken is done.

5. Put only chicken in a serving dish and add sweet peppers to skillet. Cover and cook for about 5 minutes. If sauce is more than you want, then reduce it by continuing to boil on medium high to about ⅔ its original volume.

6. Stir in pineapples and green onions. Cook only until pineapples are heated through. Put sauce over chicken, garnish with mint leaves, and serve.

Momoh Kawah Chicken

This dish is made in East, North, and West African countries. Other names may also be used.

Helpful Hint:

Serve with boiled rice.

2–3 pound broiler or frying chicken, cut up and washed
salt to taste
fresh palm oil or groundnut (peanut oil), amount desired
1 large white onion, chopped
fresh ginger, finely chopped and to taste
2 large tomatoes, chopped
3 tablespoons tomato paste
2 cloves garlic, crushed
1 sweet pepper, chopped
fresh hot peppers, chopped and to taste

1 pound gbuhen (asparagus) (break off tough ends; wash and cut stalks into 1-inch pieces)
¾ pound okra (wash and remove ends; cut into ⅓-inch slices)
2 small zucchini (wash each and remove both ends; slice into ⅓-inch portions)
4 green onions, chopped
1 cup fresh chopped poponda (basil)
½ cup green peas for garnishing; (cook in water only until bright green, drain)

1. Add salt to chicken and mix.
2. Add oil to heated skillet and lightly brown chicken. Stir in white onions and ginger and cook until onions are tender.
3. Stir in rest of ingredients except *gbuhen* (asparagus), okra, zucchini, green onions, *poponda* (basil), and cooked green peas.
4. Stirring occasionally with a wooden spoon, cook about 20–25 minutes until chicken is about ¾ done.
5. Stir in rest of ingredients except green peas. Mixing occasionally, continue to cook until chicken is done and *gbuhen* (asparagus) is tender. Put in a serving dish, garnish with peas, and serve.

Baindu Koma Chicken in Kobo Kobo Seafood Sauce

❧

This dish is prepared in many West African countries; local names may be used.

Helpful Hints:

a. Peel *kobo kobo* (eggplants) just before cooking to keep them from turning dark.
b. Serve with boiled rice, cooked green bananas, or boiled plantains.

3-pound broiler or frying chicken, cut up
2 large tomatoes, chopped
3 tablespoons tomato paste
ground cumin to taste
2 cloves garlic, crushed
fresh ginger, chopped and to taste
fresh hot pepper, chopped and to taste
½ cup roasted sesame (grind into paste; mix with ½ cup water)

salt to taste
1 medium kobo kobo (eggplant), peeled and cut into cubes
⅓ pound medium fresh shrimp, cleaned and deveined
1 pint fresh oysters
4 small cleaned soft-shell crabs (optional)
1 bunch green onions, chopped
chopped parsley for garnishing

1. Remove excess chicken fat and skin as desired; wash and season with salt.

2. Put chicken in saucepan and add all ingredients except shrimp, oysters, crabs, *kobo kobo* (eggplant), green onions, and parsley. Mix, cover, and bring to a boil.

3. Stirring occasionally, cook on low heat 20–25 minutes, until chicken is almost done.

4. Stir in *kobo kobo* (eggplant), cover and cook about 8 minutes or until *kobo kobo* is almost done.

5. Gently stir in rest of ingredients except parsley. Cook 8 minutes or only until done.

6. Put chicken and sauce in a serving dish. Garnish with crabs and parsley in that order and serve hot with rice.

Yehjembehgoi's Coconut-Groundnut Curry Chicken

ை

This is a very special dish made in East, West, and South African countries. Why not discover the taste for yourself?

Helpful Hints:

a. This dish can also be cooked in an oven. (See note below.)
b. Serve with cooked green bananas, plantains, cassava, roasted breadfruit, or boiled rice.

2½-pound broiler or frying chicken, cut up
salt to taste
curry powder to taste
2 cups coconut milk; use store bought or see How to Make Coconut Milk (p. 239)
⅓ cup groundnut (peanut) butter (mix with coconut milk)
grated fresh ginger to taste
¼ pound white mushrooms, sliced
1 sweet bell pepper, chopped
fresh hot peppers, chopped and to taste

1 large onion, chopped
2 large tomatoes, chopped
3 tablespoons tomato paste
groundnut (peanut) oil, amount desired
4 green onions, chopped
1 cup fresh poponda (basil), chopped
roasted groundnuts (peanuts) for garnishing
shredded fresh coconut for garnishing
chopped parsley for garnishing

1. Remove excess chicken fat and skin as desired. Wash and put in cooking pot with water, and season with salt. Cover and bring to a boil.

2. Stir in all ingredients except green onions, parsley, *poponda* (basil), groundnuts, and coconuts for garnishing. Mixing occasionally and making sure liquid does not boil over, continue to cook until chicken is done.

3. Gently stir in green onions and fresh *poponda* (basil), and cook 2 more minutes.

4. Put chicken in a serving dish; reduce sauce by continuing for 10 minutes longer if desired and spoon it over chicken. Garnish with groundnuts (peanuts), coconuts, and parsley in that order and serve hot.

Note: When cooking in an oven, arrange chicken in a casserole dish. Add rest of ingredients except groundnuts (peanuts), coconuts, and parsley. Cover and cook in oven at 375 degrees until thickest piece of chicken is fork tender. Take it out, garnish with groundnuts, coconuts, and parsley in that order, and serve hot.

African Chicken Peppersoup

Africans believe that chicken peppersoup has genuine medicinal value. They serve it to the sick to help improve some health conditions. New mothers are given chicken peppersoup to help secrete breast milk. Those who are well also eat it because it is good and simply delicious.

Helpful Hint:

Although this is a spicy dish, use only the amount of spices you feel comfortable eating.

3-pound broiler or frying chicken, cut up
salt to taste
chicken or vegetable broth or water
1 large onion, chopped
1 green sweet pepper, chopped
2 large tomatoes, chopped
3 tablespoons tomato paste
2 cloves garlic, crushed

fresh hot peppers, chopped and to taste
3 whole cloves
1 small cinnamon stick
grated fresh ginger to taste
juice of 1 lime
grated peel of same lime
½ cup uncooked rice
chopped green onions for garnishing

1. Remove excess chicken skin and fat as desired. Wash chicken and put in a cooking pot. Add salt and water or broth, mix, and bring to a boil.
2. Stir in rest of ingredients except green onions. Add water or broth so that it is 2 to 3 inches above chicken.
3. Cover and cook on reduced heat, stirring occasionally. When

soup is done, there should be plenty of broth. Turn off heat and keep warm.

4. When serving put soup in a bowl, garnish with chopped green onions, and serve hot.

Kenya's Coconut Curry Chicken

Beautiful Kenya is a country in East Africa. Like all African countries, the people speak several tribal languages. While English is the official language, Swahili is the national language.

My Kenyan friends are beautiful, intelligent, gentle, and kind. They are also great cooks. Coconut curry chicken is one of many dishes they enjoy eating.

People from Cameroon, Cape Verde, Gambia, Ghana, Guinea, Ivory Coast, Liberia, Mali, Mozambique, Nigeria, Senegal, Sierra Leone, and South Africa cook a similar dish. We hope you too will enjoy making and eating it.

Helpful Hints:

a. This dish is at its best when just cooked.
b. Serve with boiled rice, cooked green bananas, plantain, sweet or white potatoes, or bread of choice.

3-pound broiler or frying chicken, cut up
salt to taste
groundnut (peanut) oil, amount desired
1 large white onion, chopped
grated fresh ginger to taste
½ cup whole kernel corn
2 cloves garlic, crushed
1 sweet bell pepper, chopped
2 cups coconut milk; use store bought or see How to Make Coconut Milk (p. 239)

2 large tomatoes, chopped
curry powder to taste
fresh hot peppers, chopped and to taste
⅓ cup shredded fresh coconut
2 carrots, peeled and chopped
chunks of butternut squash, amount desired
3 green onions, chopped
chopped fresh parsley for garnishing

1. Remove excess chicken fat and skin as desired. Wash chicken, cut into small pieces, and season with salt.

2. Add oil to skillet heated over medium heat, stir in chicken, white onions, and ginger. Cook and stir until onions are tender.

3. Stir in rest of ingredients except green onions, parsley, corn, butternut squash, and carrots.

4. Stirring occasionally, cook for 20–25 minutes or until chicken is almost done. Stir in the remaining ingredients except parsley. Continue to cook 10 minutes or until chicken is done. Put in a serving dish, garnish with parsley, and serve hot.

The Mushroom Story

By chance I walked into a small Italian grocery store. When I saw *kpohwoh* for the first time in America, I became so excited that I said aloud, "*Kpohwoh!*" Holding the box of mushrooms in my hands, I went to the lady at the check-out counter and said, "I want this box of African mushrooms. How much are they?" Calm and collected, she peered at me over her eyeglasses for what seemed a long time. When she spoke, there was no change in her facial expression.

"It is not African," she said. "It is Italian. The name is portabella."

I turned around to make sure she was not talking to another person.

"Ma'am," I said, "I don't think you understand. I know that these are African mushrooms. I used to gather them in the forest with my friends in Africa."

This time, in a stronger voice, she said, "That is not African; that is Italian."

Her voice made me feel like I was breaking an unwritten law by saying that the mushrooms were from Africa. She reached out to take the box from my hand. I reluctantly gave it to her. I was already becoming protective and perhaps a little possessive of them.

Repeating, I asked, "How much are they?"

Now speaking painfully slow, as if afraid that I could not understand English well (though she herself spoke with a very heavy accent), she said, "Portabella mushrooms are seven dollars a pound, and this is a two-pound box."

A second lady who had been out of sight until now came toward us, smiling. She asked, "Did you say that you are from Africa?"

Looking at her, I said, "I said that the mushrooms are from Africa." I added, "And I am also from Africa."

She said, "You learn something new every day. I always thought that portabella mushrooms came only from Italy." She took the box from the first lady and said to me, "Please come with me." As we walked to the other end of the store where there was another cash register, she said, "Tell me more about portabella mushrooms."

I told her that they are called *kpohwoh;* that they taste more like meat than mushrooms; that they grow wild in many parts of Africa; and that I used to gather baskets of them from the forest with my friends. I added, "And we never paid a cent for them; they were always there for the taking."

She laughed and said, "Well, this is America. We pay for everything here. Portabella mushrooms are very expensive. Only people with lots of money can afford to eat them." Then she said, "I'll tell you what. Pay two dollars, and I'll let you have the box because I have learned from you today."

I gave her the money, said thanks, and added, "I am Zainabu. What's your name?" She said that her name was Mary Ann, and we shook hands.

Only people with lots of money can afford to eat them? I could not help but smile. That means every single person in my village in Africa is a multimillionaire and more. Then I thought about it for a moment. "They are rich!" I said aloud. "They are very rich. Far more than they'll ever know." As I walked away, I felt like I was carrying something more precious than two pounds of solid gold. I was holding in my hand something that reconnected me with my past. For that moment I was again a little girl in West Africa. I was in the rain forest with my friends gathering *kpohwoh* mushrooms, berries, and wild fruits. We were collecting snails and baby turtles for pets; we were watching the monkeys play with their young as they made funny faces. We were playing forest games, fishing with our hands in the ponds, and laughing our heads off.

Two pounds of mushrooms brought all of that back to me and much more. I could not buy that with any amount of money in the world. Despite my having just a couple of dollars left in my wallet, I felt richer than I have ever felt in my entire life. Then reality hit, reminding me to hurry and cash my meager part-time paycheck before the banks closed. But the realization that money had very little to do with real wealth was again mine, and I was very happy for that.

I cooked some of the *kpohwoh* that day with some chicken, fresh palm oil, tomatoes, and fresh broad beans. I also cooked some asparagus with it, the closest thing to *gbuhen*. My grandmother always cooked *kpohwoh* with *gbuhen*. It was very good. I kept some uncooked portion of it in the refrigerator for a long time, knowing that it was no longer good to eat. But I kept it just the same because it reminded me of home and my past.

Do you remember who said that it was not possible to go back home again? For some of us, that is true. In my case, I'll never go back home because I really never left.

Maama Lahun's Chicken in Kpohwoh Plasas

This dish is from Sierra Leone, West Africa. Grandmother made it often.

Helpful Hints:

a. Asparagus, which looks like *gbuhen,* will be used in this dish. *Kpohwoh* is the Mende name for portabella mushrooms.
b. Serve with boiled rice.

2–3 pound broiler or frying chicken
fresh palm oil or groundnut
  (peanut) oil, ¼ cup or amount
  desired
1 large white onion, chopped
fresh ginger, chopped and to taste
1 pound cherry tomatoes, crushed
½ pound kpohwoh (portabella)
  mushrooms, cleaned and chopped
1 pound gbuhen (asparagus)
  (remove tough ends; wash; chop
  into ⅓-inch portions)

½ pound okra (clean; remove
  ends; and cut into ½-inch slices)
1 cup fresh broad lima beans
2 tablespoons tomato paste
fresh hot peppers, chopped and
  to taste
salt to taste
1 small bunch fresh spinach,
  washed, drained, and
  chopped
4 green onions, chopped

1. Remove excess chicken fat and skin if desired, and wash chicken. Cut it into small portions and season with salt. Add oil to heated skillet; stir in chicken, white onion, and ginger. Cook until onions are tender.

2. Stir in tomatoes and mushrooms. You may add ⅓ cup of water. Cover and cook until chicken is about three-quarters done. (Add a little water if needed.)

3. Add rest of ingredients except spinach and green onions. Mix, cover, and continue to cook on medium heat until beans are done.

4. Gently stir in spinach and green onions, and cook 6 minutes more. Remove from heat and serve with rice.

Fish and Seafood

Fish is one of nature's almost-perfect foods. It is high in protein, low in cholesterol, oil, and calories; the taste is great; and it takes just minutes to prepare.

It is important to get the freshest fish possible. Of course, that really means one that is alive, which is not easy to get in many cities. The next best thing is to know how to make a good selection. There are certain qualities to look for when buying. If you follow our guidelines, anyone can purchase good-quality fish in his or her town.

GOOD-QUALITY FISH GUIDELINES

1. Fresh fish has a clean, fresh smell. Do not buy fish that has an offensive, rotten odor.
2. The fish should feel firm when touched and springy when pressure is applied.
3. The eyes are clean, clear, and normal looking. Don't buy fish with sunken or bloodshot eyes.
4. Cooked fresh fish tastes delicious.

In Africa, where there are probably more beautiful tropical fish than anywhere on earth, people use every opportunity to enjoy their beauty. For example, when the Mendes speak of a beautiful thing or a beautiful lady, they say, "It is as beautiful as [or she is as beautiful as] fish in water." A very beautiful lady may be called *manye*, which means female or lady fish. Of course, if one has not seen beautiful African fish in their natural habitat, it would be a little difficult for one to appreciate that saying or fully understand the concept.

Here are some exciting and delicious African fish dishes. Please enjoy them.

NGOKAH (TILAPIA)

Both African and American farmers now find themselves going after the same catch. Not too long ago, *ngokah* (tilapia) was only found in African fresh waters. This fish is especially abundant in the Nile River and all along the region. The delicate and delicious perch-like fish has found its way to America and around the world.

    Ngokah (tilapia), sometimes called "Nile perch," is very easy to raise. California solar aqua farmers are successfully raising it. From their farms it is shipped to some of the best supermarkets across the nation, bringing this once "only in Africa" fish to the American people also.

Ngokah (Tilapia) in Coconut Lime Sauce

This dish is made in many African countries; other herbs and spices may also be used.

Helpful Hints:

a. Cook each fish whole, with or without the head.
b. Do not overcook fish.
c. Serve with boiled rice or cooked green bananas.

groundnut (peanut) oil,
  amount desired
1 white onion, chopped
2 cups Liiyah Coconut Milk
  (recipe follows)
2 cloves garlic, crushed
grated peel of 1 lime
juice of same lime
1 cup sliced mushrooms
fresh ginger, finely chopped
  and to taste

fresh hot peppers, chopped
  and to taste
salt to taste
chopped fresh parsley for
  garnishing
2 medium ngokah (tilapia) or
  number desired, cleaned
2 green onions, chopped

1. Add oil and white onions to heated skillet over medium heat, mix, and cook until onions are tender.

2. Stir in rest of ingredients except fish and green onions. Bring to a boil but do not allow it to boil over.

3. Lay fish side by side in liquid, cover, and cook only until fish flakes easily when fork tested.

4. Remove each whole, put on a serving platter, and keep warm.

5. Reduce sauce if needed and stir in green onions. Spoon sauce over fish, garnish with parsley, and serve hot.

Liiyah Coconut Milk

Helpful Hints:

a. Use fresh coconut if possible.
b. When it is removed from shell, peel away the dark skin before cutting coconut into small portions or cubes.

coconut   *2–3 cups of water*

1. Put both ingredients in blender and blend. (In Africa, coconut is grated and water added.)

2. Remove from blender and use amount desired.

Mbola in Spinach Sesame Plasas

Fish is cooked in a special spinach sesame sauce, the way the farmer's wife prepares it on many small farms across Africa.

Helpful Hints:

a. Do not overcook fish.
b. Serve with boiled rice.

sesame oil, amount desired
4 white mushrooms, chopped
fresh ginger, ground or finely
   chopped and to taste
1 bunch green onions, chopped
   (keep white part in one bowl
   and green part in another)
1 red sweet bell pepper, chopped
fresh hot peppers, chopped
   and to taste
salt to taste

1½ pounds fresh spinach,
   washed, well drained, and
   chopped
1 cup cooked, fresh, broad lima
   beans (cook according to
   package directions and drain)
⅓ cup roasted and ground
   sesame seeds
4 medium mbola fillets,
   cut into desired portions

1. Add to skillet oil, mushrooms, ginger, white portion of green onions, peppers, and salt. Stir, cover, and cook for 3 minutes over medium heat.

2. Add rest of ingredients except fish and 1 tablespoon of ground sesame.

3. Using a wooden spoon, mix well all of the ingredients.

4. Lay fish over mixture, cover, and cook only until fish easily flakes when fork tested.

5. Remove fish and put in a bowl. Increase heat and reduce liquid if so desired. Put spinach in a serving dish and arrange fish over it. Sprinkle with rest of sesame and serve hot.

Mbola in Okra and Pumpkin Leaf Sauce

This delicious and nutritious dish is prepared in most West African countries, South Africa, and Zimbabwe.

Helpful Hints:

a. The longer okra is cooked, the less slimy and less bright green it becomes.

b. Fresh palm oil is the color of a bright red tomato. If it is heated at about 380 degrees or higher temperature, the oil loses its color in only a few minutes.

c. Serve with boiled rice.

*fresh palm oil or groundnut
  (peanut) oil, amount desired*
1 medium white onion, chopped
1 large tomato, chopped
hot peppers, chopped and to taste
fresh ginger, chopped and to taste
2 cloves garlic, crushed
3 white mushrooms, sliced
*1 pound fresh or frozen okra,
  washed (remove ends and
  cut each into ⅓-inch slices)*

salt to taste
*½ pound young pumpkin leaves,
  broccoli, or fresh spinach
  (washed, drained, and chopped)*
4 green onions, chopped
3 tablespoons tomato paste
*1½ pounds mbola fillet
  cut into bite-size portions*

1. Add oil, white onions, tomato, tomato paste, peppers, ginger, garlic, mushrooms, okra, and salt to a skillet that is over medium heat and mix. Cover and cook, stirring occasionally, until okra is almost done.

2. Stir in rest of ingredients, cover, and cook. (Do not mix again so that fish does not fall apart.) Cook only until fish flakes easily when fork tested. Put in a serving dish and serve with rice.

Ngokah Nikilii Woundu Gbotoh
(Perch in Raw Peanut Sauce)

Ngokah is a perch-like fish, abundant in African waters. This dish is prepared in Central, East, and West African countries.

Helpful Hints:

a. Unroasted groundnut (peanut) sauce is delicious, white, and creamy like milk and cream sauce.
b. Use skinless raw peanuts, well ground.
c. Use brook trout instead of *ngokah*.
d. The more peanuts used, the thicker the sauce becomes.
e. Serve with boiled rice.

peanut oil, amount desired
¼ pound pearl onions

ground fresh ginger to taste
1 red sweet bell pepper, chopped

3 green onions, chopped
fresh hot peppers, chopped and
to taste
⅓ to ½ cup raw groundnuts
(peanuts), mixed with 1 cup
water

4 medium fresh ngokah or brook
trout, cleaned (do not cut up)
salt to taste
grated peel of 1 lime
⅓ cup parsley, chopped
chopped mint leaves for
garnishing

1. Add oil to heated skillet that is over medium heat. For about 3 minutes stir and cook pearl onions, ginger, and sweet peppers.

2. Stir in salt and peanut mixture and bring to a gentle boil.

3. Lay each whole fish in skillet, cover, and cook only until fish flakes easily when tested with a fork.

4. Put fish in a serving dish and keep warm. Add to sauce rest of ingredients except mint leaves, and reduce sauce to amount desired.

5. Spoon sauce over fish, garnish with mint leaves, and serve with rice.

Tuna Ndehma

Tuna is found in most African waters, including those around Ndehma, home of the Conjor family, a well-known family who has lived in the area for generations.

Helpful Hints:

a. If possible, use fresh tuna in dish.
b. Do not overcook fish.
c. Serve with boiled green bananas, plantains, or rice.

groundnut (peanut) oil, amount
desired
1 white onion, chopped
grated fresh ginger to taste
2 cloves garlic, crushed
2 cups Liiyah Coconut Milk
(p. 62)

2 green mangoes, peeled (remove
meat and cut into chunks)
1 red sweet bell pepper,
chopped
grated peel of 1 lemon
fresh hot pepper to taste
salt to taste

*2 pounds fresh tuna, cut into
    bite-size pieces*
3 green onions, chopped

*chopped poponda (fresh basil)
    leaves for garnishing*

1. Add oil to heated skillet that is over medium heat. Stir and cook white onions and ginger until onions are tender.

2. Stir in rest of ingredients except tuna, green onions, and *poponda* (fresh basil) leaves. Cook for about 6 minutes. (Do not let pot boil over.)

3. Add tuna and green onions. Cook only until fish flakes easily when tested with a fork.

4. If sauce is more than desired, remove fish from skillet, put in a serving dish, and keep warm. Reduce sauce to desired amount; spoon sauce over fish, garnish with *poponda* (fresh basil) leaves, and serve.

Tuna in Mushroom Shrimp Boya

This dish is prepared in many African countries with little changes. People who do not eat shrimp cook without adding them; and local herbs and spices may be used.

Helpful Hints:

a. If possible, use fresh fish, not canned.
b. Serve with boiled rice.

*groundnut (peanut) oil,
    amount desired*
1 white onion, chopped
1 sweet bell pepper, chopped
*fresh hot peppers, chopped
    and to taste*
*½ pound kpohwoh (portabella)
    mushrooms, chopped*
*2 large tomatoes, seeds
    removed and chopped*
*fresh ginger, finely chopped
    and to taste*

*1 pound tuna steak, cut into
    bite-size portions*
*1 pound large shrimp, deveined
    (do not remove shells)*
2 tablespoons tomato paste
3 green onions, chopped
*1 cup poponda (fresh basil)
    leaves, chopped*
salt to taste
*roasted groundnuts (peanuts)
    for garnishing*

1. Add oil to a heated skillet. Stir in and cook white onions, sweet and hot peppers, mushrooms, tomatoes, and ginger for about 8 minutes.

2. Stir in rest of ingredients except groundnuts (peanuts). Cook only until fish flakes easily when fork tested. Remove from heat and put in a serving dish. Garnish with roasted groundnuts (peanuts) and serve hot.

Sole in Curry Tomato Sauce

This dish is from East, North, and South Africa.

Helpful Hints:

a. Remove tiny bone structure at center line of each fillet before cooking.
b. Serve with cooked rice.

⅓ *cup shredded fresh coconut*
1 white onion, thinly sliced
2 large fresh tomatoes, cut in
chunks
curry powder to taste
2 cups fish broth
olive oil to taste
2 cloves garlic, crushed
4 button mushrooms, each
cut in half
1 red sweet pepper, thinly
sliced lengthwise

fresh hot peppers, chopped and
to taste
grated fresh ginger to taste
grated peel of 1 lime or 3 fresh
lime leaves
salt to taste
1 pound fillet of sole, cut up
1 pound scallops; if large sea
scallops, cut each in half
3 green onions, chopped
chopped parsley for garnishing

1. Add to pot all of the ingredients except fish, scallops, green onions, and parsley. Cook until white onions are tender.

2. Stir in fish, scallops, and green onions. Cook only until fish flakes easily when fork tested. Put everything except the liquid in a serving dish.

3. If liquid is more than desired, reduce sauce and spoon it over fish; garnish with parsley and serve.

Beh Beh in Notoh Kibongii Plasas
(Flounder in Oyster Tomato Sauce)

This flounder-like fish is found in African waters. South and West African countries are home for this dish.

Helpful Hint:

Serve with boiled rice or cooked green bananas.

groundnut (peanut) oil,
   amount desired
1 white onion, chopped
1 pound beh beh (flounder)
   fillets or amount desired,
   cut up
1 pint fresh notoh (oysters)
2 large tomatoes, chopped
2 tablespoons tomato paste
3 green onions, chopped

2 cloves garlic, crushed
1 teaspoon fresh ginger, chopped
1 large sweet bell pepper, chopped
ground cumin to taste
ground black pepper to taste
fresh hot peppers, chopped and
   to taste
salt to taste
chopped parsley for garnishing

1. Add oil, white onion, ginger, peppers, and tomatoes to a heated skillet that is over medium heat. Stir and cook until onions are tender.

2. Stir in rest of ingredients except fish, oysters, green onions, and parsley. Cover and cook for about 7 minutes, stirring often.

3. Add fish, oysters, and green onions; stir and cook only until fish flakes easily when tested with a fork. Put in a serving dish, garnish with parsley, and serve hot.

Labonii (Halibut) in Creamy Corn Sauce

People from Central, South, and West African countries cook this delicious, halibut-like fish found in African waters.

Helpful Hints:

a. To make creamy sauce, corn must be cooked before partially crushing it in a blender. African women would crush it between two stones or in a wooden mortar with a pestle *(kondeh keh ngeteh)*. You may also use cream-style corn from the can.
b. Serve with boiled rice, cooked green bananas, or plantains.

corn oil, amount desired
1 white onion, chopped
1 sweet green bell pepper,
*   chopped*
fresh hot peppers, chopped
*   and to taste*
1 large tomato, chopped
fresh ginger, finely chopped
*   and to taste*
1½ cups cooked kernels of
*   corn, partially crushed*

1 cup coconut milk; use store
*   bought or see How to Make*
*   Coconut Milk (p. 239)*
2 cloves garlic, crushed
salt to taste
1½ pounds labonii (halibut)
*   fillets, cut into desired portions*
½ pound shrimp, cleaned and
*   chopped*
3 green onions, chopped
chopped parsley for garnishing

1. Add oil to a skillet that is over medium heat. With a wooden spoon, mix and cook white onion, peppers, tomato, and ginger until onion is tender.
2. Stir in rest of ingredients except fish, shrimp, green onions, and parsley. Cover and cook for about 8 minutes. Add about ⅓ cup water if needed.
3. Stir in fish, shrimp, and green onions. Cook only until fish flakes easily when fork tested. Put in a serving dish, garnish with parsley, and serve.

Manaamu Fry Fish with Hot Curry Fish Sauce

This dish is prepared in many African countries. In each country, it may be called by a different name, and is prepared using local herbs and spices.

Helpful Hints:

a. *Manaamu* is a delicious fish with a delicate taste. Please use local fish fillets of choice in dish.
b. *Mbagbehnyeh* is broken rice. To be able to coat fish well with it, fish must be moist. (Do not towel dry before coating.) Other choices of flour to use are rice flour and cornmeal.
c. For a crisp, crunchy fried fish, coat one piece at a time, immediately drop it in hot oil, and do not crowd fish.
d. Serve with boiled plantain or cooked green bananas and Hot Curry Fish Sauce (recipe follows).

oil for deep frying, about 3 inches deep
rice flour or cornmeal
ground hot pepper to taste
ground fresh ginger to taste
salt to taste

4 serving portions of fish fillet of choice, seasoned with salt
1 cup mbagbehnyeh; see How to Make Mbagbehnyeh (Broken Rice) (p. 225)

1. Put oil in a kettle that is over medium heat. Heat to 375 degrees, or use Suma's Onion Oil Test (p. 228).

2. In a bowl, mix together mbagbehnyeh, pepper, ginger, and salt. Coat fish with mixture and fry until golden brown. Remove from oil, drain, and serve with Hot Curry Fish Sauce.

Hot Curry Fish Sauce

Helpful Hint:

Make sauce only as hot as you like it.

groundnut (peanut) oil, amount
* desired*
⅓ cup chopped fresh hot pep-
* pers or to taste*
1 cup fish fillet, finely chopped
1 large white onion, chopped

1 bunch green onions, chopped
6 tablespoons tomato paste
1 large fresh tomato, chopped
curry powder to taste
salt to taste

1. Add oil to heated skillet that is over medium heat, stir in all ingredients.
2. Stirring often, cover and cook until onions are tender.
3. Remove fron heat and serve with fish.

Bonthe Shebro Swordfish in Crabmeat Sauce

I dedicate this dish to the memory of Mr. Senesie, the elderly gentleman who went to the wharf very early each morning and bought fresh fish for the girls at the school.

This is an elegant West African dish that is easy to prepare. Swordfish is found in many African waters, including Shebro Island waters. Bonthe Shebro is a small island in Sierra Leone, West Africa. I went to Minnie Mull Memorial School, a United Brethren in Christ boarding school for girls in Bonthe Shebro. At the middle school, fresh swordfish was served at least three times a week.

Helpful Hints:

a. Do not overcook fish and seafood.
b. Serve with Ngeh Ngeh Pahnwah Rice (Green Check Rice) (p. 139) or plain boiled rice.

groundnut (peanut) oil,
  amount desired
1 white onion, chopped
2 cloves garlic, crushed
fresh ginger, finely chopped
  and to taste
3 large fresh tomatoes, chopped
1 red sweet bell pepper, chopped
fresh hot peppers, chopped
  and to taste

salt to taste
1½ pounds swordfish steak,
  cut into bite-size portions
⅔ pound crabmeat
2 cups fresh pineapple chunks
1 bunch green onions, chopped
  1 inch long
grated peel of 1 lime
1 kiwi or kiwi-like fruit, peeled
  and sliced for garnishing

1. In heated skillet, combine oil, white onion, garlic, ginger, tomatoes, peppers, and salt. Stir, cover, and cook for about 7 minutes, mixing often.

2. Stir in rest of ingredients except kiwi. Without again mixing, cover and cook only until fish flakes easily when tested with a fork.

3. Put all in a serving dish, garnish with kiwi, and serve hot.

Tehkuh in Notoh Poponda Sauce
(Smelt in Oyster Basil Sauce)

The small, smelt-like fish with the great taste is abundant in African waters, and it is prepared in many parts of Africa. *Tehkuh* is not only a good source of protein, it also supplies a good amount of calcium to the diet. Like smelt, the bones are small, soft, and full of calcium. Because one eats the bones along with the fish, one also takes in a substantial amount of calcium.

Helpful Hints:

a. Use smelts in place of *tehkuh* in dish.
b. This dish can also be cooked in an oven if so desired. Put all ingredients except parsley in an oven dish and mix well. Cover and cook in a 375-degree oven until done. Garnish with parsley and serve with boiled rice.

fresh palm oil, olive oil, or
   groundnut (peanut) oil
   amount desired
1 large white onion, thinly sliced
2 stalks celery (trim each root
   end and wash; very thinly
   slice each stalk crosswise)
1 large tomato, chopped
fresh ginger, finely chopped
   and to taste
1 sweet bell pepper, chopped
fresh hot peppers, chopped and
   to taste

ground black pepper to taste
salt to taste
2 pounds **tehkuh** (smelts),
   cleaned
1 pint fresh oysters
4 tablespoons tomato paste
1 cup fresh poponda or basil,
   chopped
4 green onions, chopped
ground cumin to taste
chopped parsley for garnishing

1. Add oil, white onion, celery, tomatoes, ginger, peppers, and salt to heated skillet. Stir, cover, and cook for about 7 minutes, mixing often.

2. Stir in rest of ingredients except parsley. Without again mixing, cover and cook only until fish is done, about 5 minutes.

3. Spoon into a serving dish, garnish with parsley, and serve hot.

Deep-Fried Tehkuh (Smelts) with Hot Curry Fish Sauce

Helpful Hints:

a. Fish must be moist when it is put in *mbagbehnyeh* mixture. Other flour choices are rice flour and cornmeal.
b. Make Hot Curry Fish Sauce (p. 71) to serve with fish.
c. Serve with boiled plantain, cooked rice, or bread of choice.

1 cup or more mbagbehnyeh
   mixture, rice flour, or cornmeal
ground hot pepper to taste
ground black pepper to taste
grated fresh ginger to taste
grated lime peel

juice of same lime
salt to taste
oil for deep frying, about 3
   inches deep
3 pounds tehkuh (smelts),
   cleaned

1. Put in a mixing bowl all ingredients except oil and smelts and mix well.

2. Heat oil to 375 degrees in a skillet or use Suma's Onion Oil Test (p. 228).

3. Coat fish with flour, put in hot oil (do not crowd fish), and fry until golden.

4. Remove it from oil, drain, and arrange in a serving dish. Top with Hot Curry Fish Sauce and serve.

Butterfish and Seafood in Nonoh Sauce

This dish is prepared in many African countries using local *nonoh* (African yogurt), herbs, and spices.

Helpful Hints:

a. Use plain yogurt instead of *nonoh*.
b. Serve with cooked rice.

groundnut (peanut) oil, amount desired
1 white onion, chopped
1 red sweet bell pepper, chopped
fresh hot peppers, chopped and to taste
fresh ginger, finely chopped and to taste
3 white mushrooms, sliced
1 cup coconut milk; use store bought or see How to Make Coconut Milk (p. 239)

salt to taste
2 pounds butterfish or fish of choice, cut up
¼ pound scallops, chopped
¼ pound shrimp, cleaned, deveined and chopped
1 cup nonoh (plain yogurt)
3 green onions, chopped
2 cloves garlic, crushed
chopped mint leaves for garnishing

1. Put oil, white onions, peppers, ginger, and mushrooms in a heated skillet that is over medium heat. Stir and cook for about 7 minutes.

2. Add coconut milk and salt and bring to a gentle boil. (Don't let pot boil over.)

3. Put fish in liquid, cover, and cook only until it flakes easily when fork tested.

4. Put only fish in a serving dish and keep warm. If sauce is more than you want, reduce by cooking longer to lower volume to amount desired.

5. Stir in rest of ingredients except mint leaves. Bring to a gentle boil and cook only for about 3 to 4 minutes.

6. Remove from heat and spoon sauce over fish. Garnish with mint leaves and serve hot.

Manye Salmon Iepapa (Patties) with Mangoes

This dish is to remember beautiful Manye Daramy.

This dish is from many countries in Africa. It is elegant, delicious, and easy to make. Many also use local fish, herbs, and spices.

Helpful Hints:

a. Use center cut of salmon because it is easy to flake. If so desired, other kinds of fish may also be used.
b. Make larger *iepapa* (patties) because smaller ones dry easily.
c. Hot pepper and ginger can irritate the skin. We suggest that you use gloves when making *iepapa*.

2 pounds center cut salmon (flake it with a fork; don't use skin and bones)
1 egg, lightly beaten (use half in dish)
grated peel of 1 lime
3 green onions, chopped
curry powder to taste
grated fresh ginger to taste
salt to taste
groundnut (peanut) oil, amount desired
2 tablespoons unground roasted sesame seeds

parsley leaves to line serving platter
2 large tomatoes, seeds removed and chopped
1 large green mango and 1 ripe, firm one, peeled (cut meat into chunks, keep green ones separate from ripe ones)
1 green sweet pepper, chopped
hot peppers, chopped and to taste
juice of half lime
chopped parsley for garnishing

1. Put in a mixing bowl fish flakes, egg, and half each of lime peel and green onions; add some curry, ginger, salt, and both peppers. Mix well and make *iepapa* (patties).

2. Add oil to heated skillet that is over medium heat. Sprinkle both sides of each *iepapa* with roasted sesame, lightly pressing down so that sesame seeds do not fall off.

3. Lay each *iepapa* in skillet and cook on one side, turn over, and cook on the other side. Cooking time depends on thickness of *iepapa*. Do not overcook.

4. Remove from skillet and arrange on a platter lined with parsley and set aside.

5. Add to same skillet more oil as needed. Stir in tomatoes, green mangoes, peppers, and salt. Cook for about 3 minutes.

6. Stir in rest of ingredients, cover, and heat through. Garnish *iepapa* with mango mixture and parsley in that order and serve.

Great Scarcies Fish Balls

This and other kinds of fish balls are commonly made in many African countries.

Helpful Hints:

a. Use any fish of choice.
b. Prepare Hot Curry Fish Sauce (p. 71) to spoon over fish balls.
c. Hot pepper and ginger can irritate the skin and mucous membranes. You may need to use gloves when making this dish.
d. Serve with cooked rice.

2 pounds fish fillet of choice, coarsely ground
⅓ cup groundnut (peanut) butter
4 green onions, finely chopped
grated fresh ginger to taste
2 cloves garlic, crushed
1 cup mushrooms, chopped

fresh hot peppers, chopped and to taste
salt to taste
groundnut (peanut) or vegetable oil for frying
chopped parsley for garnishing

1. Put in a mixing bowl all ingredients except oil and parsley, and mix. Shape by spoonfuls into balls or egg shapes.

2. Add oil to skillet, about 1 inch deep. Heat to 375 degrees or see Suma's Onion Oil Test (p. 228).

3. Fry balls until golden. Remove from oil, drain, and arrange in a serving dish. Spoon Hot Curry Fish Sauce over balls, garnish with chopped parsley, and serve with rice.

Nile Fish Balls

Fish is plentiful along the River Nile, including Nile perch (tilapia). This and many other fish dishes are prepared in the region. The use of domestic herbs and spices help to celebrate and promote local flavor. Please enjoy this great dish.

Helpful Hints:

a. Use Nile perch (tilapia) or white fish of choice to make dish.
b. Serve with boiled rice, cooked green bananas, boiled plantains, white or sweet potatoes, cassava, or bread of choice.

2 pounds Nile perch (tilapia) fillet or white fish of choice, coarsely ground
1 cup partially ground, uncooked, fresh or frozen corn
1 to 2 tablespoons cornmeal
3 green onions, chopped
½ cup poponda (fresh basil), chopped
ground fresh ginger to taste
1 beaten egg

fresh hot peppers, chopped and to taste
grated peel of 1 lemon
salt to taste
4 cups or more fish stock (see How to Make Fish Stock, p. 78)
juice of same lemon
chopped green onions for garnishing

1. Put in a mixing bowl all ingredients except fish stock, lemon juice, and green onions and mix well. Shape by spoonfuls into fish balls.

2. Bring to a gentle boil fish stock, lemon juice, salt, and pepper.

3. Drop balls, one at a time, into liquid, and simmer until corn-meal is cooked.

4. Put balls and broth in a serving dish, garnish with chopped green onions, and serve.

How to Make Fish Stock

It is not necessary to use fish stock in every fish dish. But when it is needed, it helps to give the dish its identity.

Helpful Hints:

a. Fish trimmings, such as bones, heads, and tails; and vegetables, herbs, and spices make the best fish stock.
b. Make stock the way you like it. Add only the herbs and spices you like in the amount you want. Then cook slowly to bring out the goodness.

fish trimmings, amount desired
vegetables (celery, etc.)

herbs and spices (parsley, onions, peppers, etc.)
water

1. Put all ingredients except water in a large, heavy saucepan.
2. Cover with water so that water is about 2 inches above the rest of ingredients. Cover and bring to a boil. Simmer for 20–30 minutes and allow to cool. Run broth through a strainer that is lined with cheesecloth and use as needed.

Variations:

How to Make Chicken Stock: Put in pot chicken bones, ends of wings, backs, and other unwanted parts. Cover with water and bring to a boil. Simmer for about a half hour, cool, and strain.
How to Make Beef Stock: Put beef bones in a pot, cover with water, and simmer for about a half hour. Cool and run broth through a strainer.

How to Make Vegetable Stock: Put vegetable trimmings in a pot. Cover with water and cook for about 20 minutes. Cool and run through a lined strainer.

How to Make Shrimp Broth: Put in a pot shrimp heads, shells, tails, and water (amount desired). Cook for about 20 minutes, drain, and use broth.

African Fisherman's Hot Pepper Soup

This dish is to honor fishermen from Africa and around the world who work hard daily for their catch.

Helpful Hints:

a. African fishermen first sell their catch, then they bring home whatever is not sold. That is why this dish has anything and everything caught in the net, which is the beauty of the dish.

b. Save all shellfish trimmings to make Makasii Shellfish Stock (recipe follows); it is a good source of calcium.

c. As the name indicates, this is a spicy hot dish. Make it only as hot as you want it. Use only the ingredients you want in the amount you want to eat.

d. This dish is served with cooked green bananas, boiled plantain, or boiled rice.

groundnut (peanut) oil, amount desired

1 large white onion, chopped

grated fresh ginger to taste

2 large tomatoes, chopped

⅓ pound small button mushrooms, sliced

1 sweet bell pepper, chopped

fresh hot peppers, chopped and to taste

6 cups plus Makasii Shellfish Stock or liquid of choice

½ pound fish steak of choice, cut up

1 pound crawfish (clean; save heads and other trimmings)

6 small soft-shell crabs (clean; save trimmings)

1 medium lobster (clean; save head and other trimmings)

6 large sea scallops, each cut into two

¼ pound medium shrimp (clean; save trimmings)

½ pint fresh oysters
6 green onions, chopped
3 tablespoons tomato paste

juice of 1 lemon
grated peel of same lemon
salt to taste

1. Add to cooking pot oil, white onion, ginger, chopped tomatoes, mushrooms, and sweet and hot peppers. Stir and cook until white onions are tender.

2. Add Makasii Shellfish Stock and bring to a boil.

3. Stir in rest of ingredients and bring to another boil. Cook for about 6 minutes and serve hot.

Makasii Shellfish Stock

This fish stock is high in calcium, requires no cooking time, and it is very easy to make.

crawfish heads, shells, and
other trimmings
lobster heads, shells, and
other trimmings

crab shell and other trimmings
shrimp heads, shell, and other
trimmings
water

1. Crush all trimmings. (African women crush them in a wooden mortar with a wooden pestle.) Put in a mixing bowl, add water (amount desired), and mix.

2. Line a strainer with cheesecloth and strain mixture through before using stock.

Shenge Red Snapper in Coconut Lemon Sauce

Red snapper is found in African waters, including those around Shenge's Shebro country. This is the home of paramount chief

Madam Honoria Bailor Caulker of Sierra Leone, West Africa. The Shebros and many other tribes enjoy this dish. We hope you do, too.

Helpful Hints:

a. Cook fish with or without the head, and do not overcook.
b. Serve with boiled rice.

2 medium red snappers, each cleaned and cut in half (do not fillet fish)
salt to taste
3 white mushrooms, sliced
grated fresh ginger to taste
grated peel of 1 lemon
juice of same lemon
2 cups Liiyah Coconut Milk (p. 62)

2 cloves garlic, crushed
fresh hot peppers, chopped and to taste
1 red sweet bell pepper, chopped
4 green onions, chopped
thinly sliced fresh coconut for garnishing
chopped parsley for garnishing
lemon wedges

1. Season fish with salt and set it aside. Put in saucepan all ingredients except sliced coconut, parsley, fish, green onions, and lemon wedges. Bring to a boil over reduced heat and cook for about 7 minutes.
2. Add fish and green onions. Cook only until fish easily flakes when tested with a fork.
3. Put fish only in a serving dish. Reduce sauce as desired and spoon it over fish. Garnish with coconut and parsley in that order and serve with lemon wedges.

Red Snapper in Pumpkin Seed Poponda Sauce

This dish is served in many countries in Africa.

Helpful Hints:

a. May also use other fish of choice.
b. Serve with cooked green bananas or boiled rice.

groundnut (peanut) oil,
 amount desired
1 white onion, chopped
fresh ginger, chopped and
 to taste
1 red sweet pepper, chopped
fresh hot peppers, chopped
 and to taste
½ cup raw pumpkin seeds,
 shelled (grind well and
 mix with 1 cup water)
2 cloves garlic, crushed

salt to taste
2 pounds red snapper fillets,
 cut up
½ pound large shrimp, each
 deveined but not shelled
3 green onions, chopped
1 cup fresh poponda (fresh
 basil), chopped
4 chunks fresh pineapple
4 chunks medium ripe mango
chopped parsley for garnishing

1. Put oil, white onion, ginger, and peppers in a heated skillet; stir and cook until onions are tender.

2. Stir in rest of ingredients except fish, shrimp, green onions, basil, parsley, mangoes, and pineapples.

3. Bring to a boil and cook for about 7 minutes.

4. Add to skillet rest of ingredients except parsley. Cover and cook only until fish flakes easily when tested with a fork.

5. Remove from heat and put in a serving dish, garnish with chopped parsley, and serve hot.

African Kpee Kpee (Electric Catfish) Fried Fish

This fish has a powerful, built-in electricity that is ready to be delivered on demand. The words *kpee kpee* are the Mende verbal expression of the feel of electricity as it travels through the body. Nature equipped the fish with what I call a shocking defense mechanism. The high electric voltage compels anyone to immediately drop the fish when it transmits severe electric shock on contact.

When I was growing up, I went fishing with Grandmother, other female relatives, and friends. I caught in my little fishing net (*mbehbeh*) a smooth-skinned, seemingly helpless but fast-moving fish. It was large enough to cause some excitement. Little did I know that I was about to get the shock of my life. I grabbed it in the net with my right hand and let out a loud yell that brought all of the women running in my direction. I did not need to explain what had happened. The way I held my right hand, supported by my left, said it all. For a long time I heard stories about that day's event. Like any fish story, most of them were not quite the way I had remembered it.

This dish is from West African countries. Other names may be used for the same dish and fish.

Helpful Hints:

a. Use *kpee kpee* or other catfish of choice because they all are very delicious.
b. Other ingredients you can add to fish before frying are as follows: other herbs and spices of choice; roasted sesame seeds; dry rice flour; dry cornmeal.
c. Spoon Kpee Kpee Hot Sauce (recipe follows) over fish and serve with cooked green bananas, plantain, boiled rice, or bread of choice.

grated peel of 1 lime
juice of same lime
ground hot pepper to taste
grated fresh ginger to taste
salt to taste

2 pounds catfish fillets or
amount desired
groundnut (peanut) oil or vegetable oil of choice
rice flour

1. Put in a mixing bowl all ingredients except oil and rice flour and mix well.
2. Add oil to heated skillet, about 3 inches deep. Heat it to 375 degrees or use Suma's Onion Oil Test (p. 228).
3. Dust each piece of fish with flour, drop it in oil (do not crowd), and fry until golden. Remove from oil, drain, and serve with Kpee Kpee Hot Sauce (p. 84).

Kpee Kpee Hot Sauce

Helpful Hint:

Make only as spicy as you want it.

⅓ *cup ground fresh hot*
   pepper or to taste
6 green onions, chopped
1 large white onion, chopped
fresh ginger, finely chopped
   and to taste

1 large tomato, chopped
3 tablespoons tomato sauce
salt to taste
sesame or groundnut (peanut)
   oil, amount desired

1. Put all ingredients in a heated pot that is over medium heat, stir, and cover.
2. Cook and stir often until onions and peppers are done. Spoon sauce over *kpee kpee* and serve hot.

Ngakui in Komafaleh Hondii Plasas
(Crabmeat in Mushroom Spinach Sauce)

This special mushroom dish is prepared in many parts of Africa. Very often the *komafaleh* mushrooms would be coarsely ground before they are cooked with seafood or meat of choice.

Helpful Hints:

a. Because *komafaleh* mushrooms are not readily available, use mushroom of choice, coarsely ground. Do not soak them or overcook spinach and crabmeat.
b. Serve with boiled rice.

fresh palm oil or groundnut
   (peanut) oil, amount desired
1 white onion, chopped

1 red sweet pepper, chopped
fresh hot peppers, chopped
   and to taste

1½ pounds mushrooms of choice,
    cleaned, coarsely ground
4 tablespoons tomato paste
1 pound fresh or canned
    ngakui (crabmeat), picked
1 pint fresh oysters

1 cup fresh or frozen cooked lima
    beans (cook according to pack-
    age directions and drain)
4 green onions, chopped
½ pound fresh spinach, washed,
    drained, and chopped
salt to taste

1. Put oil, white onion, sweet and hot peppers, mushrooms, and tomato paste in a heated skillet that is over medium heat. Mix often and cook uncovered until almost all liquid is gone.

2. Stir in rest of ingredients and cook only until spinach is cooked but still bright green. Remove from heat and serve hot.

Kpohwoh (Portabella) Mushrooms Stuffed with Crabmeat

Helpful Hints:

a. This can be served as a side dish or with bread of choice.
b. It can also be oven cooked. After mushrooms are stuffed, arrange them in a greased baking dish. Sprinkle with rest of bread crumbs and cheese in that order. Bake uncovered at 375 degrees until done; uncover, bake a few more minutes, and serve hot.

4 medium kpohwoh (porta-
    bella mushrooms)
sesame oil, olive oil, or butter,
    amount desired
salt to taste
1 pound crabmeat, picked
⅔ cup dry bread crumbs

⅓ cup sesame seeds, roasted
    and ground
3 green onions, chopped
1 clove garlic, crushed
fresh ginger, chopped and to taste
fresh hot peppers, chopped and
    to taste
½ cup grated cheese of choice

1. Wipe mushrooms with a damp cloth. Remove and chop stems. Brush the inside and outside with oil or butter and season with salt.

2. Put in a mixing bowl chopped mushroom stems, crabmeat, ⅓ cup bread crumbs, sesame, onions, garlic, ginger, salt, peppers, and butter and mix well. Use ¼ of mixture to stuff each mushroom shell.

3. Add oil to skillet that is over medium heat and arrange mushrooms in skillet. Sprinkle with rest of bread crumbs and cheese in that order.

4. Cook for about 20 minutes, partially covered. Then uncover and cook only until moisture in skillet dries up. Remove from heat and serve hot.

5. You may also arrange mushrooms in an oiled baking dish. Cook in an oven at 370 degrees for 30–40 minutes. Serve hot.

Shrimp and Crab Guyoo Guyoo

This dish is prepared in many parts of Africa. It is the kind of food one would take time to eat and relax on a carefree day. Please enjoy it.

Helpful Hints:

a. Fresh crabs and shrimp are recommended for dish.
b. Serve with roasted breadfruit or bread of choice.

12 soft-shell crabs, cleaned
1–2 pounds large fresh shrimp, deveined but not shelled
*1 cup **poponda** or fresh basil, chopped*
5 green onions, chopped
sesame oil, amount desired

ground hot peppers to taste
2 cloves garlic, crushed
curry powder to taste
salt to taste
⅓ cup roasted and coarsely ground sesame seeds
lemon wedges

1. Add to skillet about 2 tablespoons of water and all ingredients except sesame. Cover, bring to a boil, and cook for about 5 minutes.

2. Uncover and sprinkle with sesame. Increase heat, use two

wooden spoons to stir, and cook until crabs and shrimp are well coated with sesame and there is no liquid left.

3. Remove from heat, put in a *kalabash* or serving platter, and serve with lemon wedges.

Shrimp Gbuhen (Asparagus) Okra Sauce

This dish is from Central, South, and West Africa.

Helpful Hints:

a. The longer you cook okra, the less slimy and less green it becomes.
b. *Gbuhen,* which grows in the African rain forest, looks like asparagus, which will be used in the dish.
c. Serve with boiled rice.

1 large white onion, chopped
groundnut (peanut) oil,
*   amount desired*
1 pound fresh okra (wash,
*   remove ends, and cut into*
*   ½-inch slices)*
1 pound asparagus (wash, re-
*   move tough ends of spears, and*
*   chop into ⅓-inch-long sections)*
2 large fresh tomatoes, chopped
3 tablespoons tomato paste
1 green sweet bell pepper, chopped
fresh ginger, finely chopped
*   and to taste*

2 cloves garlic, crushed
3 large white mushrooms, sliced
⅓ cup (groundnut) peanut butter,
*   mixed with ½ cup water*
fresh hot peppers, chopped and
*   to taste*
grated peel of 1 lime
salt to taste
2 pounds fresh large shrimp,
*   shelled and deveined*
¼ cup roasted, chopped ground-
*   nut (peanut) for garnishing*
chopped parsley for garnishing

1. Cook white onions in oil until they are tender. Stir in rest of ingredients except shrimp, chopped groundnut, and parsley.

2. Cover and cook; stirring often, continue to cook until *gbuhen* (asparagus) are tender.

3. Stir in shrimp and cook for about 8–10 minutes or until they are just done.

4. Remove from heat and put in a serving dish. Garnish with chopped peanuts and parsley in that order, and serve hot with rice.

Shrimp Coffee Rice

ගග

This dish is prepared in different parts of Africa. It is special, unique, and delicious.

Helpful Hint:

Serve rice with Parsley Shrimp Tomato Sauce (recipe follows).

*groundnut (peanut) oil,
    amount desired*
2 cups uncooked regular rice
1 large white onion, chopped
fresh ginger, chopped and to taste
1 cup shredded fresh coconut
*1 cup strong brewed coffee, or
    mix 1 cup hot water with
    amount of instant coffee
    desired*

*fresh hot peppers, chopped and
    to taste*
salt to taste
3 cups water
*1 pound medium fresh shrimp,
    cleaned and deveined*

1. Put oil, rice, onion, and ginger in a heated rice-cooking pot that is over medium heat. Mix with a wooden spoon for about 6 minutes.

2. Stir in rest of ingredients except shrimp. When mixture comes to an active boil, lower heat and put on lid. Cook until rice absorbs about ⅔ of the liquid.

3. Stir in shrimp, cover, and cook over reduced heat until rice is done.

4. Arrange rice in a serving dish. Spoon Parsley Shrimp Tomato Sauce over rice and serve hot.

Parsley Shrimp Tomato Sauce

Helpful Hints:

a. Do not overcook shrimp.
b. Sauce may be served with other kinds of boiled rice.

2 large tomatoes, finely chopped
½ cup fresh parsley, chopped
1 white onion, chopped
groundnut (peanut) oil,
  amount desired
fresh hot peppers, chopped
  and to taste

fresh ginger, chopped and to
  taste
1 sweet pepper, chopped
salt to taste
1 cup fresh shrimp, chopped
3 green onions, chopped

1. Put all ingredients except shrimp and green onions in a heated skillet. Stir often and cook for about 6 minutes.

2. Stir in shrimp and green onions. Cook a few more minutes and remove from heat. Spoon sauce over rice and serve hot.

South African Lobster Aiesha

This classic, elegant dish is prepared in Central, South, and West Africa and is known as much for its looks as for great taste.

Helpful Hints:

a. If frozen lobster tails are used, thaw before cooking.
b. Serve with roasted breadfruit, cooked green bananas, boiled rice, or bread of choice.

2 quarts water
salt to taste

4 fresh or frozen South African
  rock lobster tails (or use other
  lobster tails of choice in
  amount desired)

groundnut (peanut) oil, butter,
  or olive oil, amount desired
3 green onions, chopped
2 large fresh tomatoes, seeded
  and chopped
2 tablespoons tomato paste
1 medium green sweet pepper,
  chopped
fresh hot peppers, chopped and
  to taste

2 cloves garlic, crushed
fresh ginger, finely chopped and
  to taste
1 pound medium shrimp,
  cleaned and deveined
3 large sea scallops, chopped
4 chunks fresh pineapple for
  garnishing
lemon wedges for garnishing
chopped parsley for garnishing

1. In a pot bring water and salt to a rapid boil. Put lobster tails into boiling water. With lid in place, cook for about 10 minutes or until lobsters are done the way you like them.

2. Remove from water and cool enough so that tails feel comfortable to handle.

3. Lay each tail on its back. With a sharp knife, cut shell and some of meat at center, all the way to tail end. (Meat and shell at the back are left intact.) Pull shells apart slightly to expose more of meat.

4. Add oil to skillet that is over medium heat. For 4 minutes stir and cook in oil all ingredients except shrimp, scallops, green onions, pineapple, parsley, and lemon.

5. Stir in shrimp, scallops, and green onions. Cook 3 more minutes or until shrimp and scallops are done to your liking.

6. Put some of shrimp sauce in a serving platter. Arrange lobster tails over sauce and put rest of sauce over them. Garnish with pineapple, lemon wedges, and parsley in that order and serve.

Oyster Coconut Curry

This dish is made in East, West, and South African countries with possible use of other seafoods, herbs, and spices.

Helpful Hint:

Serve with boiled rice.

*groundnut (peanut) oil, ¼ cup
    or amount desired*
1 large white onion, chopped
*1 pound medium button mush-
    rooms, cleaned (each cut in half)*
1 sweet pepper, chopped
*fresh hot peppers, chopped and
    to taste*
*2 pints large fresh oysters
    (drain and save juice)*

*1 cup Liiyah Coconut Milk
    (p. 62)*
⅓ cup shredded fresh coconut
curry powder to taste
grated peel of 1 lime
*juice of same lime or amount
    desired*
salt to taste
3 green onions, chopped
chopped parsley for garnishing

1. Add oil, white onion, mushrooms, and peppers to heated skillet that is over medium heat. Stir and cook until onions are tender.

2. Stir in oyster juice and rest of ingredients except oysters, green onions, and parsley. Stirring often, cook until liquid is reduced to desired amount.

3. Add oysters and green onions; cook 8 minutes or only until oysters are done just the way you like them.

4. Put in a serving dish. Garnish with parsley and serve hot.

Fish and Scallops in Igusii Sauce

This dish is prepared in Central, South, and West African countries. Other seafoods may also be used.

Helpful Hints:

a. *Igusii* are protein-rich seeds that look like pumpkin or squash seeds. The raw seeds are crushed and used as sauce thickener in many African dishes. Unroasted, shelled pumpkin seeds are used in this dish. The result is a delicious, rich, white sauce without milk or cholesterol.

b. Serve with boiled rice.

1 pound sea scallops
*1 pound fish steak of choice,
    cut up*

salt to taste
*groundnut (peanut) oil,
    amount desired*

1 *white onion, chopped*
1 *small red sweet pepper,*
    chopped
fresh ginger, finely chopped
    and to taste
½ *cup shelled, raw pumpkin*
    seeds, well ground
fresh hot peppers, chopped and
    to taste

2 *cloves garlic, crushed*
1 *cup plus fish stock, water, or*
    coconut milk; use store bought
    or see How to Make Coconut
    Milk (p. 239)
4 *green onions, chopped*
chopped fresh parsley for
    garnishing

1. If large sea scallops are used, cut each in half. Mix together scallops, fish, and salt and set aside.

2. Add oil, white onions, sweet peppers, and ginger to heated skillet that is over medium heat. Cook and mix for about 5 minutes.

3. Mix ground pumpkin seeds with liquid and add them to skillet; also add rest of ingredients except scallops, fish, green onions, and parsley. Bring to a boil and cook for about 6 minutes.

4. Stir in green onions, fish, and scallops. Cook only until scallops are done the way you like them.

5. If liquid is more than desired, put everything in a serving dish except liquid, boil it down to lower volume. Spoon it over scallops and fish. Garnish with parsley and serve.

Mattru Jong Oyster Balls with Oyster Sauce

Oyster balls are truly African, prepared in many countries. They are delectable, special, and easy to make.

Helpful Hints:

a. Prepare Mattru Jong Oyster Sauce (recipe follows) to mix with oyster balls.

b. Hot pepper and ginger can irritate the skin and mucous membranes. We suggest that you use gloves when making balls.

c. Serve with boiled rice.

3 pints fresh oysters drained,
   coarsely ground or chopped
   (save juice to add to Mattru
   Jong Oyster Sauce)
⅓ cup groundnut (peanut) butter
1 cup mushrooms, finely chopped
3 green onions, chopped
fresh ginger, finely chopped
   and to taste

grated peel of 1 lime; use only
   half (save other half to add to
   Mattru Jong Oyster Sauce)
fresh hot peppers, finely chopped
   and to taste
salt to taste
groundnut (peanut) or corn oil
   for frying

1. Put all the ingredients except oil and oyster juice in a mixing bowl, mix, and shape by spoonfuls into balls.

2. Heat oil (about 2 inches deep) to 375 degrees in a skillet over medium heat. Use Suma's Onion Oil Test (p. 228) as needed. Fry balls until golden on all sides.

3. Remove from oil, drain, and set aside.

Mattru Jong Oyster Sauce

Helpful Hint:

Sauce without oyster balls may also be served with boiled rice.

groundnut (peanut) oil,
   amount desired
1 white onion, thinly sliced
fresh ginger, finely chopped
   and to taste
1 clove garlic, crushed
1 large tomato, chopped
reserved oyster juice
reserved ½ grated peel of lime
3 green onions, chopped
3 tablespoons tomato paste
1 cup poponda or fresh basil,
   chopped

3 white mushrooms, sliced
fresh hot peppers, chopped and
   to taste
salt to taste
1 pint fresh oysters, drained
   (save liquid)
Mattru Jong Oyster Balls
roasted groundnuts (peanuts)
   for garnishing
chopped parsley for garnishing

1. Add oil, white onion, ginger, garlic, and chopped tomato to heated skillet that is over medium heat. Cook and stir until onions are tender.

2. Stir in rest of ingredients except parsley, groundnuts (peanuts), and oysters. Bring to a boil and cook for about 2 minutes. Stir in oyster and cook another 2 minutes.

3. Gently stir in oyster balls and heat through. Put in a serving dish, garnish with groundnuts and parsley in that order, and serve hot.

GREAT EGYPT, ONE GLORY OF AFRICA

I have met a number of people who, for one reason or another, were not aware that ancient Egypt—land of biblical times, home of the Pharaohs, the pyramids, papyrus, and early civilization—is in Africa.

One summer I wore a comfortable African outfit and went to the school library. There I met a lady who later told me that she was a graduate student in history. During our conversation the friendly student said, "I like to talk with people from foreign countries because I always learn from them." Continuing, she added, "My boyfriend is from Egypt. But I believe this is the first time that I have ever met an African." I did not tell her that her boyfriend was as much an African as I was because I did not want her to feel embarrassed. A middle-aged pastor once said to me, "Until a few years ago, I did not know that Egypt is in Africa."

Recipes from Egypt do belong in an African cookbook because Egypt has always been part of the African continent. Please enjoy the dishes.

Lamb

One way Egyptians enjoy eating lamb is by cooking it with okra. As you may know, okra is a well-known and -liked vegetable from Africa. Algerians, Ethiopians, Libyans, Moroccans, Sudanies, Tunisians, and people from all of North, Central, East, South, and West African countries like to eat lamb cooked with okra.

Lamb in Okra Mint Sauce

Helpful Hints:

a. Young and tender okra is always best for cooking.
b. This dish is served with steamed *cous cous*, bread of choice, or boiled rice.

olive oil, amount desired
1 pound boneless lamb or
*   amount desired, cut up*
1 large white onion, chopped
2 large tomatoes, chopped
3 tablespoons tomato paste
3 cloves garlic, crushed
fresh hot pepper, chopped
*   and to taste*

ground black pepper to taste
salt to taste
2 pounds fresh okra (wash,
*   remove ends, and cut into*
*   ⅓-inch slices)*
4 green onions, chopped
mint leaves, chopped and to taste
chopped fresh parsley for
*   garnishing*

1. Add oil to preheated skillet that is over medium heat. Lightly brown meat in oil, add white onion, and cook for about 4 minutes.

2. Stir in all ingredients except okra, green onions, parsley, and mint leaves. Stirring occasionally, cover and cook until meat is more than half done. Add a little water if needed.

3. Add okra and cook until meat is done.

4. Stir in green onions and mint, and cook a few more minutes. Put in a serving dish, garnish with parsley, and serve hot.

Lamb in Kobo Kobo Mushroom Sauce

This dish is prepared in many countries in Africa. Many use local herbs and spices.

Helpful Hints:

a. To keep it from turning dark, peel *kobo kobo* (eggplant) just before cooking it.
b. Serve with boiled rice or bread of choice.

1 large young kobo kobo (egg-plant)
groundnut (peanut) oil, amount desired
1 pound boneless lamb or amount desired, cut up
½ pound pearl onions
6 large white mushrooms, sliced
2 cloves garlic, crushed
1 sweet red bell pepper, chopped

grated peel of 1 lime
3 tablespoons tomato paste
1 fresh tomato, chopped
grated fresh ginger to taste
fresh hot peppers, chopped and to taste
salt to taste
4 green onions, chopped
chopped fresh mint leaves for garnishing

1. Peel *kobo kobo* (eggplant) and cut into cubes.
2. Add oil to heated skillet that is over medium heat. Cook and stir meat until light brown.
3. Stir in pearl onions and cook until onions are tender. Add rest of ingredients except *kobo kobo*, green onions, and mint leaves. Stirring occasionally, continue to cook until meat is almost done.
4. Stir in *kobo kobo* and green onions. Cook only until *kobo kobo* and meat are done. Put in a serving dish, garnish with mint leaves, and serve hot.

Fatmata's Lamb and Shrimp in Curry-Coconut Sauce

This dish is to remember Fatmata Fulamusu Kallon.

This special lamb dish is prepared in East, West, and South African countries. Local herbs and spices are often used.

Helpful Hints:

a. To toast coconut slices, add just enough groundnut (peanut) oil to coat bottom of heated skillet that is over reduced heat. Lay coconut slices in skillet. Lightly brown one side, turn, and brown the other side. (Watch carefully because coconut burns easily.) Remove from oil and drain well.
b. Serve dish hot with African Rice Balls (p. 152), garnished with toasted coconut slices.

groundnut (peanut) oil,
amount desired
1 pound boneless lamb or
amount desired, cut up
1 large white onion, chopped
grated fresh ginger to taste
2 cups coconut milk; use store
bought or see How to Make
Coconut Milk (p. 239)
curry powder to taste
1 sweet bell pepper, chopped
2 large tomatoes, chopped

3 tablespoons tomato paste
fresh hot peppers, chopped and
to taste
12 thinly sliced fresh coconut
slices toasted in oil (see Help-
ful Hints above)
salt to taste
10 large shrimp, shelled and
deveined
3 green onions, chopped
chopped parsley for garnishing

1. Add oil to heated skillet that is over medium heat. Cook and stir meat in oil until light brown on all sides.
2. Stir in white onions and ginger; cook until onions are tender. Add to meat all ingredients except shrimp, toasted coconut, green onions, and parsley.
3. Cover and cook, stirring occasionally, until meat is tender. Stir in shrimp and green onions, cook a few more minutes or until shrimp are done.

4. Remove from heat and put in a serving dish. Garnish with parsley and serve.

Lamb and Mint in Green Peas

∾

This dish is served in many parts of Africa.

Helpful Hints:

a. Cook peas only until they are tender but bright green. (Do not overcook.)

b. Serve with boiled rice, cooked green bananas, or plantains.

sesame oil, amount desired
⅓ pound pearl onions
1 pound boneless lamb or amount desired (cut into bite-size portions)
fresh ginger, chopped and to taste
2 large fresh tomatoes, chopped
3 tablespoons tomato paste
4 large fresh mushrooms, chopped
2 cloves garlic, crushed

fresh hot peppers, chopped and to taste
ground black pepper to taste
salt to taste
3 cups fresh or frozen green peas
fresh mint, chopped and to taste
4 green onions, chopped
¼ cup roasted and ground sesame for garnishing

1. Add oil, pearl onions, meat, and ginger to skillet that is over medium heat. Stir and cook until onions are tender.

2. Stir in rest of ingredients except peas, ground sesame, mint leaves, and green onions. Cover and cook, stirring occasionally, until meat is tender.

3. Add peas, mint, and green onions. Cook only until peas are tender but bright green. Remove from heat and put in a serving dish, garnish with sesame, and serve hot.

Lamb Langoyama

This dish is prepared in Central, South, and West African countries. Many people enjoy eating it, and it is easy to make. Try it.

Helpful Hints:

a. Peel *kobo kobo* (eggplants), cut into slices, and put in a colander. Sprinkle with salt and set colander over a bowl to catch liquid. Allow to drain for about half an hour. Then put *kobo kobo* in a clean cloth and gently wring or squeeze out as much liquid as possible before cooking it.
b. When it is time to add salt, don't forget that you already added some salt to eggplant.
c. Serve with boiled rice or bread of choice.

groundnut (peanut) oil, amount desired
1 pound ground lamb or amount desired
1 medium white onion, chopped
1 sweet red bell pepper, chopped
fresh hot peppers, chopped and to taste
2 cups **kpohwoh** (portabella) mushrooms, chopped
grated fresh ginger to taste
2 cloves garlic, crushed

2 large kobo kobo (eggplants); peel and squeeze out liquid (see Helpful Hints above)
1 bunch green onions, chopped
4 tablespoons tomato paste
salt to taste
⅔ cup roasted groundnuts (peanuts), chopped
⅔ cup fresh coconut, shredded
chopped fresh mint leaves for garnishing

1. Add oil, meat, white onion, peppers, mushrooms, ginger, and garlic to a heated skillet that is over medium heat. Stir and cook until onions are tender and most of liquid is gone.

2. Stir in rest of ingredients except mint leaves, coconut, and groundnuts (peanuts). Cook for about 10 minutes or until *kobo kobo* is done or becomes soft.

3. Add coconut and nuts and heat through. Put in a serving dish, garnish with mint leaves, and serve hot.

Asmaow's Lamb with Mango Fahnima

This dish is prepared in most African countries. Many use local herbs and spices.

Helpful Hint:

This dish can be served with boiled rice, cooked green bananas, or roasted breadfruit.

1½ pounds boneless lamb leg, cut into cubes
¼ cup roasted sesame seeds
salt to taste
grated fresh ginger to taste
groundnut (peanut) oil, ¼ cup or amount desired
⅓ pound pearl onions
2 large tomatoes, seeds removed and cut into chunks
1 sweet pepper, chopped
fresh hot peppers, chopped and to taste
3 large medium ripe mangoes, peeled and meat cut into chunks
1 bunch green onions, chopped
fresh poponda (basil), chopped and to taste
chopped mint leaves for garnishing
3 tablespoons tomato paste
honey to taste

1. In a bowl, combine meat, sesame seeds, salt, and some of the ginger.

2. Add oil to a heated skillet that is over medium heat and lightly brown meat. Stir in about 3 tablespoons of water, cover, and cook on reduced heat 10–12 minutes or until meat is tender.

3. Put meat in a bowl and set it aside. Return same skillet to heat and add some oil as desired. Stir in pearl onions and rest of ginger. Cook 3 minutes or until onions are tender.

4. Stir in tomatoes and peppers. Cover and cook for about 5 minutes. Add all ingredients except meat, honey, and mint leaves. After mixing, cover and cook until thoroughly heated through.

5. Add honey to taste and gently stir in meat. Cook 3–5 minutes or only until mangoes are just done. Put in serving dish, garnish with mint leaves, and serve.

Ndodeh (Pork)

As you probably know, there are wild and domesticated pigs in Africa. Both animals look alike and taste much the same.

Pork and Chicken in Poponda Sauce

Helpful Hints:

a. When a recipe calls for hot peppers and fresh ginger, remember that fresh ginger is spicy hot by nature. The more mature the ginger, the more spicy it will taste.
b. Because *poponda* is not readily available, fresh basil, the closest ingredient in aroma, is often used.
c. Serve with boiled rice.

fresh palm oil or groundnut (peanut) oil, amount desired
1 pound lean pork steak or amount desired, cut up
1 pound boneless chicken thighs, cut up
salt to taste
1 large white onion, chopped
½ pound fresh button mushrooms, each cut in half
⅓ cup fresh ginger strips (julienne) or to taste

2 cloves garlic, crushed
1 red bell pepper, cut in ¼-inch strips, lengthwise
2 large tomatoes, cut into chunks
3 tablespoons tomato paste
fresh hot peppers, chopped and to taste
3 green onions, chopped
1 cup fresh poponda (basil), chopped

1. Add oil to a preheated skillet that is over medium heat. Season pork and chicken with salt and brown in oil.

2. To meat add white onion, mushrooms, ginger, and garlic. Mix, cover, and cook for 5 minutes.

3. Stir in rest of ingredients except green onions and *poponda* (basil).

4. Cover and cook, stirring occasionally, until both pork and chicken are tender.

5. Stir in green onions and *poponda* (basil). Remove from heat and serve hot.

Pork and White Snapper in Coconut-Lime Sauce

൭

This dish is prepared in Central, East, and South Africa with possible use of other meats, herbs, and spices.

Helpful Hint:

Serve with boiled rice.

groundnut (peanut) oil,
  amount desired
1 white onion, chopped
⅓ pound kpohwoh (porta-
  bella) mushrooms, chopped
fresh ginger, chopped and
  to taste
1 pound boneless pork, cut
  into pieces (season with salt
  just before cooking)
2 cups Liiyah Coconut Milk
  (p. 62)

1 large fresh tomato, chopped
1 sweet bell pepper, chopped
grated peel of 1 lime
juice of same lime
fresh hot peppers, chopped and
  to taste
salt to taste
1 pound snapper fillet, cut up
curry powder to taste
3 green onions, chopped
chopped coriander for garnishing

1. Add oil, white onion, mushrooms, and ginger to skillet. Cook and stir until onions are tender.

2. Stir in rest of ingredients except fish, green onions, coriander, and curry. Bring mixture to a boil.

3. Cover and cook until pork is almost done. Stir in all ingredients except coriander and green onions. Cook only until fish flakes easily when tested with a fork. If sauce is more than you desire, put meat and fish in serving dish and reduce it to your liking.

4. Stir in green onions and spoon sauce over meat. Garnish with coriander and serve hot with rice.

Pork Spareribs and Cabbage in Groundnut Sauce

ை

This dish is prepared in Central, South, and West African countries with possible use of other meats, herbs, and spices.

Helpful Hints:

a. We try to cook with as little animal fat as possible. Do the same only if you want. Cut spareribs into individual portions and remove excess fat. Brown ribs and drain fat before adding cooking liquid.
b. Serve with cooked green bananas, plantains, potatoes, or boiled rice.

1 medium head green cabbage
2 pounds spareribs or amount
desired
salt to taste
1 large white onion, chopped
⅓ cup groundnut (peanut) but-
ter mixed with 1 cup water

2 large tomatoes, chopped
2 cloves garlic, chopped
1 sweet pepper, chopped
fresh hot peppers, chopped and
to taste
roasted groundnuts (peanuts) for
garnishing

1. Remove root end of cabbage; wash and cut it into wedges. Add to pot spareribs, salt, and cover with water. More water may still be needed.
2. With lid in place, bring pot to a boil. Stirring occasionally, cook on low heat until meat is about three-quarters done.
3. Stir in rest of ingredients except nuts for garnishing; continue to cook until meat is done and tender.
4. Put in a serving dish, garnish with groundnuts (peanuts), and serve hot.

Njeh (Goatmeat)

Goatmeat in Ohleleh Shrimp Sauce

If you have never eaten goatmeat, cook it in this unusual bean sauce and see how delicious they are together.

Helpful Hints:

a. When adding liquid to beans, it is suggested that hot—not cold—liquid is slowly stirred in until sauce is desired thickness.
b. Serve with boiled rice.

*2 pounds boneless goatmeat
 or amount desired
fresh palm oil or groundnut
 (peanut) oil, amount desired
1 white onion, chopped
2 large fresh tomatoes, chopped
1 sweet bell pepper, chopped
fresh hot peppers, chopped
 and to taste
3 large white mushrooms,
 chopped*

*2 cloves garlic, crushed
2 cups or more warm liquid (water,
 chicken broth, or coconut milk)
¼–⅓ cup ohleleh beans; see
 How to Prepare Ohleleh
 Beans (p. 30)
1 cup fresh shrimp, chopped
3 green onions, chopped
3 tablespoons tomato paste
ground black pepper to taste
salt to taste*

1. Cut up meat and season with salt.
2. Add oil to heated skillet over medium heat and brown meat in oil. Stir in onion, tomatoes and paste, peppers, mushrooms, and garlic. Cover and cook, mixing occasionally, until meat is almost tender, adding some liquid as needed.
3. Put skillet contents in a pot and set it aside. Add more oil to same skillet. Using a wooden spoon, stir in beans and continue stirring until beans separate.
4. Slowly add hot liquid and stir at the same time until sauce is desired thickness.

5. Stir in meat and rest of ingredients. Bring to a boil and cook until meat is done. Remove from heat and serve hot.

Wild Game

BIRDS

In order to safely and freely move around in the African rain forest, one must learn some basic skills. This is as important and necessary as it is for city dwellers to know how to cross busy streets.

The young African male must go on hunting trips with the elders and *kamajohs* (professional hunters), and he learns safe hunting rules from them. Among many things, he is taught that one does not kill just for the sake of pleasure. "When an animal is killed," he is told, "it must always be done in a spirit of respect for all forms of life. The animal's life is taken away so that people may eat and live." He also learns to protect and keep the forest alive by not abusing or misusing its plants, rivers, animals, and all that make up the environment.

Doohwee in Plantain Poponda Sauce (Duck in Plantain Basil Sauce)

This dish is prepared in many African countries, with possible use of other herbs and spices.

Helpful Hint:

Serve with boiled rice.

2 cups water, 1–2 cups broth,
  or coconut milk
salt to taste
2 wild mallard ducks, cleaned
  and cut up
fresh palm oil or groundnut
  (peanut) oil, ¼ cup or
  amount desired
1 large ripe plantain, peeled
  and chopped
½ pound pearl onions
fresh ginger, finely chopped
  and to taste

2 cloves garlic, crushed
3 large tomatoes, chopped
1 large sweet bell pepper, chopped
fresh hot peppers, chopped and
  to taste
ground black pepper to taste
5 green onions, chopped
1 cup **poponda** (fresh basil),
  chopped
chopped fresh mint leaves for
  garnishing

1. To skillet add water, salt, and duck. Stirring occasionally, cover and cook until meat is about half done. Empty skillet contents into a bowl and return skillet to heat.

2. Add oil, plantain, pearl onions, and ginger to skillet. Stir and cook for 10–12 minutes.

3. Add just meat to skillet. If necessary, remove excess oil from duck broth before adding stock to skillet and more liquid as needed. Stir in rest of ingredients except basil, mint, and green onions.

4. Stirring occasionally, cover and continue to cook until meat is tender.

5. Add green onions and *poponda* (basil), and cook a few more minutes. Put in a serving dish, garnish with mint leaves, and serve.

Hokay in Mushroom Tomato Plasas

This pheasant-like game bird is a favorite dish of many people who work on small farms and live in little villages.

Helpful Hints:

a. Use pheasant or pheasant-like game in dish.
b. Chicken may also be used if so desired.
c. Serve with boiled green bananas, sweet potatoes, or boiled rice.

2 pheasants, cleaned and cut
   into pieces
salt to taste
dry or fresh hot peppers to taste
1 sweet bell pepper, chopped
2 cups or more water
1 pound mushrooms, sliced
1 pound pearl onions
2 cloves garlic, crushed
2 large kibongii (tomatoes),
   chopped

2 whole cloves
ground cumin to taste
¼ cup roasted and ground
   sesame seeds for garnishing
⅓ cup cooked black-eyed peas for
   garnishing (cook according to
   package directions and drain)
½ cup green onions, chopped

1. Put in pot meat, salt, and peppers and mix. Bring to a boil and cook for 5 minutes.

2. Stir in water and rest of ingredients except green onions, black-eyed peas, and ground sesame. With lid in place and stirring occasionally, cook until meat is done.

3. Stir in green onions and cook for 3 more minutes. Put in a serving dish. Garnish with black-eyed peas and sesame seeds in that order and serve hot.

Kohkohyeh Potoh Potoh

This small quail-like bird is plentiful, and it is served in many countries in Africa.

Helpful Hints:

a. Quails, rock cornish hens (game hens), or other small hens may also be used in this dish.

b. Serve with cooked green bananas, roasted breadfruit, or bread of choice.

c. Spicy Hot Groundnuts (Peanuts) (p. 14) should be made in advance.

3 kohkohyeh or cornish hens
salt to taste

groundnut (peanut) oil, ¼–⅓ cup
   or amount desired

curry powder to taste
fresh ginger, grated and to taste
1 large white onion, thinly sliced
1 red sweet bell pepper, sliced
   lengthwise
4 white mushrooms, sliced
fresh hot peppers, chopped and
   to taste
ground cimingii (cinnamon)
   to taste
2 large tomatoes, seeds removed
   and chopped

9 large fresh shrimp, shelled and
   deveined
3 green onions, chopped
2 large, ripe, and firm mangoes
   (peel and cut meat into chunks)
Spicy Hot Groundnuts (Peanuts)
   for garnishing
chopped fresh parsley for
   garnishing
2–3 tablespoons water

1. Wash each bird, split from front neckline all the way down, leaving back intact. Remove chest bone, widen cavity by pulling chest walls apart, but do not sever.

2. Rub birds inside and outside with salt, oil, curry powder, and ginger in that order. Add oil to heated skillet and lay bird in skillet, front side down.

3. Cook and brown, turning once. Add water, cover and cook until meat is tender. Uncover and cook 7 more minutes. Lay birds side by side on serving platter and keep warm.

4. Add rest of ingredients except mangoes, shrimp, nuts, parsley, and green onions to same skillet and add more oil as needed. Cook and mix often until onions and peppers are tender.

5. Stir in shrimp, green onions, and mangoes. Cook only until shrimp are done 7–9 minutes or the way you like them. Put ⅓ of shrimp mixture in each bird cavity, garnish with nuts and parsley, and serve.

COOKING WITH WILD GAME

Ndopah with Greens

Grandmother always cooked *ndopah* (venison) in a clay pot (*poh-veh*) with a handful of sun-dried beans. I later found out that a clay pot is very good for maintaining even temperature. African sun-dried beans and venison take about the same amount of cooking time to become tender. Grandmother tested the beans, which was easier to do. If they were cooked, the meat was also done.

This dish is from all countries in Africa. *Ndopah* (venison), cooked with greens, is common in the African diet.

Helpful Hints:

a. Grandmother believed that this meat should not be cooked in a hurry. To bring out the great natural flavor, it should be cooked slowly, in lots of liquid, until it is tender.
b. Fresh greens must be soaked in plenty of cold water for about an hour before washing. To remove insects that may be present on the leaves, add some salt to soaking water. Wash well and chop before cooking.
c. If possible, mix together kale, mustard greens, and collards to make the dish more interesting.
d. To keep it from turning dark, *kobo kobo* (eggplant) should be washed and cut into chunks just before cooking. (Do not peel unless so desired.)
e. Serve with cooked green bananas or boiled rice.
f. When one simmers greens, the fibers break down; this will result in a softer texture. Boiling greens, however, allows the fibers to remain firm and whole.

2 pounds ndopah (venison) or amount desired, cut up
fresh ginger, finely chopped and to taste
ground black pepper to taste
4 cups plus broth or water

3 pounds greens, cleaned and chopped
1 pound whole fresh okra, washed and each top end removed

½ *cup sun-dried okra (optional)*
½ *pound pearl onions*
1 *pound cherry tomatoes, crushed*
1 *large kpohwoh (portabella) mushroom, chopped*

1 *medium kobo kobo (eggplant), cut into chunks (do not peel)*
whole dry hot peppers to taste
fresh palm oil or sesame oil, ¼ *cup or amount desired*
salt to taste
2 *cups cooked broad lima beans (cook according to package directions, drain)*

1. Add to pot meat, ginger, black pepper and water. Mix, cover, and bring to a boil.
2. Cover over reduced heat, stirring occasionally, until meat is almost done. (Add more liquid as needed.)
3. Stir in rest of ingredients except cooked beans. Increase heat to medium so that the pot is boiling. Continue to cook until meat is done.
4. Stir in beans and cook a few more minutes before serving it hot.

SEHJEH (RABBIT)

An almost countless rabbit population exists in the African wild. To those who are unfamiliar with the taste of this meat, it may surprise you to know that it tastes like chicken, yet it is different. Rabbit is delicious and easy to cook. We hope you enjoy it.

Sehjeh Kondiyama

This is a delicious rabbit dish prepared in Central, East, and West African countries. This dish may also have other names.

Helpful Hint:

Serve with boiled rice.

*fresh palm oil or groundnut
    (peanut) oil, amount desired*
1 sehjeh (rabbit) cut up
1 large white onion, chopped
*fresh ginger, finely chopped and
    to taste*
2 large tomatoes, chopped
3 tablespoons tomato paste
3 cloves garlic, crushed
4 large white mushrooms, sliced

ground black pepper to taste
salt to taste
*1 each large red, yellow, and
    green sweet bell peppers (cut
    each pepper into 1-inch cubes)*
1 cup fresh spinach, chopped
3 green onions, chopped
*chopped fresh mint leaves for
    garnishing*

1. Add oil to heated skillet that is over medium heat. Brown meat on all sides, drain, and set it aside.

2. Adjust the amount of oil, stir in white onion and ginger, and cook until onions are tender.

3. Return meat to skillet; stir in rest of ingredients except sweet peppers, spinach, mint leaves, and green onions. Stirring occasionally and adding as little water as needed, cover and continue to cook until meat is almost done.

4. Stir in the remaining ingredients except chopped mint. Cook only until peppers are done the way you like them. Put in a serving dish, garnish with chopped mint leaves, and serve hot.

Sehjeh in Okra Plasas

This dish is prepared on small farms and in little villages in most countries in Africa.

Helpful Hint:

Serve with boiled rice.

fresh palm oil or vegetable oil,
   amount desired
1 sehjeh (rabbit), cleaned and
   cut up
1 large white onion, chopped
4 green onions, chopped
fresh ginger, finely chopped
   and to taste
2 large tomatoes, chopped
3 cloves garlic, crushed
salt to taste

¼ pound kpohwoh (portabella)
   mushrooms; cleaned and chopped
2 pounds okra, cleaned and ends
   removed (do not slice)
2 cups cooked fresh lima beans
3 tablespoons tomato paste
1 sweet bell pepper, chopped
ground cumin to taste
fresh hot peppers, chopped and
   to taste

1. Add oil to a heated skillet that is over medium heat. Brown meat in oil; remove from oil, drain, and set it aside.

2. Adjust the amount of oil, stir in white onion and ginger, and cook until onions are tender. Stir in tomatoes, garlic, salt, hot pepper, and meat. Stirring occasionally, cover and cook until meat is almost done.

3. Stir in rest of ingredients and continue to cook until meat is done. Remove from heat and serve hot.

Other Varieties of Meat

Heart and Mushroom Sokotoh

This is one of the less tender meats, and it should be cooked slowly in lots of liquid until it is tender. Slow cooking also helps to bring out the wonderful flavor of this meat.

Helpful Hints:

a. To prepare this dense muscle for cooking, cut it in half lengthwise. Remove blood vessels, fat, and other unwanted parts. Wash well under running water before cooking it.
b. Serve with boiled rice.

1 heart (lamb, beef, etc.), prepared for cooking
fresh palm oil or groundnut (peanut) oil; amount desired
1 large white onion, chopped
1 pound white mushrooms, cleaned and sliced
fresh ginger, chopped and to taste
4 green onions, chopped
2 large tomatoes, chopped
3 tablespoons tomato paste

2 cloves garlic, crushed
3 whole cloves
grated peel of 1 lime or 3 fresh lime leaves
fresh hot peppers, chopped and to taste
salt to taste
½ cup green peas, for garnishing (cook only until bright green, drain, and set aside)
chopped mint leaves for garnishing

1. Put meat in a heavy saucepan and cover with water. Bring to a boil, then add salt. With lid in place, cook over reduced heat until meat is tender.
2. Take meat out of broth and allow to cool. Cut it into 2-inch strips lengthwise, then cut each strip into ⅓-inch slices, or cut it as desired.

3. Add oil to preheated skillet that is over medium heat. Stir in white onion, mushrooms, and ginger. Cook until onion is tender.

4. Stir in meat and rest of ingredients except peas; also add some broth, amount desired. (Save rest of broth for another dish.)

5. Cover and cook for another 10–12 minutes. Remove from heat and put in a serving dish. Garnish with peas and mint leaves in that order and serve.

Liver in Onion Curry Sauce

Not only is liver delicious, it is also a very good source of iron. This dish is prepared in many parts of Africa with possible use of local herbs and spices.

Helpful Hints:

a. If you like to peel away the thin membrane before cooking liver, that is your option.

b. Fresh liver is preferred, but if it is frozen, thaw it slowly before cooking.

c. Lamb or calf liver may be used.

d. Overcooking toughens liver.

e. Serve with cooked green bananas, boiled rice, or bread of choice.

groundnut (peanut) oil, amount desired

1 large white onion, thinly sliced

1 red sweet bell pepper, sliced lengthwise

1 pound liver of choice or amount desired, cut into bite-size portions

curry powder to taste

fresh ginger, finely chopped and to taste

fresh hot peppers, chopped and to taste

ground black pepper to taste

salt to taste

⅓ cup roasted groundnuts (peanuts)

chopped green onions (only green part) for garnishing

1. Add oil to preheated skillet that is over medium heat. Stir and cook white onions and sweet peppers until onions are tender. Put mixture in a bowl and set aside.

2. Adjust oil amount, stir, and cook liver and rest of ingredients except groundnuts and green onions. Cook only until liver is done as desired.

3. Stir in onion mixture and groundnuts and heat through. Put in a serving dish, garnish with green onions, and serve hot.

Liver and Mushrooms in Oyster Sauce

This dish is served in many parts of Africa.

Helpful Hint:

Serve dish with steamed *cous cous* or boiled rice.

sesame oil, amount desired
1 large tomato, seeds removed
  and chopped
½ pound white mushrooms,
  thinly sliced
1 sweet green pepper, chopped
fresh hot peppers, chopped
  and to taste
1 pound calf's or lamb's liver,
  cut into bite-size portions

1 pint fresh oysters, drained
6 green onions, chopped at
  1-inch length
grated peel of 1 lemon
½ juice of same lemon
salt to taste
chopped parsley for garnishing
¼ cup roasted and ground
  sesame seeds for garnishing

1. Add oil, tomatoes, mushrooms, and peppers to a preheated skillet that is over medium heat; stir and cook until most of liquid is gone.

2. Stir in rest of ingredients except parsley and sesame seeds. Mix and cook only until liver and oysters are done as desired.

3. Put in a serving dish. Garnish with parsley and sesame before serving.

Chicken Liver and Shrimp

Helpful Hints:

a. Do not overcook.
b. Serve with boiled rice, cooked green bananas, or bread of choice.

*groundnut (peanut) oil,
    amount desired*
1 large white onion, thinly sliced
1 sweet red bell pepper, chopped
*fresh hot peppers, chopped and
    to taste*
grated fresh ginger to taste
3 tablespoons tomato paste
*1 pound chicken liver, cut each
    into two pieces*

*½ pound whole small fresh
    shrimp, cleaned and deveined*
grated peel of 1 lime
1 cup fresh spinach, chopped
ground black pepper to taste
salt to taste
*chopped green onions for
    garnishing*

1. Add oil, white onion, peppers, ginger, and tomato paste to a preheated skillet that is over medium heat. Stir and cook until onions are tender.
2. Stir in rest of ingredients except green onions. Mix and cook until liver is done as desired.
3. Put in a serving dish, garnish with green onions, and serve hot.

Beef Tongue and Poponda Lalehun

This dish is prepared in East, South, and West African countries with possible use of local herbs and spices.

Helpful Hints:

a. More time is needed to cook beef tongue than lamb or pork tongue because it is longer.

b. This dish may be served with boiled rice, cooked potatoes, or cooked green bananas.

1 beef tongue
salt to taste
groundnut (peanut) oil,
  amount desired
2 large tomatoes, chopped
1 sweet bell pepper, chopped
fresh hot peppers, chopped and
  to taste
fresh ginger, chopped and to taste
lemongrass, chopped and to
  taste, or 3 fresh lime leaves

1 bunch green onions, chopped
2 tablespoons tomato paste
ground cumin to taste
*1 cup fresh **poponda** (basil) leaves,*
  chopped or grated rind of lime
roasted groundnuts (peanuts)
  for garnishing
fresh pineapple chunks
chopped parsley for garnishing

1. Put meat and salt in a heavy cooking pot, cover with water, and bring to a boil. With lid in place, cook slowly about 3–4 hours or until meat is tender.

2. Remove meat from broth and keep meat in a bowl of cold water for about 15 minutes or longer. With a knife, peel off skin, cut away area of attachment, and remove any unwanted parts.

3. Cut meat into desired slices across the grain. Heat skillet over medium heat. Add oil and meat. Cook and mix often until meat is light brown. Add tomatoes, ginger, lemongrass, and salt. Cook 10–12 minutes.

4. Stir in pineapples and the rest of ingredients except roasted groundnuts (peanuts) and parsley. Cover and cook for about 10 more minutes.

5. Put in a serving dish, garnish with groundnuts (peanuts) and parsley in that order before serving it hot.

Kidneys in Kidney Beans

This is a dish rich in protein and iron. It is also inexpensive and delicious!

Helpful Hints:

a. May use beef, lamb, or pork kidneys.
b. Serve with boiled rice or cooked green bananas.

1 pound lamb kidney
salt to taste
ground black pepper to taste
groundnut (peanut) oil, ¼ cup
  or amount desired
1 large white onion, chopped
4 cups cooked kidney beans
  (cook according to package
  directions and drain)

4 green onions, chopped
2 large tomatoes, chopped
3 tablespoons tomato paste
fresh hot peppers, chopped
  and to taste
3 whole cloves
some water as needed

1. Wash kidneys and remove white veins and unwanted parts. Cut into smaller pieces, add salt and pepper, and mix.

2. Add oil to preheated skillet that is over medium heat. Stir in kidneys and white onion. Cook until onion is tender.

3. Stir in rest of ingredients, cover, and cook until kidneys are done, about 25 minutes. Remove from heat and serve.

Pig's Feet with Green Bananas and Plantains

You can always count on Africans to make a great dish out of anything that is edible. We do not believe in wasting anything, no matter how small.

Pig's feet are delicious if cooked right. They must be cooked slowly in lots of liquid to awaken the true flavor.

Helpful Hints:

a. If you want to have an easier job of cutting, cook pig's feet whole and then cut at each joint.
b. Peel and slice green bananas and plantains just before cooking to keep them from turning dark.

2 pig's feet, cut up or whole
1 large white onion, cut in half
1 small cinnamon stick
salt to taste
¼ pound bone-in pork, cut up
fresh ginger, chopped and to taste
2 large tomatoes, chopped
3 whole cloves

whole, dry hot peppers to taste
2 green bananas (peel, cut into
   1-inch slices)
2 almost ripe plantains (peel,
   cut into 1-inch slices)
2 green onions, chopped, for
   garnishing

1. Put pig's feet, white onion, cinnamon stick, and salt in cooking pot, cover with water, and bring to a boil. Put cover in place and cook on low heat until meat is about half done.

2. Stir in pork and the rest of ingredients except plantains, bananas, and green onions. Continue to cook until meat is almost done.

3. Add bananas and plantains and cook until meat is done. Banana is tender after 10–12 minutes. Put in a serving dish, garnish with green onions, and serve hot.

Dambo (Chitterlings) Pepper Soup

This meat has a delicate flavor all its own. In order to enhance it, cook it slowly with some meat from the same animal.

Helpful Hints:

a. It is always good to cook several pounds of *dambo* (chitterlings) at the same time. A large portion is lost when thick layers of fat, etc. are cut away in the cleaning process. Also, because *dambo* takes hours to cook, cook more than one meal's worth to save time and energy.

b. *Dambo* is not easily cut, even when the knife is sharp. Slowly cook it in plenty of liquid until it is tender and easily chewed. Then cut it up to serve.

c. Remember that this is hot pepper soup, but make it only as spicy hot as you like it.

d. In Africa *dambo* dishes are made from beef, lamb, goat, and wild animals. But pork *dambo* is great. Please use what you like.

e. Serve with boiled green bananas, boiled plantain, cooked cassava, boiled rice, or bread of choice.

6 pounds dambo (chitterlings) or amount desired	*whole dry hot peppers to taste*
salt to taste	*⅓ pound white mushrooms, sliced*
2 large white onions, whole fresh ginger, chopped and to taste	*3 cloves garlic, crushed*
	3 whole cloves
1 pound bone-in pork, cut up	*grated peel of 1 lime*
3 large tomatoes, chopped	*juice of same lime*
1 large sweet bell pepper, chopped	*3 fresh lime leaves (optional)*
	1 bunch green onions, chopped

1. Clean *dambo* (chitterlings) and wash well. Put in cooking pot, cover with water, and bring to a boil. Stir in salt, white onions, and ginger. Cover and cook over reduced heat, stirring occasionally, until *dambo* are more than ¾ done.

2. Stir in rest of ingredients except green onion. Continue to cook over reduced heat until *dambo* and pork are done.

3. Remove *dambo* from broth and cool. Cut into bite-size portions, return it to the broth, and stir in green onions. Cook 5 more minutes and serve hot.

Giiben: A Special Frog and Childhood Disease Story

Today most African children are not immunized against childhood diseases. When I was growing up in Sierra Leone, West Africa, still fewer children were ever immunized. It would be correct to say that during those years, most children had all of the common childhood diseases. Parents gave them the native medicines they had, all the love and support humanly possible, then they watched helplessly while each disease followed its natural course.

I was attacked by nearly all of the many childhood diseases, and I can recall little details about all of them. Yet I clearly remember when I was sick with whooping cough. My cousin, Meme, who is my same age, also got the disease at the time I did. When we were not coughing, Grandmother was giving us medicines. She brought home at least ten different kinds a day, or so it seemed. Some medicines she rubbed on our chests and backs; others we drank, and we ate some more. For the inhalants she boiled many different kinds of leaves in a large pot of water. We then inhaled the warm steam, breathing it deep into our lungs, while we had a heavy cloth thrown over our heads.

It is almost impossible to remember all of Grandmother's medicines that she gathered during my growing years. But I remember one for whooping cough because it was so delicious. After the men brought home some special frogs (*giiben*) they caught in the swamp, Grandmother cleaned them and washed them with a special homemade soap and fresh lime juice. (The lime juice got rid of the slimy secretion on the skin.) She then smoked them over the fire until the skin was almost dry. (It was believed that the frog skin had more medicinal value than its other parts.) She cooked the smoked frogs with roasted sesame seeds ground into paste (*mandeh gbotoh*). This she served with soft cooked rice (*mbagboleh*). Only those who had whooping cough were supposed to eat what I now believe to be a delicacy as well as medicine. Unfortunately, the cough often did not allow us to eat much, and it was difficult to keep down what little we could eat.

Malaria is not considered a childhood disease. I think of it as the ancient plague that visited Africa in mosquito clothing, and it never left. Malaria and malaria-related complications have killed more of Africa's children than any other disease. This illness can be life-threatening, even for people who are in good health, if it is not treated. For Africa's children and the elderly, often malnourished and suffering with other untreated health conditions, malaria may cause death, and it often does.

There were talks about the possibility of adding antimalarial drugs to salt, similar to iodizing salt. The argument was that most Africans like salt in their diet. Therefore, if antimalarial drugs were added to salt, the population could take the drugs prophylactically, with little or no problems. The trouble is that this plan has been in the talking stage for as long as I can remember.

Grandmother's medicines must have worked for me, because I am able to tell my story. I wonder how many children could not tell theirs because they did not live. I hope the time will soon come when all the children of the world will be immunized against each and every childhood disease. I also hope that malaria will soon be a thing of the past, not only in Africa, but in the entire world.

Let me quickly add that in the past many people in the field of medicine worked very hard to give medical help to the people of Africa. There are stories of medical doctors and nurses, both foreigners and natives alike, who gave their lives while working with Africa's sick. Today many people continue to work in Africa, helping the sick. We thank all of you so very much. Without your endless efforts and hard work, health conditions in Africa would be much worse than they presently are, something hard to imagine.

I dedicate the children's health story section of the book to the memory of Grandmother, Maama Lahun, my private physician. She was always on call and did not once ask for a fee. Grandmother was far more than a willing, loving, tireless worker and supporter; she was great!

Another person to whose memory I also dedicate the same section of the book is Dr. Mabel Irine Silver. She was an Evangelical United Brethren (now United Methodist) missionary from America. She spent a lifetime at Rotifunk, Sierra Leone, West Africa, healing the sick. Dr. Silver may have treated hundreds of thousands of Africa's sick; from malnourished children to leprosy patients, Dr. Silver treated all of them. She always called each patient brother this or sister that. A leprosy patient once said, "I like to come because I am always treated with respect. Here people talk to me like I am a real person."

Each morning Dr. Silver opened the clinic with a short Bible reading and prayer. She and her helpers then went to work. They saw to the needs of each person until the last patient was taken care of. Those who could afford it paid a small fee for treatment and medicine. The people who had no money were also seen and given medication. Of course emergency patients were brought in at all hours of the day, seven days a week. Sometimes patients came from countries other than Sierra Leone, and they were all taken care of.

During the later part of Dr. Silver's practice, patients who had surgical needs were referred to Dr. Guess's and Dr. Harris's part of the clinic, under the watchful eyes of Miss Esther L. Megill, the missionary laboratory technician, who worked with Dr. Silver for many years. One day an emergency patient, who was also pregnant and at full term, was brought to the clinic. The patient was prepared for emergency surgery if it was needed. Dr. Guess was examining the patient when her uterus ruptured. They immediately did an emergency cesarean section, followed by a hysterectomy, saving both forty-year-old mother and her only child.

The people came because they truly believed that if they saw Dr. Silver, they would be made well again, no matter how sick they had become. Around the country Dr. Silver's other name was "Dr. Savior." Sick persons told their families, "If you just take me to Dr. Savior, I know she will make me well again." Yet each morning during Bible reading and prayer time, Dr. Silver told her patients, "I ask you to believe in the Lord Jesus Christ, the one and only true Savior. He is able and willing to heal your heart, mind, body, and soul."

Frog Legs in Sesame-Coconut Sauce

One day I was in an expensive supermarket. In the frozen food section I found some skinless frog legs. They cost a lot more money than I was willing to pay. I was told, "They are raised just for the table, and it is a very expensive undertaking." I asked myself, "Why would anyone use money and time to raise frogs, 'a very expensive undertaking,' and sell only the legs? What about the other parts of the frogs?" That explains why the dishes call only for frog legs, because one can get only those in America.

Helpful Hints:

a. To make sesame paste, roast sesame seeds and grind into paste. Raw sesame has a bitter taste. Roasting removes almost all of the bitterness; the seeds also grind better.
b. Serve with boiled rice.

1 medium white onion, chopped
fresh ginger, chopped and to taste
2 cloves garlic, crushed
2 cups coconut milk (mix it
with sesame paste)
salt to taste
15 jumbo frog legs or number
desired
⅓ cup sesame paste

1 large tomato, seeds removed
and chopped
1 cup fresh mushrooms, chopped
fresh hot peppers, chopped and
to taste
fresh mint leaves, chopped and
to taste
2 green onions, chopped

1. Put in a heavy pot white onion, ginger, garlic, coconut milk, and salt. Bring to a boil and cook over reduced heat until onions are tender.

2. Add to pot rest of ingredients except green onions and mint. Continue to cook until frog legs are done.

3. Put only meat in serving dish. If sauce is more than you want, reduce it or boil it down to desired amount.

4. Stir in mint and green onions and cook one minute. Spoon sauce over meat and serve.

Frog Legs with Pineapples

ᏬᏬ

Helpful Hint:

Serve with boiled rice, cooked green bananas, or boiled plantains.

½ cup or more rice flour
¼ cup roasted sesame seeds
ground black pepper to taste
salt to taste
groundnut (peanut) oil
15 jumbo frog legs, seasoned
  with salt
1 white onion, thinly sliced

1 red sweet pepper, sliced
  lengthwise
grated peel of 1 lime
fresh hot peppers, chopped and
  to taste
3 green onions, chopped
4 chunks of fresh pineapples
chopped parsley for garnishing

1. Mix together flour, sesame seeds, black pepper, and salt.

2. Heat oil (about ½-inch deep) to 375 degrees in skillet over medium heat. Use Suma's Onion Oil Test as needed (p. 228). Roll each frog leg in flour mixture and drop it into hot oil. Fry until golden on all sides.

3. Fork test legs for tenderness. If not tender enough, put lid in place and cook until tender.

4. Remove from skillet and drain; arrange in a serving dish and keep warm.

5. Remove oil and keep about ¼ cup in skillet. Stir in rest of ingredients except pineapple, green onions, and parsley. Cook until onions are tender.

6. Stir in green onions and pineapples and heat through. Spoon over frog legs, garnish with parsley, and serve hot.

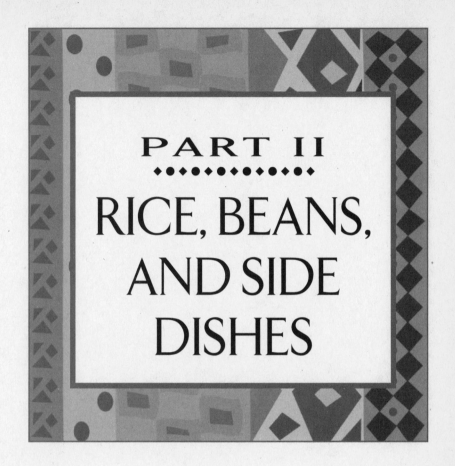

PART II
RICE, BEANS, AND SIDE DISHES

Mbah (Rice)

More people eat *mbah* (rice) than any other grain. Even in America many families now serve rice at least once a week, something unheard of not so long ago. If breakfast cereal is included, that number is much higher.

Mende is an African tribe whose home is in Sierra Leone, West Africa. Not only do the Mende people eat rice more often than most people do, they also have an interesting and unique relationship with it. To a Mende, rice is much more than just food. Let me explain what I mean. On any given day a Mende person may eat a complete meal consisting of meat, potatoes, some corn, and fresh fruits. After the meal is over, if he is asked, "Have you eaten?" he would reply, "I have not eaten yet. But I did eat some meat, potatoes, some corn, and fresh fruits." Strange as this may sound to you, in his mind he has not truly eaten yet. He has just had a snack or something to hold him over until he eats the real thing—rice. His stomach may be full, but if it is not full of rice with sauce, he has not had real food. There will still be another kind of emptiness in the stomach, but more important, in the mind. Only rice fills that emptiness.

Statements such as "Father is the breadwinner in our family," or "I work very hard to put bread on the table," do not mean much to the Mende's way of thinking. On the other hand, sayings such as "Your father always worked hard to make sure that each child's bowl is full of rice every day," and "As long as she lived, your mother filled your bowl with rice and plenty of love" are more meaningful to the Mende person.

Once I spoke with an American missionary. At the time of our conversation he and his family worked among the Mende tribe. I said something like, "Rice is what the Mende people know. To them it is more than just food. They believe that it not only meets

129

their physical need, but it also meets some of their psychological, emotional, and even spiritual needs. In the Mende person's way of thinking, only rice keeps body and soul together. Therefore, it makes sense to use rice in the celebration of the holy eucharist instead of bread, which is foreign to them. Rice could readily become a symbol of a never-changing and always-providing God who satisfies their spiritual hunger, similar to the way rice satisfies their physical hunger." I continued, "If Jesus had lived in Mende land, and we know that He used everyday, simple objects to illustrate eternal truth, He would have probably said to the Mende people, 'I am the rice of life.' " Jesus is the only giver of the kind of nourishment that takes care of spiritual hunger, the way rice takes care of the physical hunger of the Mende people.

The Mendes also believe that the only farmer is the rice farmer. One may grow fruits, vegetables, or cash crops such as coffee and cocoa. Or one may even raise chicken, sheep, and cattle. But if one does not grow rice, one is not a true farmer. When it is finally harvest time (*mbah leh kpehleh*) in Mende, or Kwanzaa in other parts of Africa, everyone helps to gather the valuable crop—rice. On a large farm special musicians are invited. Their music is designed to help the reapers harvest the rice faster. There is much work, but there is also plenty of excitement and food. This is the only time in the year when the women do not measure rice before they cook it. If the lady of the farm is asked, "How many hands of rice do you want cooked?" The common reply would be, "Enough to fill the pot," no matter how large that pot may be.

At night the harvest moon is beautiful and so bright that children play games with their shadows. The women spin cotton into thread and tell children's stories to teach life's lessons. The men work on looms they have helped to make, as they arrange intricate patterns and weave beautiful country cloths.

The drums are heard far away. Soon the sound is heard much closer as it becomes more inviting. Everyone is busy putting away unfinished items. The village gathering place has become alive again. There is laughter everywhere; dancing has begun. Mothers, fathers, young lovers, and children dance to their heart's content while grandmothers and grandfathers enjoy the gentle breeze of sweet harvest.

Recipes for some of the best Mende and other African rice dishes follow. Please enjoy them.

RICE COOKING TIPS

Anyone can cook great rice dishes if one only follows a few rice cooking tips.

1. Always use a heavy pot with a well-fitted cover. The heavier the pot, the more moist heat it retains, and the better the result.
2. Except for very few exceptions, cooking water must start to boil before rice is added to it. Mix with a wooden spoon as soon as rice is added to boiling water. Then increase heat to quickly bring the water back to boiling. This is important because boiling water seals the outside of each grain, preventing it from breaking before the core is done.
3. When the water starts to actively boil again, reduce the heat and put the cover in place. Cook on reduced heat until done.
4. Do not mix more than two times. Too much mixing breaks the outside of each grain, making the rice sticky before it is done.
5. Open the pot as few times as possible. Moist heat is vital to cooking rice.
6. The ratio of regular rice to cooking water is 1 cup uncooked rice to 2 cups water. For very firm rice (*Waajama* or *Vai* style) the ratio is 1 cup uncooked regular rice to 1 ¾ cups water. But the rice is cooked longer with moist heat.
7. One more way to ensure good results is by the use of Wokie's Two-Finger Rice Test, which follows. Please use it often.

WOKIE'S TWO-FINGER RICE TEST

This test lets the cook know whether or not the rice is done, and whether or not more liquid is needed to complete the cooking process.

1. When in doubt about the doneness of the rice, use a spoon to remove a few grains of rice from pot. Squeeze grains between thumb and index finger.
2. If rice feels hard and there is little or no water present, it means that the rice is not done. It also means that there is a need to add some hot or boiling water to rice. Mix after water is added, cover, and continue to cook on reduced heat until rice is done. The

amount of water to be added depends on how much rice is in the pot. Add from a few tablespoons up to ¼ cup boiling water at a time.

JOLLOFF RICE

This popular African festive rice dish is enjoyed by people from Guinea, Liberia, Senegal, Sierra Leone, Tanzania, Zambia, and most African countries. Various kinds of meats, herbs, and spices are used in a variety of jolloff rice dishes.

Two-Pot Jolloff Rice

ᏉᎧ

The rice is cooked in two steps. In step one the sauce is prepared. In step two the rice is cooked with about ⅓ of the sauce in a second pot; hence the name Two-Pot Jolloff Rice.

Helpful Hints:

a. Chicken and beef are often used for meat, but use any meat combination desired.
b. First cook sauce, which will enable you to cook the rice with some of the sauce.
c. Use Suma's Onion Oil Test (p. 228) and Wokie's Two-Finger Rice Test (p. 131) as they are needed.
d. Jolloff Rice Sauce may also be served with plain, boiled rice.

Jolloff Rice Sauce (Pot One)

ᏉᎧ

2–3 pound broiler or frying chicken
salt to taste
groundnut (peanut) oil, ½ cup or amount desired

3 small kpogii (taro) or white potatoes, each peeled and cut in half
½ pound boneless beef, cut up
2 large white onions, chopped

2 large tomatoes, chopped
6 tablespoons tomato paste
2 sweet bell peppers, chopped
6 large white mushrooms,
  sliced
3 cloves garlic, crushed
fresh ginger, finely chopped
  and to taste
ground cloves to taste

½ teaspoon ground semengii
  (cinnamon) or to taste
ground cumin to taste
½ teaspoon nutmeg or to taste
ground black pepper to taste
fresh hot peppers, chopped
  and to taste
½ pound large fresh shrimp,
  cleaned and deveined
1 bunch green onions, chopped

1. Remove excess chicken skin and fat as desired. Wash and cut chicken in desired portions. Add salt, mix, and set it aside.

2. Add oil to heated skillet that is over medium heat. Lightly brown potatoes in oil, remove, and set aside. Do the same with the beef and chicken in that order.

3. Adjust oil to ¼ cup or amount desired. Stir in white onions and cook until they are transparent. Stir in chicken, beef, tomatoes, tomato paste, and salt.

4. With lid in place, cook (adding more water as needed) for about 20 minutes or until meat is about half done. Stir in rest of ingredients except green onions and shrimp.

5. Continue to cook, stirring occasionally, until chicken and meat are done. Gently stir in shrimp and green onions, and cook only 7 more minutes. Remove from heat and keep sauce warm.

6. Put about ⅓ of meat and sauce in another pot that is suitable for cooking rice. Add enough water to bring it to 3⅔ cups liquid. (This is used to cook Jolloff Rice, recipe follows.)

Jolloff Rice (Pot Two)

Helpful Hints:

a. A pot suitable for cooking rice is heavy and has a well-fitted lid. Because less liquid is used to cook rice, cook it longer with moist heat.

b. Use long or short grain regular rice as desired.

*3⅔ cups sauce and water
　mixture (from pot one)
3 tablespoons tomato paste
salt and pepper to taste*

*2 cups uncooked regular rice
chopped fresh parsley for
　garnishing*

1. Add to pot all ingredients except rice and parsley, and bring to a boil. Using a wooden spoon, stir in rice. Increase heat and bring to a quick boil.
2. Stir one more time, cover, and cook on reduced heat until rice is done.
3. Arrange rice in a serving platter, put some of meat and sauce over rice, and garnish with parsley. Put rest of meat and sauce in another serving dish and serve with rice.

Did You Know?

Do you know how many kinds of rice there are? Experts tell us that over three thousand varieties of rice grow around the world. In Africa we have *gbongoh, gotoh, kpangula, maalah, mlanje, waga, yakah,* and much more. The African people enjoy eating all of them. While one says, "regular rice," there is nothing regular about rice.

Okra and Rice Pandanga

This easy-to-make, moist, and delicious rice dish is from Central, South, and West African countries.

Helpful Hints:

a. Also make Komafalii Kibongii Chicken Sauce (recipe follows) to serve with rice.
b. This dish is at its best when just cooked.

*groundnut (peanut) oil, ¼-
　⅓ cup or amount desired
2 cups uncooked regular rice
1 large white onion, chopped*

*1 pound ground chicken
fresh ginger, finely chopped
　and to taste
5 tablespoons tomato paste*

2 cups cooked black-eyed
  peas (cook according to
  package directions and
  drain)
¼ pound fresh okra (wash;
  remove ends; and cut into
  ⅓-inch slices)
3 whole cloves
4 white mushrooms, sliced
2 cloves garlic, crushed

ground black pepper to taste
fresh hot pepper, chopped
  and to taste
salt to taste
3¾ cups water or chicken
  broth
roasted groundnuts (peanuts)
  for garnishing
chopped green onions for
  garnishing

1. Add oil to a heated rice cooking pot that is over medium heat. Add rice and stir for 5 minutes with a wooden spoon. Stir in white onions, chicken, and ginger. Mix 3–5 more minutes.

2. Add remaining ingredients except green onions and chopped nuts, and bring to a boil.

3. Cover and cook over reduced heat until rice is done.

4. Arrange it in a serving platter, garnish with nuts and green onions, and serve hot with Komafalii Kibongii Chicken Sauce (recipe follows).

Komafalii Kibongii Chicken Sauce

Komafalii are delicious African mushrooms that grow on dead trees in the forest. They are often coarsely ground and cooked with fish, meat, or chicken.

This dish is from West Africa.

Helpful Hints:

a. Use coarsely ground mushrooms of choice instead of *komafalii*.
b. Mushrooms have great capacity to absorb liquid; do not soak them in water unless they are dry.
c. This sauce is also great with plain boiled rice.

groundnut (peanut) oil, ¼ cup
  or amount desired

1 white onion, chopped
½ pound ground chicken

1 pound mushrooms of choice,
*   cleaned and coarsely ground*
fresh ginger, chopped and to
*   taste*
1 large tomato, chopped
3 tablespoons tomato paste
3 green onions, chopped

1 bell pepper, chopped
fresh hot peppers, chopped
*   and to taste*
salt to taste
chopped parsley for
*   garnishing*

1. Add oil to heated skillet that is over medium heat. Stir in white onions, chicken, mushrooms, and ginger. Mix and cook until onions are tender.

2. Add remaining ingredients except parsley. Cook, stirring often, until done. Put in a serving dish, garnish with parsley, and serve.

My Mother's Coconut Rice

My mother's coconut rice;
What a wonderful surprise!
As white as grated coconut;
Spongy, juicy, and sweet.
Soft in my mouth,
As creamy as coconut butter;
Stirring excitement, joy, and laughter.
Nutty is the savor,
Tender sweet flavor,
Like the warm affection from above,
Like my mother's gentle tender love.

COCONUT RICE AND THE OCCASIONS

Coconut rice is one of my favorite dishes. Many of my best childhood memories are associated with it. Any time Mother cooked it, something special was taking place. She prepared it to celebrate our coming home from boarding schools, for good grades, school graduations, and many other occasions. That was why I cooked it as the main course for about 250 people who were guests at our African wedding ceremony.

To make the dish I asked the butcher at the supermarket for ground chicken. He replied, "Lady, you don't know what you're talking about. I have never seen or heard of ground chicken in my entire life. Maybe where you come from they grind chicken, but in America we don't." Saying those words, he walked away. I had to grind all the chicken I needed by myself. That was then. Today the best supermarkets in the country carry ground chicken all the time, making it easy to prepare this dish.

Mother's Coconut Wedding Rice

This dish is from Sierra Leone, West Africa. People from many African countries also cook coconut rice, possibly using other meats, local herbs, and spices.

Helpful Hints:

a. Make Mamokoh's Chicken Balls without the sauce. (p. 229)
c. Use Wokie's Two-Finger Rice Test (p. 131) as needed.
d. Make Mother's Coconut Wedding Rice Sauce (recipe follows) to serve with rice.

Mamokoh's Chicken Balls

Use ⅓ to cook with rice, ⅔ to make sauce

3¾ cups coconut milk
1 white onion, chopped
5 white mushrooms, sliced
1 sweet bell pepper, chopped
fresh hot peppers, chopped
*   and to taste*
2 cloves garlic, crushed
2 cups uncooked regular rice
*   (long or short grain)*

fresh ginger, chopped and to
*   taste*
salt to taste
sliced fresh coconuts for
*   garnishing*
chopped fresh parsley for
*   garnishing*

1. Put coconut milk, onion, mushrooms, and peppers in a heavy pot and bring it to a boil over medium heat. (Do not allow to boil over.) With a wooden spoon stir in rice and bring to an active boil.

2. Add ⅓ of chicken balls and rest of ingredients except coconut slices and parsley. When it comes to a good boil, reduce heat, cover, and cook until rice is done.

3. Arrange rice in a serving platter and put some sauce over it. Garnish with coconut slices and chopped parsley in that order. Serve rest of sauce along with rice.

Mother's Coconut Wedding Rice Sauce

Helpful Hint:

The sauce may also be served with plain boiled rice and other rice dishes.

*groundnut (peanut) oil, ¼ cup
 or amount desired*
1 white onion, chopped
4 white mushrooms, sliced
*chicken balls left to make
 sauce (⅔)*
1 cup or more coconut milk
*1 large tomato, remove seeds
 and chop*
*1 small kobo kobo (eggplant)
 (peel and slice just before
 cooking)*

1 clove garlic, crushed
*fresh ginger, chopped and to
 taste*
grated peel of 1 lime
*fresh hot peppers, chopped
 and to taste*
1 sweet bell pepper, chopped
salt to taste
4 green onions, chopped

1. Put oil, white onion, and mushrooms in a cooking pot. Stir and cook until onions are tender.

2. Stir in rest of ingredients except green onions and chicken balls.

3. Cook 10–12 minutes until *kobo kobo* (eggplant) is done. Stir in green onions and chicken balls. Cook only 1 or 2 more minutes.

4. Remove from heat and serve with rice.

THE PAHNWAHS

Pahnwah means rice and other grains dressed in bright colors from leafy vegetables, fruits, and nuts. African women skillfully add these to rice and other grains to enhance taste, texture, color, and smell.

Ngeh Ngeh Pahnwah Rice
(Green Check Rice)

Ngeh ngeh is an African leafy vegetable. When cooked, it is brilliant green like spinach and slimy like okra. The Vai women in Liberia and the Waajama Mende women in Sierra Leone enjoy cooking with it. When it is added to cooked rice, *ngeh ngeh* changes the rice into a bright, beautiful, spinach-green color with white specks all over. If done correctly, the finished rice looks like a green and white checkerboard or the look of a green-and-white-checked fabric pattern. Women in other West African countries may also cook rice in this manner.

   Ngeh ngeh leaves are not readily available outside of Africa. Okra together with spinach are used. The result is not only good, it is better than the real thing. The okra and spinach together are more nutritious than just the *ngeh ngeh* leaves. As you know, most supermarkets sell okra and spinach all year round.

Helpful Hints:

a. Use frozen spinach and frozen okra.
b. In order that the rice may mix well with the sauce, cook firm—not soft—rice.
c. Serve rice with Jolloff Rice Sauce (p. 132).
d. Use Wokie's Two-Finger Rice Test (p. 131) as needed.

2 cups uncooked regular rice   *3½ cups water*
   (long or short grain)

1. Bring water to a boil in a heavy, rice-cooking pot over medium heat. Add rice and mix. Increase heat and bring water to a quick boil.

2. With a wooden spoon, mix, cover, and cook on reduced heat until rice is done.

3. Remove all of rice from pot and put into a mixing bowl, then add sauce (recipe follows) and mix.

Ngeh Ngeh Pahnwah Sauce (Green Check Rice Sauce)

8 frozen okra
½ cup water
½ pound frozen spinach
  (thaw before use)

pinch of baking soda (use
  no more)

1. In a pot, bring water to a boil over medium heat. Add okra to water. Cover and cook 10–14 minutes or until okra is tender. Drain all of water except about ¼ cup.

2. Mix spinach and baking soda. Add spinach to cooked okra. Mix and cook on low heat for 8–10 minutes.

3. Remove from heat and put in a mixing bowl. Mix with a wooden spoon into a smooth sauce or *plasas* while it is still warm.

4. Add mixture a spoonful at a time to rice that is already in a mixing bowl, and mix. Repeat until you get desired shade of green. Put rice in a serving dish and serve hot with Jolloff Rice Sauce.

Note: The sauce can also be pureed in a blender. Do so with care so that sauce is not too smooth, an undesired characteristic.

Bondoh Pahnwah Rice
ᏳᎤ

This is a simple rice and okra dish, a favorite of many West African tribes.

Helpful Hints:

a. The rice must be firm because it is *pahnwah,* and okra is added.
b. Serve with Serabu Seafood Plasas (p. 148).

3½ cups water
2 cups uncooked, long grain,
  regular rice

6 whole okra, each top end
  removed
salt to taste

1. Bring water to a boil in a heavy, rice-cooking pot. Add rice, mix, and increase heat to bring to a quick boil.
2. Cover and cook on reduced heat until about half of liquid is absorbed. Add okra to rice without mixing it. Cover and continue to cook on reduced heat until rice is done, 20–25 minutes.
3. Put okra in a mixing bowl; with a wooden spoon crush okra until it is as smooth as possible.
4. Put all of rice and salt in another mixing bowl. Add to rice some of the okra mixture and mix. Repeat until you have added as much okra as you would like. Put rice in a serving dish and serve hot.

Cabbage Coconut Rice
ᏳᎤ

This dish is from Benin, Burundi, Kenya, Mozambique, South Africa, and Tanzania.

Helpful Hints:

a. If possible, use shredded fresh coconut.
b. Serve with Kobo Kobo (Eggplant) Chicken Sauce (p. 142).

groundnut (peanut) oil,
    amount desired
2 cups uncooked regular rice
    (long or short grain)
1 onion, chopped
1 small cabbage, shredded
¾ cup fresh coconut, shredded
ground hot pepper to taste

2 cups coconut milk; use store
    bought or see How to Make
    Coconut Milk (p. 239)
fresh ginger, finely chopped
    and to taste
salt to taste
1¾ cups water

1. Add oil, rice, and onion to a heated pot that is over medium heat. Stir with a wooden spoon until onions are transparent.

2. Add rest of ingredients, mix, and bring to a boil. Mix again, cover, and cook on reduced heat until rice is done. Serve hot with sauce.

Kobo Kobo (Eggplant) Chicken Sauce

This dish is from North, East, and West African countries.

Helpful Hint:

To keep it from turning dark, peel *kobo kobo* (eggplant) just before cooking it.

groundnut (peanut) oil, ¼ cup
    or amount desired
1 white onion, chopped
¾ pound ground chicken
ground fresh ginger to taste
fresh hot peppers, chopped
    and to taste
1 red sweet bell pepper,
    chopped
1 medium kobo kobo (egg-
    plant) peeled and cut into
    1-inch cubes

4 large white mushrooms,
    chopped
1 large tomato, chopped
3 tablespoons tomato paste
curry powder to taste
salt to taste
4 green onions, chopped
1 cup fresh parsley, chopped

1. Add oil to a heated skillet that is over medium heat. For 5 minutes stir in and cook onions, chicken, ginger, and peppers.

2. Stir in rest of ingredients except green onions and parsley. Cook only until *kobo kobo* (eggplant) is tender, about 8 minutes. Stir in green onions and parsley. Remove from heat and serve.

Sakitomboh Rice

This dish is from Central, East, and West African countries. Other names may also be used for the same dish.

Helpful Hints:

a. *Sakitomboh* (cassava leaves) are rich in vitamins, minerals, and very high in fiber. The leaves are ground and cooked with rice in this dish.

b. Other leafy vegetables that can be used are chopped mustard greens, collards, turnip greens, kale, sweet potato leaves, spinach, and lettuce. The last three leafy vegetables become less identifiable if they are finely chopped or cooked too long.

c. Chop all leaves only after they are soaked and washed well—not before. Soaking helps to loosen sand and dirt on leaves. Adding salt to soaking water kills insects, and they will fall off in the washing process.

d. Serve with Kobo Kobo (Eggplant) Chicken Sauce (p. 142).

groundnut (peanut) oil, ¼ cup
  or amount desired
3¾ cups water
2 cups uncooked regular rice
  (long or short grain)
1 onion, chopped
1 pound ground cassava leaves
  or chopped greens of choice

ground hot peppers to taste
2 large tomatoes, cut in chunks
salt to taste
roasted groundnuts (peanuts)
  for garnishing

1. Add oil, rice, and onions to a heavy rice-cooking pot that is over medium heat. Stir until onions are tender. Add liquid and bring to a boil.

2. Stir in rest of ingredients except nuts, and bring to another boil. Put lid in place and cook on reduced heat until done.

3. Put rice in a serving dish, garnish with nuts, and serve with Kobo Kobo (Eggplant) Chicken Sauce (p. 142).

Hondii (Spinach), Beans, and Curry Rice
೦೦

This dish is from Benin, Burkina Faso, Malawi, Mozambique, Rwanda, Senegal, Sierra Leone, and Tanzania. Enjoy this simple and delicious dish.

Helpful Hint:

Serve with Serabu Seafood Sauce (p. 120).

3½ cups broth or water
2 cups uncooked long grain
  rice
curry powder to taste
groundnut (peanut) oil, ¼ cup
  or amount desired
salt and pepper to taste
½ pound fresh hondii
  (spinach), washed, drained,
  and chopped

1 cup cooked fresh or frozen
  broad or lima beans
  (cook according to
  package directions and
  drain)
roasted groundnuts for
  garnishing

1. Stir rice in boiling water or broth, increase heat, and bring it to a quick boil.

2. Add all of the ingredients except *hondii* (spinach), beans, and groundnuts. Mix and bring to another boil. Cover and cook over reduced heat until rice is about half done.

3. Stir in rest of ingredients except groundnuts. Cover and continue to cook on reduced heat until rice is done. Put in a serving platter, garnish with nuts, and serve with Serabu Seafood Sauce.

Avocado Sesame Rice

This dish is prepared in many African countries. It is easy to make, delicious, and elegantly attractive.

Helpful Hints:

a. To keep avocado from turning dark, peel and add it to rice just before serving.
b. Serve with Shrimp Mango Chicken Kabaltii (p. 146).

2 cups uncooked long-grain rice
sesame oil, amount desired
salt to taste

2 ripe avocados
⅓ cup roasted, partially ground sesame seeds

1. Cook rice according to package directions or see Rice Cooking Tips (p. 131).
2. Put all of cooked rice except ½ cup into a mixing bowl. Add oil and salt and mix well.
3. Peel one avocado and cut into small pieces. Add some to rice and mix. Repeat until rice is the shade of color desired.
4. Put the green rice in a serving platter. Peel the second avocado, slice, and use it to garnish rice. Also garnish dish with white rice and sesame seeds, in that order. Serve while it is still hot.

Green Mango Rice

Africans enjoy cooking with fruits. This dish is prepared in several countries. If the right mangoes are used, rice should have a tangy taste. In order to balance flavor, it is served with Shrimp Mango Chicken Kabatii (see p. 146). The two together create a great sweet and sour taste, one your family and guests will enjoy.

Helpful Hints:

a. It is necessary to use green, tart, and firm mangoes. They are also the only kind that can be easily shredded. Or peel each, remove meat from seed, and chop.
b. Because there is less than 4 cups of liquid to cook 2 cups of rice, cook rice a little longer with moist heat 20–30 minutes or until done.

*groundnut (peanut) oil, ¼ cup
  or amount desired*
*2 cups uncooked regular rice
  (long or short grain)*
*3½ cups water, broth, or co-
  conut milk*
2 cloves garlic, crushed

*fresh hot peppers, chopped
  and to taste*
*fresh ginger, finely chopped
  and to taste*
salt to taste
*4 cups shredded or chopped
  green mangoes*
4 green onions, chopped

1. Add oil and rice to a heavy pot that is over medium heat. With a wooden spoon stir it for about 5 minutes.

2. Stir in rest of ingredients except mangos and green onions. Bring to a full boil. Mix again and put lid in place. Cook on reduced heat until about half of liquid is gone.

3. Add mangoes and green onions, and mix so that they are evenly distributed. Cover and continue to cook on reduced heat until rice is done. Serve while it is hot.

Shrimp Mango Chicken Kabatii

Helpful Hints:

a. Mangoes must be ripe, sweet, and firm.
b. Shrimp Mango Chicken Kabatii may also be served with other rice dishes.

*2 large ripe, firm mangoes
groundnut (peanut) oil, ¼ cup
  or amount desired*

*1 white onion, chopped
fresh ginger, finely chopped
  and to taste*

*1 pound boneless chicken
    breast, cut up*
1 sweet bell pepper, chopped
*fresh hot peppers, chopped
    and to taste*
1 large fresh tomato, chopped
salt to taste
3 tablespoons tomato paste

*1 kpohwoh (portabella) mush-
    room, chopped*
grated peel of 1 lime
*1 pound fresh large shrimp,
    cleaned and deveined*
3 green onions, chopped
*chopped fresh parsley for
    garnishing*

1. Peel each mango and cut meat into chunks.

2. Add oil to a heated skillet that is over medium heat. Stir and cook white onion and ginger until onion is tender. Add chicken, peppers, tomato, and tomato paste, and salt. Mix and cook for about 3 minutes.

3. Stir in rest of ingredients except shrimp, mangoes, parsley, and green onions. Continue to cook, stirring often, until chicken is almost done.

4. Add shrimp, mangoes, and green onions. Cover and cook 3 minutes or until shrimp is done the way you like them.

5. Arrange rice in a serving platter. Spoon some of sauce over it and garnish with parsley. Serve it with rest of sauce.

Note: Beef, lamb, goatmeat, pork, and fish can also be used in this dish.

Sweet Potato Rice Luyalah

This dish is moist and delicious every time. It is prepared in Central, East, and West African countries. Other kinds of meats, herbs, and spices may also be used.

Helpful Hints:

a. Use Wokie's Two-Finger Rice Test (p. 131) as needed.
b. Serve with Serabu Seafood Plasas (p. 148).

*groundnut (peanut) oil, ¼ cup
   or amount desired*
*2 cups uncooked regular (long
   or short grain) rice*
1 white onion, chopped
*3½ cups water or liquid of
   choice*
4 white mushrooms, sliced
1 cup shredded fresh coconut
grated fresh ginger to taste

*fresh hot peppers, chopped
   and to taste*
salt to taste
*2 medium sweet potatoes,
   shredded (shred after peeling)*
*½ pound medium-size shrimp,
   cleaned and deveined*
*½ pound sea scallops (if too
   large, cut each into 2 pieces)*
4 green onions, chopped

1. Put oil, rice, and white onion in a rice-cooking pot that is over medium heat. Mix with a wooden spoon until onions are transparent. Add liquid and bring it to a full boil.

2. Stir in rest of ingredients except shrimp, scallops, sweet potatoes, and green onions. Cover and cook on reduced heat until about half of liquid is gone.

3. Gently stir in rest of ingredients. With lid in place, continue to cook until rice is done. Serve hot with Serabu Seafood Plasas (recipe follows).

Serabu Seafood Plasas

This dish is from Burkina Faso, Senegal, Nigeria, Liberia, and Sierra Leone.

Helpful Hints:

a. Don't overcook seafood.
b. *Plasas* can also be served with plain boiled rice.

*groundnut (peanut) oil, ¼ cup
   or amount desired*
1 white onion, chopped
*1 large tomato, seeds removed
   and chopped*

*½ pound small fresh shrimp,
   cleaned and deveined*
½ pound small scallops
¼ pound crab meat
2 tablespoons tomato paste

3 green onions, chopped
hot fresh peppers, chopped
and to taste
2 cloves garlic, crushed

3 white mushrooms, chopped
salt to taste
chopped parsley for
garnishing

1. Add oil, white onion, and tomatoes to a heated skillet over medium heat; stir and cook until onions are transparent.

2. Stir in rest of the ingredients except parsley; cook 3–5 minutes.

3. Spoon sauce over rice, garnish with chopped parsley, and serve hot.

SIERRA LEONE

Sierra Leone is a former British colony. This small country, about the size of the state of Connecticut, has the third largest natural harbor in the world. With a yearly rainfall from 80 to 144 inches, there are large rivers such as Jong, Great Scarcies, and Moa. Some of these rivers feed the majestic and breathtaking Becongoh Falls in the Mondema-Kono area.

Sierra Leone means "Lion Mountains," because some of the mountains along the coast look like lions chasing one another. Real lions indeed dwell on these beautiful mountains. Elephants, buffalo, and the world's largest and most impressive troop of monkeys roam the lush mountains, hills, and valleys. Migratory birds of many kinds come from afar to enjoy the abundant food supply, have their young, and watch them rapidly grow. Then they are ready to fly again to the other side of the Atlantic Ocean.

The Creoles, Fula, Kissi, Kono, Limba, Madingos, Mendes, Temnes, Shebro, and Susus are some of the tribes who call Sierra Leone home. The people are soft-spoken, have quick smiles, and are somewhat shy, kind, and friendly by nature. They are intelligent and very interested in education. One of the oldest and most prestigious colleges in all of Africa is Sierra Leone's Fourah Bay College. In the past many students came from Ghana, Liberia, Nigeria, and many other African countries to the college for education. In 1887, the Women's Missionary Society of the Evangelical United Brethren Church in America sponsored Harford School for Girls. The Albert Academe, a school for boys, was also established by the E.U.B. Church, now United Methodist Church. Other schools, such as the Minnie Mull Memorial School for Girls, by United Brethren in Christ Church; Holy Rosary, by the Roman Catholic Church; Freetown Secondary School for Girls (F.S.S.G.); Bo Secondary School for Boys; and many more have all worked hard to help educate the people.

Sierra Leone Nyandeh
(Sierra Leone Beauty)

This beautiful dish from Sierra Leone has a festive look with an elaborate display of colors. It is sure to please both family and guests.

Helpful Hint:

Hands must be clean and wet when making rice balls or when molding them in egg-shape form. (Cooked rice does not adhere to wet hands.)

2½-pound broiler or frying chicken, cut-up
salt to taste
1 medium-size butternut squash
groundnut (peanut) oil, ¼ cup or amount desired
1 large white onion, chopped
2 cloves garlic, crushed
3 tablespoons tomato paste
2 large tomatoes, seeds removed and chopped
fresh hot peppers, chopped and to taste
grated peel of 1 lemon
3 whole cloves

fresh ginger, finely chopped and to taste
4 cups cooked white rice (keep warm; cook rice according to directions on package)
1 red and 1 green sweet bell pepper, sliced ¼-inch wide, lengthwise
4 cups Ngeh Ngeh Pahnwah Rice (Green Check Rice) (p. 139)
4 white button mushrooms, each cut in half
4 green onions, chopped
8 large shrimp, each deveined but not shelled

*½ cup cooked black-eyed
peas for garnishing*
*½ cup cooked green peas for
garnishing; cook only until
bright green*

*cooked broccoli for garnishing;
cook 1 cluster only until
bright green*

1. Remove excess skin and fat from chicken as desired. Season with salt and set aside.

2. Peel butternut squash. Cut it open and remove seeds and fibers with a spoon. Wash, cut into equal, medium-size chunks or slices, and set aside.

3. Add oil to a heated skillet and brown chicken. Stir in white onions and cook until onions are transparent.

4. Put in skillet all of the ingredients except white and green rice, squash, shrimp, black-eyed peas, green peas, green onions, sweet peppers, broccoli, and mushrooms. Cover and cook until chicken is about half done, stirring occasionally.

5. Lay squash over chicken, cover, and cook until squash is done but firm.

6. Remove squash piece by piece, put in a bowl, and keep warm. If chicken is not done at this time, cook until it is done, adding some water as needed.

7. Arrange only chicken at center of a *kalabash* (a serving platter) lined with fresh cassava or parsley leaves.

8. Reduce sauce if it is more than you want by cooking over medium heat until liquid lessens. and keep warm.

9. With clean, wet hands, mold each spoonful of white rice into equal egg shape or balls. Do the same with green rice.

10. Arrange one green, one white ball around edge of the platter.

11. Arrange squash around platter between rice and chicken. (Don't pour sauce over rice balls, because they will crumble if wet.)

12. Put in another skillet sweet peppers, mushrooms, oil, green onions, and salt. Stir and cook for about 3 minutes. Stir in shrimp and cook only until the shrimp is just done.

13. Garnish dish with black-eyed peas, green peas, sweet peppers, mushrooms, and shrimp in that order. Shave with a knife only the green part of broccoli and sprinkle it over the entire dish. Serve hot with the chicken sauce.

African Rice Balls

ꙮ

This is a simple, attractive way Africans present rice.

Helpful Hints:

a. When making rice balls both hands must be clean and wet because cooked rice does not stick to wet hands.
b. You can make balls all white, all green, or some of each. They can also be all round or some made into an egg shape.
c. Rice ball stuffing should be as liquid free (water and oil) as possible. Liquid can cause balls to become crumbly.
d. Stuffing suggestions: Cooked shrimp, oysters, fish, chicken, fruits, and vegetables.

4 cups cooked white rice
4 cups cooked green rice; see
* Ngeh Ngeh Pahwah Rice*
* (Check Green Rice) (p. 139)*
salt to taste

cooked broccoli for garnishing
* (cook head part of broccoli*
* in water until bright green;*
* chop and use to garnish)*
chopped sweet red peppers
* for garnishing*
a bowl of water

1. Clean and wet both hands. Shape rice by the spoonful into balls or an egg shape.
2. Arrange balls on a warm serving platter. Sprinkle with chopped broccoli and red sweet peppers, and serve with Jolloff Rice Sauce. (p. 132)

Variation:

Stuffed African Rice Balls: After rice is made into a ball, press thumb about two thirds of the way through ball. Fill hole with stuffing of choice, squeeze ball together, and reshape.

Tiiwee Rice

෬

This is cooked rice wrapped in edible leaves. They are attractive and nutritiously delicious.

Helpful Hints:

a. Suggested leaves are fresh spinach, lettuce, and other edible leaves of choice. Wash, remove long stems, and towel dry before use.
b. Rice mixture must be hot; this makes the leaves wilt when the rice is wrapped.
c. Use a ratio of 3 cups cooked rice to ⅔ cup grated fresh coconut, or amount desired.

groundnut (peanut) oil,
  amount desired
3 cups cooked rice or amount
  desired

⅔ cup grated fresh coconut
salt and pepper to taste
1 pound fresh spinach leaves,
  washed and towel dried

1. Put oil, rice, coconut, salt, and pepper in a skillet that is over medium heat. Mix until mixture is heated through.

2. Lay out one or two leaves on a clean, dry plate. Put a spoonful of mixture at center of leaf. Fold so that left side of leaf is over rice, right side completely over folded left side; top end is over center, and bottom is pulled over top.

3. You now have rice packaged in a *tiiwee.* Lay it on the fold in a bowl. If rice is warm enough, the leaf will wilt and keep each *tiiwee* folded.

4. Repeat until all of rice is wrapped. Set bowl over a pot of hot water until ready to serve.

Groundnut Pineapple Rice Salad
◔◔

Helpful Hint:

This dish is made in Algeria, Egypt, Ethiopia, Morocco, and South Africa. It can be served at room temperature or chilled.

olive oil, amount desired
sugar to taste
honey to taste
juice of 2 fresh lemons
salt to taste
3 cups cooked rice (cook according to package directions)
⅓ cup roasted and chopped groundnuts (peanuts)
⅓ cup fresh coconut, shredded
⅓ cup sweet red pepper, chopped
⅓ cup sweet green pepper, chopped

⅓ cup dates, chopped
2 cups fresh pineapple chunks, drained
⅓ cup black olives, chopped
3 green onions, chopped
1 cup cooked small shrimp
1 cup cooked, cubed chicken breast
fresh ginger, finely chopped and to taste
hot fresh peppers, chopped and to taste
chopped parsley for garnishing

1. Put oil, sugar, honey, lemon juice, and salt in a mixing bottle and mix well.
2. In a large bowl, combine the remaining ingredients except parsley, and pour the oil mixture over it.
3. Using two wooden spoons, toss and arrange salad in a serving dish. Garnish with parsley and serve cold or at room temperature.

Chick Peas Mango Rice Salad

Helpful Hint:

This North African rice salad can be served chilled or at room temperature.

olive oil to taste
juice of two fresh lemons
honey to taste
sugar to taste
salt to taste
3 cups cooked rice
2 cups cooked and drained
  chick peas (cook chick peas
  according to package
  directions)

2 ripe, firm mangoes; peel
  each, remove meat, and cut
  into chunks
1 sweet red bell pepper,
  chopped
3 green onions, chopped
½ cup olives, chopped
⅓ cup roasted groundnuts
  (peanuts)
ground black pepper to taste
chopped mint leaves for
  garnishing

1. Mix well oil, lemon juice, honey, sugar, and salt, and set aside.
2. Put remaining ingredients except mint leaves in a mixing bowl. Mix oil-lemon mixture again and add it to rice. Using two wooden spoons, toss until all ingredients are well coated.
2. Put in a serving dish, garnish with mint leaves, and serve chilled or at room temperature.

Madin Jan Sehddi

It is understandable that most three year olds are not too eager to eat unfamiliar foods. After all, at the tender age of three, a child has very little experience with most of the foods we have available today. I know adults who hesitate to eat something they have not had in the past.

I was surprised when my three-year-old friend asked for more *sehddi* after he ate it for the first time at our house. "I like it!" he said. "I am going to ask my mommy to make it for me. I want more." So I gave him some more. After he ate, he asked, "What do you call it?" When I did not immediately reply, he repeated in a higher tone of voice, "What do you call it?"

When Madin Jan wants something, he goes after it until he gets it. I like that in anyone, especially if that anyone is just three years old and happens to be one of my favorite people. That is why I call the dish *Madin Jan Sehddi*. Both children and adults enjoy eating it.

This rice dish is made in all countries in Africa using local fruits and spices. It may also be called by other names.

Helpful Hints:

a. Use dry fruits like raisins; fresh fruits such as crushed pineapples, chopped mangoes, and apples; shredded or grated coconut; coconut milk or other kinds of milk; ground cinnamon, ginger, and other spices.
b. Use uncooked rice or your leftover cooked rice.
c. Do not use milk and lemon juice together, except as desired.

½ cup uncooked rice or left-
   over rice, amount desired
chopped apples, amount
   desired

sugar and/or honey to taste
water, coconut milk, or other
   milk, amount desired
lemon juice to taste (optional)

1. Put rice in cooking pot and cover with water 2–3 inches above rice. Bring to a boil, mix, and cover.
2. Cook on low heat, stirring occasionally, until rice is almost as soft as pudding. Stir in apples and honey and/or sugar.
3. Continue to cook until apples are soft. Add milk or fresh lemon juice. Remove from heat and serve chilled or at room temperature.

AFRICAN RICE NOODLES

Did you know that Africans have been making noodles for a very long time? Grandmothers and granddaughters often make noodles together. This is one of those African grandmother-teaching-granddaughter things so that the "know how" is passed on and not forgotten.

Noodles are often made using rice flour, although other grain flour and corn flour can also be used. Some noodles are more time-consuming to make than others, but it is lots of fun for children to help mix the flour as they work with their hands and eat much of the mixture. It is also good hand and finger exercise for grandmothers. More important, it is a fun thing for the family to do together.

Sweet African Rice Noodles

This is a dish made in West African countries, using rice flour.

Helpful Hints:

a. The balls should be as uniform as possible, about the size of cooked chick peas.
b. Balls should be made about one hour before cooking so that they are partially dry.
c. The noodles can be made sweet by adding honey and/or sugar. Or do not make them sweet and serve with sauce.

3 cups or more rice flour   *juice of 1 lemon or to taste*
water   *honey and/or sugar to taste*

1. Put flour in a mixing bowl, sprinkle with ¼ cup of water, and mix. If most of flour is still dry, sprinkle with more water, 1–2 tablespoons at a time, and repeat until most of flour is moist and lumps are formed.

2. Mix, break lumps into smaller lumps, then sprinkle with more flour. Make even balls, sprinkle with more flour, and set aside to dry.

3. Put about 3 cups water in a pot and bring to a boil. Using a wooden spoon, stir in balls, mix often, and continue to cook on low heat until done. If sauce is not as thick as desired, mix some flour with water, slowly stirring in mixture until the desired consistency

is reached. The consistency is like medium to thick gravy with lumps.

4. Stir in lemon juice, sugar, and/or honey to taste. Remove from heat and serve hot or at room temperature.

Variations:

Non-Sweet Lehweh Noodles: Mix flour with salt to taste. Make balls like above. Add to boiling water and cook, stirring often until done. Remove from heat, drain, and serve with Serabu Seafood Sauce (p. 148).

Kawah Lehweh Noodles: This can be sweet or not, as desired. Mix flour with honey and/or sugar to taste. Add water and mix into lumps. Make lumps into the shape and size of an egg. Cook in boiling water, mixing occasionally until done. Remove from liquid and serve. If salt instead of sugar is added, cut into slices while still warm; that is when noodles are easy to cut. Arrange in a serving dish and garnish with chopped green onions or parsley. Serve warm with Serabu Seafood Sauce (p. 148).

Corn Rice Noodles: Mix ⅓ part cornmeal, ⅓ part corn flour, ⅓ part rice flour, and salt to taste. Sprinkle with water and make balls like Kawah Lehweh Noodles (p. 120). Cook in boiling water until done. Drain, slice while still warm, and serve with Serabu Seafood Plasas (p. 148).

Beans and Peas—The Poor Man's Meat

In Africa beans were sometimes called "the poor man's meat." Today the rich as well as the poor frequently have them on their dinner tables. They are nutritious, delicious, high in protein, a good source of iron, and they have no cholesterol.

There are as many kinds of beans as there are different ways of cooking them. Some African dry beans are unique and beautiful.

They almost look like painted floral designs of red, black, and white. Others look like green or yellow string beads. Some beans are cooked while they are fresh; others after they are dry; some are boiled while in their pods, some after they are peeled, and others are used in powder form—all very delicious.

The price of beans is very reasonable in many parts of the world, especially if they are bought dry and by the pound. It costs Africans no money to dry them in the hot tropical sun. When properly dried, they can easily be stored for a very long time. Serve bean dishes often because they are good for the body as well as for the pocketbook.

Chicken in Bean Powder Plasas

Africans cook beans in many ways. In this dish, common to Central, East, and West African countries, dry beans are crushed into powder and then used to make a thick sauce.

Helpful Hints:

a. Lamb, goatmeat, pork, beef, fish, and seafood may also be used in place of chicken in this dish.
b. To make beans into powder see How to Make Beans into Powder (p. 160).
c. The more bean powder is used, the thicker the sauce becomes.
d. Serve sauce with boiled rice.

2–3 pound broiler or frying chicken, cut up
salt to taste
ground black pepper to taste
fresh palm oil or groundnut (peanut) oil, amount desired
1 large white onion, chopped
2 large tomatoes, chopped
1 sweet bell pepper, chopped

fresh hot peppers, chopped and to taste
1 large kpohwoh (portabella) mushroom, chopped
¼ to ⅓ cup bean powder
4 green onions, chopped
3 tablespoons tomato paste
grated fresh ginger to taste
3 cloves garlic, chopped

1. Remove excess chicken fat and skin as desired, wash, and cut it up. Put chicken, salt, and pepper in a skillet. Cover and bring to a boil.

2. Add 2 cups water and cook until chicken is almost done.

3. Empty skillet into a bowl and return it to medium heat. Add ¼–⅓ cup of oil and white onion and cook until onion is tender.

4. Stir in tomatoes, garlic, peppers, and mushrooms. Also add all of broth and bring to a boil.

5. Slowly add bean powder as you mix with a wooden spoon until well mixed. If sauce is too thick, stir in enough hot water and bring it to desired thickness.

6. Add chicken and rest of ingredients. Continue to cook, stirring often, until chicken is done and sauce is about the consistency of thick spaghetti sauce. Serve hot with boiled rice.

How to Make Beans into Powder

½ cup broad dry beans (or amount desired)

1. Put beans in a heated skillet that is over medium heat. With a wooden spoon stir often until they are heated through. (You do not want to roast them, you just want them heated through so that they break easily.)

2. Remove from skillet and grind them into fine powder in a food processor while they are still warm.

Note: In Africa the beans are stone ground. They may also be ground in a wooden mortar *(kondeh)* with a wooden pestle *(ngeteh)*.

Beans in Bean Mushroom Sauce

This dish is prepared in most African countries using local mushrooms, herbs, and spices.

Helpful Hint:

Serve with boiled rice.

*fresh palm oil or groundnut
    (peanut) oil, amount desired*
⅓ pound pearl onions
*½ pound button mushrooms,
    cleaned and cut in half*
*1 green sweet bell pepper,
    chopped*
*fresh hot peppers, chopped
    and to taste*
salt to taste
3 large tomatoes, chopped
*½ cup ohleleh beans; see How
    to Make Ohleleh Beans (p. 30)*
*1 cup or more chicken broth
    or water*

*4 cups cooked dry beans
    (cook according to package
    directions and drain)*
2 tablespoons tomato paste
*fresh ginger, chopped and to
    taste*
ground cumin to taste
ground cinnamon to taste
curry powder to taste
*boiled or roasted groundnuts
    (peanuts) for garnishing*
*chopped green onions for
    garnishing*

1. Add to skillet oil, onions, mushrooms, peppers, salt, and tomatoes. Mix, cover, and cook until onions are tender, about 3 minutes. Put mixture into a bowl and return skillet to medium heat.

2. Put ⅓ cup of oil in skillet and stir in *ohleleh* beans. Continue to cook and stir until beans separate.

3. Stir in broth and bring to a boil. Add tomato-onion mixture and more liquid as needed.

4. Add rest of ingredients except groundnuts (peanuts) and green onions. Mix and cook until beans are well heated. Remove from heat and put in a serving dish. Garnish with groundnuts and green onions in that order and serve hot.

Note: Meat, chicken, fish, or seafood may also be added during cooking.

Jayanh Beans

Helpful Hint:

Serve with boiled rice or cooked green bananas.

*3 cups dry broad or lima
  beans (soaked in cold water
  for 2–4 hours and washed)*
*1 chicken, washed and cut
  into desired portions*
*2 large fresh tomatoes,
  chopped*
3 tablespoons tomato paste
1 large white onion, chopped
2 sweet peppers, chopped
*½ pound white mushrooms,
  sliced*

*hot peppers, chopped and to
  taste*
salt to taste
*1 medium kobo kobo (eggplant),
  cut up (need not peel
  except so desired)*
fresh **poponda** *(basil), chopped
  and to taste*
*½ cup cooked green peas for
  garnishing (cook in water
  only until bright green and
  drain)*

1. Cover beans with water and cook until almost done, drain, and set aside.

2. Add to pot all other ingredients except *kobo kobo* (eggplant), *poponda* (basil), and green peas. Stirring occasionally, cook until chicken is almost done.

3. Gently stir in beans and *kobo kobo* (eggplant) and continue to cook until both are done. Add *poponda* (basil) and cook a few more minutes. Put in a serving dish and garnish with green peas before serving.

Plain Ohleleh

This dish is made in Central, West, and South African countries. It may be referred to by other names.

Helpful Hints:

a. When fresh banana leaves are held over open fire, they become soft and pliable. *Ohleleh* is then packaged in the leaf before it is steamed. Corn husk may also be used as another wrapping material.
b. It can be served hot, but for firmness, allow dish to cool to room temperature before serving.

4 cups ohleleh beans; see
  How to Make Ohleleh
  Beans (p. 30)
fresh palm oil, sesame oil, or
  peanut oil to taste

fresh hot peppers, chopped
  and to taste
salt to taste
banana leaves or corn husk

1. Mix all ingredients except leaves in a mixing bowl. Put 1 tablespoonful on a piece of wrapper.
2. Wrap by bringing left side of leaf over mixture to right side, right side over left side, top over bottom, bottom over top, and tie with another corn husk or a string. You have just made a *tiiwee*.
3. Repeat until all of mixture is wrapped.
4. Put in a steamer, each on the folded side, and steam 3-4 hours or until beans are cooked. Turn off stove and cool to room temperature while steamer stays on top of stove. Serve while in *tiiwee*.

Variations:

Ohleleh with Fish: To bean mixture add 1 cup steamed, slightly mashed fish steak. Mix, wrap into *tiiwee*, and steam.
Ohleleh with Sesame: To bean mixture add ⅓ cup roasted and ground sesame seeds and 1 tablespoon sesame oil. Mix, wrap into *tiiwee*, and steam.

Moi Moi

6·9

Helpful Hints:

a. See How to Make Ohleleh Beans (p. 30).
b. Clean the inside of each empty fruit or vegetable can. Completely open one end and generously grease the inside.
c. May add 1 or 2 whole, hard-boiled, shelled eggs to each can before beans are steamed.

2 cups ohleleh beans
salt and chopped fresh hot
  peppers to taste
1 tablespoon vegetable oil or
  to taste
2 16-ounce empty fruit or
  vegetable cans, cleaned and
  oiled

hard boiled eggs (optional)
Enough banana leaves to
  cover both cans or 4 corn
  husks to cover each can or
  1 piece of aluminum foil
  large enough to cover open
  end of each can

1. Put in a mixing bowl beans, salt, pepper, and oil and mix. Add half of mixture to each can and add boiled eggs. Cover open end with banana leaf and secure with a string.

2. Set cans in a heavy pot, adding water to cover two-thirds the height of cans. Bring to a gentle boil and cook on low heat for about 3 hours or until beans are done.

3. Turn off heat, keep cans in cooking water, and cool *moi moi* to room temperature. Remove each can from water and open the unopened end.

4. Push steamed beans through one end, slice, and serve.

Moi Moi Mango Salad

Helpful Hints:

a. See *moi moi* recipe (opposite) and make it in advance. Also make Green Mango Sesame Honey Sauce (p. 222).
b. Use ripe, firm mangoes, amount desired; peel and cut into chunks.

1. Cut *moi moi* into cubes or slices. Put in a serving dish and add mango chunks.
2. Pour Green Mango Sesame Honey Sauce over beans, garnish with sliced kiwi, and serve.

Moi Moi with Topping

Helpful Hints:

a. Make *moi moi* in advance.
b. Use suggested topping or your own and serve: cooked chopped shrimp, grated cheese of choice, chopped fruits of choice, chopped hard-boiled eggs, chopped nuts of choice, and roasted, ground sesame.

Moi Moi Topping

1. Cut *moi moi* into bite-size pieces in different shapes.
2. Arrange on a serving platter, add topping, and serve.

Ohleleh Hot Cakes

Helpful Hints:

a. See How to Make Ohleleh Beans (p. 30).
b. Size of hot cakes depends on what is desired.
c. Dish is done very much the same as flat pancakes. More oil and time are used to make sure that beans are well done. Also cook a little more slowly on low-medium heat.

*oil of choice for frying,
  amount desired*
*ohleleh beans, 2 cups or amount
  desired*

*salt and pepper to taste
shredded vegetables of choice
  (optional)*

1. In a bowl, mix all ingredients except oil. Add oil to heated skillet and pour 1–2 tablespoons of beans. Slowly cook on one side, turn, and cook on the other side until it is done. About 8 cakes will be made.
2. Remove from skillet and serve hot with Green Mango Sesame Honey Sauce (p. 222).

Ohleleh Akara

Helpful Hints:

a. See How to Make Ohleleh Beans (p. 30).
b. Make Green Mango Sesame Honey Sauce (p. 222) to serve with dish.

*ohleleh beans, amount
  desired*

*salt and pepper to taste
oil for deep frying*

1. Add oil to heated skillet, 2–3 inches deep (see Suma's Onion Oil Test, p. 228).

2. Pour beans by spoonfuls in hot oil and fry until golden. Remove from oil, drain, and serve hot with sauce.

Fried Moi Moi with Chicken Sauce

Helpful Hint:

Do not steam beans with boiled eggs except so desired.

Moi Moi (p. 164)
2 tablespoons roasted
*   sesame seeds*
groundnut (peanut) oil
*   amount desired*
½ pound ground chicken
3 green onions, chopped
fresh ginger, chopped and
*   to taste*

fresh hot peppers, chopped
*   and to taste*
1 fresh tomato, chopped
⅓ cup fresh mushrooms,
*   chopped*
salt to taste
chopped parsley for garnishing
½ cup cooked black beans
*   for garnishing*

1. Cut *moi moi* into ⅓-inch slices. Sprinkle each slice with roasted sesame. Press both sides lightly with a spoon to push sesame seeds into beans and to keep seeds from falling off.

2. Add oil (just enough to brown beans) to a heated skillet that is over medium heat. Fry slices until light brown, turning once.

3. Remove from skillet and drain; arrange in a serving platter and keep warm.

4. Stir and cook chicken in skillet for 2 minutes. Stir in rest of ingredients except parsley and black beans.

5. Cover and cook for about 8 minutes or until done. Spoon sauce over *moi moi* and garnish with black beans and parsley in that order before serving it hot.

Oxtail with Broad Beans

Oxtail is an inexpensive cut of meat that is succulent and delicious. Other animal tails are also used in this dish on many African farms.

Helpful Hints:

a. Brown disjointed oxtail on all sides in a hot skillet, drain, and discard oil.
b. Meat should be cooked slowly in liquid.
c. Serve with boiled rice, cooked green bananas, roasted bread-fruit, or boiled plantains.

2 pounds oxtail prepared for cooking
1 large white onion, chopped
water or meat broth enough to cover meat
3 cups fresh or frozen lima beans
2 large tomatoes, chopped
⅓ cup fresh coconut, shredded

1 sweet bell pepper, chopped
2 carrots, peeled and chopped
fresh hot peppers, chopped and to taste
fresh ginger, chopped and to taste
salt to taste
4 green onions, chopped

1. Add to cooking pot meat and white onion, cover with water or meat broth, and bring to a boil.
2. With lid in place cook on low heat, stirring occasionally, until meat is almost done.
3. Stir in rest of ingredients except green onions. Continue to cook until meat and beans are done.
4. Stir in green onions and serve hot.

Awujoh Beans

Awujoh is a celebration to remember and honor somebody who has passed away. After an African person dies, the mourning period lasts for forty days. At the end of this time, the Sierra Leone Creoles would bring together family and friends, one last time, to honor the life and memory of the deceased. This is a happy occasion, even for the deceased's close relatives. They would talk about the good things that person did and how he touched and enriched others' lives. They would tell funny stories about him to emphasize that he was just like one of them, and that he lived like others did. There would be much joy, singing, and dancing.

An *awujoh* also means plenty of food. One dish that is a must at the celebration is *awujoh* beans. The two essential ingredients of the dish are black-eyed peas and fresh palm oil. Other less important ingredients, such as meat, vegetables, herbs, and spices, would also be added to complete the cooking.

Helpful Hints:

a. Use fresh palm oil or oil of choice.
b. Water in which dry mushrooms are soaked should be used to cook beans. You may also use fresh white mushrooms to taste instead of dry ones.
c. Serve with boiled rice or cooked green bananas.

1 pound dry black-eyed peas, soaked 3–4 hours
1 pound stew beef, cut up
1 large onion, chopped
½ pound cherry tomatoes, washed and crushed
⅓ cup dry tomatoes
1 sweet bell pepper, chopped

fresh palm oil or oil of choice, ¼ cup or amount desired
fresh hot peppers, chopped and to taste
½ cup dry mushrooms of choice, soaked in water for ½ hour
salt to taste

1. Put all ingredients in a heavy cooking pot. Cover with water and bring to a gentle boil.
2. With lid in place, cook on reduced heat, stirring occasionally and adding more water as needed.

3. When beans and meat are done, remove from heat and serve hot.

Beans and Coconatii

ꙮ

This unusually delicious bean dish is prepared in East, South, and West African countries.

Helpful Hints:

a. Broad lima beans are used in this dish. Other kinds of beans, dry or fresh, may also be used as desired.
b. When dry beans are cooked, they keep longer if they are kept in the cooking water until they are used.
c. This dish can be served with cooked green bananas, cooked ripe plantain, boiled rice, or as desired.

groundnut (peanut) oil, ¼-⅓ cup or amount desired
1 medium white onion, chopped
4 cups cooked broad lima beans (cook according to package directions and drain)
¾ cup fresh coconut, shredded
1 red sweet bell pepper, chopped
ground cumin to taste
fresh ginger, chopped and to taste
fresh hot peppers, chopped and to taste
salt to taste
½ cup roasted or boiled groundnuts (peanuts)
1 bunch green onions, chopped
½ cup cooked corn for garnishing
chopped parsley for garnishing
¼ cup of water

1. Add to heated skillet oil and white onion. Mix and cook until onion is tender.
2. Stir in rest of ingredients except groundnuts, corn, green onions, and parsley. Cook for about 7 minutes. Gently stir in groundnuts and green onions and remove from heat.
3. Spoon onto a serving platter, garnish with corn and parsley, and serve hot.

Mango and Honey Beans

This dish is prepared in many parts of Africa. It is very delicious and easy to make.

Helpful Hints:

a. This dish tastes great the next day, so cook it a day ahead if you can. Just heat and serve.
b. Serve it as you like; that's the beauty of it.

1 pound dry kidney beans
2 large fresh tomatoes,
  chopped
1 large onion, chopped
sesame oil to taste (about
  ¼ cup, optional)
fresh ginger, chopped and
  to taste
ground cinnamon to taste
ground hot peppers to taste

grated peel of 1 lime
juice of same lime
salt to taste
3 medium ripe mangoes
  (peel each, remove meat from
  seed, and cut into chunks)
honey ¼ cup or to taste
poponda (fresh basil), chopped,
  for garnishing
½ cup green onions, chopped

1. Rinse beans and put in a heavy cooking pot, cover with water, and bring to a gentle boil. Turn off heat and let beans stay on stove for about 2 hours. Drain and return to same pot.

2. Add 2–3 cups water and rest of ingredients except mangoes, honey, green onions, and *poponda* (basil). Mix, cover, and bring to a boil. Stirring occasionally, cook on reduced heat until beans are almost done 20–30 minutes, adding more water as needed.

3. Stir in mangoes, honey, and green onions and cook until they are heated through. Remove from heat and put in a serving dish, garnish with *poponda*, and serve hot.

Mama Lango Yogboh Beans and Sweet Potatoes

This is a meal in itself, the kind that is very satisfying. Mama Lango Yogboh knew that and served it often. Many Africans who work on the land and live in small villages also enjoy serving it.

Helpful Hints:

a. Kidney beans are used in this recipe, but use any kind of beans you like.
b. This is a hearty, spicy dish. Use only the amount of herbs and spices that please your taste buds.
c. Shred fresh coconut and add it to skillet that is over medium to low heat. Stir often with a wooden spoon until it is roasted and light brown, about 3 minutes.

1 pound dry kidney beans
2–3 pound broiler or frying chicken, chopped
salt to taste
fresh palm oil or groundnut (peanut) oil, ¼ cup or amount desired
1 large white onion, chopped
2 large tomatoes, chopped
3 tablespoons tomato paste
1 green sweet bell pepper, chopped
fresh ginger, chopped and to taste

2 whole cloves
curry powder to taste
fresh hot peppers, chopped and to taste
shredded roasted coconut for garnishing
chopped green onions for garnishing
ground black pepper to taste
2 pounds sweet potatoes, peeled and shredded or cut into chunks just before cooking

1. Wash beans and put in a heavy cooking pot, cover with water, and slowly bring to a gentle boil. Cook until they are more than half done; turn off heat and keep covered pot on stove until you are ready to use beans.

2. Remove excess skin and fat from chicken as desired. Wash, cut it into small pieces, and season with salt and pepper.

3. Add oil to heated skillet that is over medium heat and stir in chicken and white onion. Cook only until onion is tender.

4. Drain beans and add them to chicken; also add about 2 cups water and rest of ingredients except potatoes, coconuts, and green onions. Cover and cook, stirring occasionally, until chicken and beans are almost done.

5. With a wooden spoon stir in potatoes. Without again mixing, continue to cook until chicken and beans are done. Put in a serving dish, garnish with coconut and green onions, and serve hot.

Beans in Plantain Curry Sauce

This special dish is from Central, East, and South Africa. Try it!

Helpful Hints:

a. Use any kind of beans desired.
b. Serve with boiled rice.

sesame oil, ¼ cup or amount
  desired
2 ripe but firm plantains,
  peeled and chopped or sliced
1 large white onion, chopped
fresh ginger, finely chopped
  and to taste
2 large tomatoes, chopped
curry powder to taste
salt to taste
fresh hot peppers, chopped
  and to taste
4 cups cooked kidney beans
  (cook according to package
  directions and drain)

1–2 pounds chicken breast,
  cut into bite-size portions
3 green onions, chopped
3 tablespoons tomato paste
⅓ cup roasted and ground
  sesame seeds
½ cup cooked green peas for
  garnishing (cook in water
  only until bright green;
  drain and set aside)
½ cup of water

1. Put oil, plantains, white onion, and ginger in a heated skillet. Cook and stir until onion is tender, about 3–4 minutes.

2. Stir in rest of ingredients except green peas and kidney beans.

Cover, and cook 15–20 minutes or until chicken is done. Stir in beans and heat through.

3. Put in a serving dish, garnish with green peas, and serve hot.

Beans in Squash Plasas

This dish is from most countries in Africa.

Helpful Hints:

a. Pinto beans are used in this recipe, but use any kind desired.
b. This dish is served with cooked rice; boiled green bananas; boiled, baked, or fried plantains.

1 medium butternut squash
fresh palm oil or groundnut (peanut) oil, ¼ cup or amount desired
1 pound boneless goatmeat or beef; cut into bite-size portions
1 large onion, chopped
2 celery stalks, washed and cut into very thin slices
1 large tomato, chopped

3 tablespoons tomato paste
1 sweet bell pepper, chopped
2 whole cloves
fresh or dried hot peppers to taste
salt to taste
4 cups cooked pinto beans (cook according to package directions and drain)
chopped parsley for garnishing

1. Peel squash and cut in half, lengthwise. Spoon out seeds and fibers before washing. Cut it into desired chunks and set aside.

2. Add oil to a heated skillet that is over medium heat. Brown meat, stir in onion, and cook until onion is tender, about 3–4 minutes.

3. Stir in rest of ingredients except squash, beans, and parsley. Also add some water as needed. Cover and cook, stirring occasionally, until meat is almost done.

4. Gently stir in squash and beans. Without again mixing, cover and continue to cook until meat and squash are done. Put in a serving dish, garnish with parsley, and serve hot.

Groundnut-Coconut Shrimp Beans

This dish is made in Central, South, and West Africa. It is delicious and nutritious.

Helpful Hints:

a. In Africa, beautiful broad beans of many colors are often used in this dish. Please use fresh or frozen lima beans.
b. Serve with boiled rice or cooked green bananas.

groundnut (peanut) oil, amount desired
1 large white onion, chopped
2 cups **kpohwoh** *(portabella) mushrooms, chopped*
3 cups fresh or frozen lima beans
⅓ cup groundnut (peanut) butter (mix with coconut milk below)
2 cups coconut milk; use store bought or see How to Make Coconut Milk (p. 239)

3 large tomatoes, chopped
1 sweet bell pepper, chopped
2 cloves garlic, crushed
fresh ginger, chopped and to taste
fresh hot peppers, chopped and to taste
salt to taste
1 pound medium shrimp, shelled and deveined
3 green onions, chopped
chopped parsley for garnishing

1. Add oil, white onion, and mushrooms to a heated heavy pot that is over medium heat. Stir with a wooden spoon and cook until onion is tender, 3–4 minutes.
2. Stir in rest of ingredients except shrimp, green onions, and parsley. Mix, cover, and cook until beans are almost done, adding more liquid as needed.
3. Add shrimp and green onions, and cook only until beans are done. Put in a serving dish, garnish with parsley, and serve hot.

Okra Bean Soup

This dish is as African as it can get. It is made in all countries in Africa. We hope you enjoy it as much as we do.

Helpful Hints:

a. Black-eyed peas are most often used in this dish. Use beans of your choice, however.
b. Use fresh or frozen okra as desired.
c. Serve with boiled rice.

1 pound stew meat, cut up
1 pound dry black-eyed peas
1 large onion, chopped
2 large fresh tomatoes, chopped
hot peppers, chopped and to taste

ground black pepper to taste
2 cloves garlic, crushed
salt to taste
2 pounds okra, washed, ends removed and sliced

1. Put meat in a heavy cooking pot.
2. Remove any unwanted foreign material from beans, rinse, and add to meat. Also add rest of ingredients except okra. Cover with water and bring to a boil while lid is in place.
3. Cook over reduced heat, stirring occasionally with a wooden spoon. When beans and meat are almost done, stir in okra. Continue to cook until beans and meat are done. Serve hot.

Green Beans with Tomatoes and Mushrooms

This dish is prepared in East, North, and South African countries. After you eat it, you will not want to eat green beans cooked any other way.

Helpful Hints:

a. Beans should be tender but crisp; do not overcook them.
b. They may be cut into desired portions or cooked whole.

sesame oil, ¼ cup or to taste
2 large tomatoes, chopped
1 red sweet pepper, chopped
fresh hot peppers, chopped
* and to taste*
2 cloves garlic, crushed
2 cups sliced white mush-
* rooms*

2 pounds green beans; wash
* and remove ends*
1 bunch green onions, chopped
grated peel of one lime
1 cup or more chicken broth
salt to taste
¼ cup roasted and ground
* sesame seeds for garnishing*

1. Add oil, tomatoes, peppers, garlic, and mushrooms to a heated skillet that is over medium heat. With a wooden spoon stir and cook for a few minutes.

2. Stir in rest of ingredients except sesame. Cover and cook until beans are just done and bright green, about 10 minutes. Cook longer if you want.

3. Put in a serving dish, garnish with sesame, and serve hot.

Chicken and Green Peas Fanima

People in many African countries prepare this dish not only with chicken but also with beef and fish. It is delicious, nutritious, and your family and friends will enjoy eating it.

Helpful Hints:

a. Make in advance Spicy Groundnuts (Peanuts) (p. 141) for garnishing.
b. Fresh or frozen green peas may be used in dish.
c. Serve with Ngeh Ngeh Pahnwah Rice (Green Check Rice) (p. 139) or plain boiled rice.

sesame oil, olive oil, or fresh
   palm oil, ¼ cup or amount
   desired
1 white onion, chopped
fresh ginger, finely chopped
   and to taste
2 cloves garlic, crushed
2 large tomatoes, chopped
1 pound boneless chicken
   breast or amount desired
   (cut into bite-size pieces
   and season with salt)
3 tablespoons tomato paste
1 sweet bell pepper, chopped

fresh hot peppers, chopped
   and to taste
grated peel of 1 lime
salt to taste
4 cups fresh or frozen green
   peas
1 bunch green onions,
   chopped
Spicy Groundnuts (Peanuts) (p. 14)
   for garnishing
½ cup cooked broad beans for
   garnishing (cook according
   to directions on package)

1. Add oil, white onion, ginger, garlic, and chopped tomatoes to a preheated skillet that is over medium heat. Stir and cook until onion is tender, 3–4 minutes.

2. Stir in rest of ingredients except peas, Spicy Groundnuts (Peanuts), cooked broad beans, and green onions. Cover and cook, mixing often, for about 8 minutes, or until chicken is almost done.

3. Stir in peas and green onions; cook only until peas are just done and bright green.

4. Remove from heat and put in a serving dish. Garnish with Spicy Groundnuts (Peanuts) and broad beans in that order and serve hot with rice.

Lentils and Beef in Groundnut Sauce

Lentils are one of the oldest foods known to man. In Genesis 25:33–34 we read that Esau sold his birthright to his brother, Jacob, for a bowl of lentil soup. This dish is just as delicious and enticing as the one for which Esau sold his birthright and his future.

Although lentil dishes are prepared in many parts of Africa, the people in North Africa serve this ancient food most often.

Helpful Hint:

Serve dish with boiled rice or bread of choice.

1 pound beef or amount de-
    sired, cut up
1 large white onion, chopped
1 green bell pepper, chopped
3 large tomatoes, chopped
2 cups carrots, chopped
4 large white mushrooms,
    sliced
fresh ginger, chopped and to
    taste
fresh hot peppers, chopped
    and to taste
salt to taste

3–4 cups water, or beef or
    vegetable broth
1 pound dry lentils (remove
    unwanted material and wash)
⅓ cup groundnut (peanut)
    butter mixed with half cup
    water
1 medium zucchini, cut into
    chunks
roasted groundnuts (peanuts)
    for garnishing
chopped green onions for
    garnishing

1. Put in cooking pot all ingredients except lentils, green onions, zucchini, peanuts, and peanut butter. Add water, cover, and bring to a boil.

2. On low heat cook 15–20 minutes, stirring occasionally, until meat is about half done. Add lentils and peanut butter and cook 15 minutes until meat and lentils are almost done.

3. Stir in zucchini and continue to cook until meat and lentils are done and there is sauce.

4. Put in a serving dish, garnish with nuts and green onions, and serve hot.

Lentils and Lamb in Kobo Kobo (Eggplant) Sesame Sauce

Nothing could be more hearty than this dish from North and South African countries. Find out for yourself.

Helpful Hints:

a. Cut up *kobo kobo* (eggplant) just before cooking to keep it from turning dark.
b. Serve with steamed *cous cous*, boiled rice, or bread of choice.

1 large white onion, chopped
1 pound lamb or amount de-
sired, cut of choice, cut into
small pieces (cubed)
sesame oil, ¼ cup to taste
3 large tomatoes, chopped
ground cumin to taste
grated fresh ginger to taste
salt to taste
3 cups broth or water

1 pound dry lentils or amount
desired, washed
½ cup roasted and ground
sesame seeds
fresh hot peppers, chopped
and to taste
1 sweet bell pepper, chopped
1 medium kobo kobo (egg-
plant), peeled and sliced
chopped fresh parsley for
garnishing

1. Put in cooking pot all ingredients except lentils, *kobo kobo* (eggplant), peppers, mint leaves, and ground sesame.
2. With lid in place, bring to a boil and cook over reduced heat. Stirring occasionally, cook 20-30 minutes until meat is about half done.
3. Stir in rest of ingredients except *kobo kobo*, parsley, and mint leaves. Cook until meat and lentils are almost done, about 20 minutes.
4. Stir in *kobo kobo* and mint leaves. Continue to cook until *kobo kobo* is done, 10–12 minutes.
5. Put in a serving dish, garnish with parsley, and serve hot.

Chick Peas in Tomato Sauce

This dish is from East, North, and South African countries. It is delicious and easy to prepare.

Helpful Hint:

Serve with boiled rice, steamed *cous cous*, or bread of choice.

1 pound boneless chicken
   breast, cut into bite-size
   portions
1 white onion, chopped
olive oil, amount desired
2 large fresh tomatoes,
   chopped
1 sweet pepper, chopped
fresh hot peppers, chopped
   and to taste

grated fresh ginger to taste
1 cup celery, chopped
salt to taste
3 cups cooked chick peas
   (cook according to directions
   on package and drain)
1 bunch green onions,
   chopped
chopped parsley for
   garnishing

1. Add to skillet all ingredients except chick peas, parsley, and green onions. Stir, cover, and cook for about 7 minutes.

2. Stir in chick peas and green onions. Continue to cook until chicken is done. Put in a serving dish, garnish with parsley, and serve hot.

Chick Peas Mint Salad

This delicious dish is from East, North, and South African countries.

Helpful Hints:

a. Serve chilled or at room temperature.
b. If possible, use fresh lemon juice.

3 to 4 cups cooked chick peas
   (cook according to package
   directions and drain)
⅓ cup green onions, chopped
1 red sweet bell pepper,
   chopped

2 large tomatoes, cut into
   chunks
fresh mint leaves, chopped
   and to taste
1 medium cucumber, thinly
   sliced (peel if desired)

parsley, chopped and to taste
olive oil, ¼–⅓ cup or
   amount desired

juice of 2 lemons
sugar or honey to taste
salt to taste

1. Put all ingredients except olive oil, lemon juice, sugar, and salt in a bowl.
2. Mix in a bottle oil, lemon juice, sugar, and salt.
3. Add oil mixture to rest of ingredients and toss. Serve at room temperature or after salad is chilled.

Hummus

This dish is prepared in most countries in North Africa. It is also made in some other parts of Africa and may be referred to by other names.

Helpful Hints:

a. Add one of the following ingredients, to taste, after the chick peas are ground: ¼–⅓ cup sesame oil, sesame paste, ⅓ cup olive oil, or ¼–⅓ cup chicken broth (¼ cup oil must be added to broth of ¼–⅓ cup).
b. *Hummus* is used as a spread, but it can also be used as a dip by adding a little more liquid, like olive oil or lemon or lime juice.
c. When I make hummus for myself, I wash the peas without removing the skin—to make the most use of the fiber.

3 cups cooked chick peas or
   amount desired (cook
   according to package
   directions and drain)
sesame paste to taste
chicken broth to taste (add
   if mixture is too thick)

salt to taste
pepper to taste
green onions, finely chopped
   and to taste (optional)
parsley, finely chopped and to
   taste (optional)

1. Remove skin from peas and grind into a smooth paste.
2. Put paste into a mixing bowl and stir in rest of the ingredients.
3. Put in a serving dish and serve as a spread or a dip.
4. Remove skin from peas. Put all ingredients in a blender or food processor. Mix until mixture is a smooth spread.

Note: When I make *hummus* for myself, I crush the peas without removing the skin.

For Better Understanding

Most African stories are not written down. One cannot find them on shelves in local libraries. They are found on the shelves of the human mind, stored away in the hearts of the African people. They are told to children by word of mouth, at the feet of grandparents, very similar to the way I heard them when I was growing up. The stories are powerful. They capture and convey images of people and families; of harvest season and hunger periods; of animals, the rain forest, and the list goes on. This form of teaching still captivates the young mind. It helps children to learn about themselves, and it teaches them how to experience and live life fully.

There was a story of plenty and famine. It also took place in Africa a long time ago. In Genesis chapters 41 through 45, we read that there was much food in Egypt for seven years. Then a great famine came to the world. People came to Egypt to buy food "so that we may live and not die of hunger." Since that story took place, Africans have experienced more than their share of hunger. What causes it? Countless and prolonged drought, floods, and other changes in weather patterns; long and bitter, senseless wars; lack of good farming tools; and the ever-growing human population are all responsible for hunger in our world. One would have to be blind not to see the never-ending images of starving people, especially African children, on television. These children usually have enormous bellies, arms and legs that look like skeletons, and sad-looking large eyes. They have no smiles on their faces. For them a smile is a luxury; an indulgence the body, with barely enough energy to maintain life itself, cannot afford. The children may not have smiling faces, but they have great willpower. Their eyes are full of love, hope, and determination to stay alive.

Plantain and Bananas

GOLDEN FRIED PLANTAIN—THE PASSING GRADE FOR MARRIAGE

Africa has produced some of the greatest women in history. Cleopatra and Queen Nefertiti are two examples. The culture, however, has always believed that a woman's main purpose in life was to become a good wife and mother. The older female members of society saw to it that their daughters and granddaughters were ready for marriage when the time came, usually soon after puberty. They also prepared them to be able to successfully manage future childbearing pain. For example, when young women saw their mothers and grandmothers open hot cooking pots without the use of pot holders, they too practiced doing the same. A statement like, "Physical pain comes with the privilege of becoming a mother" was heard often enough. Girls learned to accept the fact that the only painkiller available to women during labor and delivery time was endurance. So they learned to gradually increase their pain tolerance for the time when labor and motherhood would come upon them.

Soon after a young lady was spoken for (engaged), she had to spend some time with her future mother-in-law in order to learn her style of cooking. She already understood that her cooking had to please her future husband; it had to be like his mother's cooking. Many people believe that their mothers are the world's best cooks. This may not always be true, but after a son has eaten his mother's cooking throughout his growing years, often associating happy memories with her kind of cooking, for him she indeed becomes the best cook in the world. Out of a desire to please her future husband, a young bride to be would often see the need to learn some cooking tips from her future mother-in-law.

After these ladies had met all requirements for getting married, they actually had to demonstrate their readiness, similar to taking a final exam, to show that they had learned the material well. For example, plantain was used to test their cooking skills at frying food.

Why plantain? One would have to have much cooking skill to be able to fry this fruit to a beautiful golden color. One must know the amount of oil to use. At what point is it necessary to increase or decrease the heat? When is it time to turn over the slices? Remember that all of these were carried out when the use of a cooking thermometer was out of the question. After so many years of training, the young ladies always served beautiful golden plantains with smiles, earning a passing grade to become married women.

At the young age of about 15 years, African ladies were well advanced in what modern people now call home economics (domestic science). Most often after the marriage took place, the bride came to live with her husband and his parents. They all became a big, happy family, and the parents helped to care for the grandchildren.

Fried Plantain

Plantain is served in all countries in Africa. It is most often served as a vegetable, not as a fruit.

Helpful Hint:

Green as well as ripe plantains may be fried, but they always taste better when served hot.

2 plantains or number desired	*salt to taste (optional)* *oil of choice for frying*

1. Peel each plantain and cut in one of the following ways:
   a. Cut across into 3 equal portions, then cut each piece into 3 equal parts, lengthwise.
   b. Holding a knife almost parallel to cutting surface, cut plantain on the diagonal into ⅓-inch portions.
   c. Slice across into ⅓-inch pieces.
2. Add salt if desired and mix well. Put oil (about 2 inches deep) in skillet and heat to 375 degrees, or use Suma's Onion Oil Test (p. 228) as needed.

3. Put plantains in hot oil (do not overcrowd) and fry until golden on both sides. Remove from oil, drain, and serve as a side dish or as a snack.

Variation:

Fried Banana: Use green bananas instead of plantains.

Ngehleh Feleh Plantain (Twice Fried Plantains)

Helpful Hints:

a. Ripe plantain is used in dish because it is easy to squash. It must be crushed when it is still warm.
b. Serve hot as a vegetable or as snack.

> **2 ripe plantains that are already fried; see Fried Plantain (p. 185)**
> **groundnut (peanut) oil for frying**
>
> **ground cinnamon to taste**
> **grated fresh ginger to taste**
> **sugar to taste (optional)**
> **rice or wheat flour**

1. Lay each piece on a dry, floured surface. Crush with a rolling pin so that it is flattened out but still remains intact.
2. Heat oil (¼-inch deep) to 375 degrees or use Suma's Onion Oil Test (p. 228) as needed.
3. Sprinkle each piece with cinnamon and ginger. Dust both sides with flour, and fry for a few minutes or until crisp, turning once.
4. Remove from oil and drain. Serve hot with Ginger Honey Lemon Sauce (recipe follows) or sprinkle with sugar and serve hot.

Ginger Honey Lemon Sauce

Helpful Hint:

If possible, use only fresh lemon.

honey ¼ cup or to taste   *ground hot peppers to taste*
juice of 2 fresh lemon to taste   *salt to taste*
grated fresh ginger to taste   *¼ cup oil of choice*

Put all ingredients in a bowl, mix well, and serve.

Plantain Bolah

This is a delicious, elegant, and colorful way of serving boiled plantains.

Helpful Hint:

Use medium ripe plantain in this dish; it is a little sweet and soft, just right.

**2 plantains that are cooked (see Boiled Bananas and
    Plantains, p. 191)**

1. Peel each fruit while still warm and cut into desired slices and shapes.
2. Remove a piece at center of each portion and make a hole about halfway down.
3. Fill hole with one of the following suggested foods or some of your own. Arrange on a serving platter and serve.

a. Crushed avocado, lemon juice, sugar, and salt to taste, all mixed
b. Groundnut (peanut) butter mixed with honey
c. Hard-boiled egg mixed with salt, pepper, and sesame paste

d. Grated cheese of your choice
e. Chopped mushrooms, green onions, and peppers all cooked in ¼ cup oil for 8–10 minutes
f. Jellies or jams of your choice

Note: Plantains can also be served without removing the center; just top with favorites and serve.

Hot Curry Plantain with Lamb

Helpful Hints:

a. Use plantains that are half ripe.
b. Make the recipe only as hot and spicy as you like it.

1 pound good cut of lamb, cut up	*fresh ginger, finely chopped and to taste*
1 large tomato, chopped	*salt to taste*
1 tablespoon tomato paste	*2 or 3 plantains*
curry powder to taste	*4 green onions, chopped*
fresh hot peppers to taste, chopped	*¼ cup roasted and ground sesame seeds for garnishing*
groundnut (peanut) oil, ¼ cup or amount desired	*(optional)*
ground cinnamon to taste	*chopped parsley for garnishing*

1. Peel each plantain and cut into ⅓-inch slices. Add oil to a heated skillet and stir in all ingredients except plantains, parsley, sesame, and green onions.

2. Cover and cook, stirring often, for about 8–14 minutes or until meat is almost done.

3. Stir in plantains and green onions. Cover and cook, without again mixing, until plantains are done. Put in a serving platter, garnish with sesame and parsley in that order, and serve hot.

Stuffed Plantain with Mango Plantain Chicken Plasas

Helpful Hints:

a. Use large, green plantains, or as green as possible.
b. Must serve dish while it is still hot.

2 large green plantains
1 pound ground chicken
1 ½ cups medium ripe man-
*   goes, chopped*
2 green onions, chopped

fresh ginger, finely chopped
*   and to taste*
ground hot pepper to taste
salt to taste
groundnut (peanut) oil or oil
*   of choice*

1. Peel each plantain and cut across into 3 equal portions. Using vegetable knife and a spoon, scoop so that each piece looks like a water pipe with a large hole running through. Lightly oil the inside. (Save the portion that is dug out to use in Mango Plantain Chicken Plasas.)

2. Put rest of ingredients in a mixing bowl, mix, and loosely stuff each plantain piece.

3. Fry in deep oil (about 3 inches deep) until golden on all sides. If in doubt about doneness of stuffing, cover and cook for about 3 minutes; uncover and cook another 3 minutes. Remove from oil, drain, and keep warm.

4. To prepare in oven, stuff each portion and rub with some oil. Put in a greased oven dish and bake in a 375 degree oven 45 minutes or until done.

5. Arrange on a serving platter; spoon Mango Plantain Chicken Plasas over plantains, garnish with chopped parsley, and serve while still hot.

Variation:

Baked Plain Plantain: Bake green or ripe plantains without stuffing and serve hot with Mango Plantain Chicken Plasas below.

Mango Plantain Chicken Plasas

Helpful Hint:

Use medium-ripe mangoes.

portion of plantain dug out,
  or small plantain, finely
  chopped
¾ pound chicken breast, cut
  into small portions or
  ground chicken
1 large mango, peeled and
  meat cut into chunks
1 large tomato, chopped

2 white mushrooms, sliced
fresh ginger, chopped and to
  taste
fresh hot peppers, chopped
  and to taste
groundnut (peanut) oil,
  amount desired
⅓ cup roasted peanuts, chopped
chopped parsley for garnishing

1. Put all ingredients except parsley and nuts in skillet.
2. On medium heat, cook, stirring often, until chicken and plantains are done.
3. Stir in nuts and spoon mixture over plantains. Garnish with parsley and serve hot.

BANANA AND PLANTAIN—THE TWIN FRUITS

Did you know that "banana" is an African name? It is one of two African words most frequently used by English-speaking people around the world. The other word is "safari." Banana, like plantain, originated in Africa where both grow wild and are also cultivated. Most people would find it hard to tell a banana tree and a plantain tree apart, because they look almost identical. I most certainly can't tell one from the other. After both fruits have achieved full growth, however, a plantain becomes much larger than a banana. The words of Jesus, "You will know them by their fruits," are literally true in this case.

These twin fruits are cooked and served very much the same way when they are green. Many African tribes would rather eat cooked green bananas or plantain than eat rice. They first boil them in the skin, then they peel and mash them like potatoes. They are often served with meat sauce.

Boiled Bananas and Plantains

This is one popular way Africans serve the two fruits on the farms and in small villages. They are ready in just minutes.

Helpful Hints:

a. Plantains are larger than bananas, and they take longer to cook.
b. Serve while they are still hot, because they taste better.

2 green bananas or plantains   *salt to taste*
    or amount desired
roasted ground sesame seeds
    or sesame oil to taste

   1. Cut both ends of each fruit and put in cooking pot. Add water. (It is not necessary to completely cover fruit with water.) Cook bananas and plantains separately because they do not cook at the same rate.
   2. With lid in place bring to a boil and cook over medium heat until done, or it becomes soft.
   3. Remove from pot, peel, and cut into slices. Put in a serving dish, sprinkle with roasted ground sesame seeds or sesame oil and salt, and serve hot.

Plantain and Banana Chips

These chips will be the talk of any party. Try them!

Helpful Hints:

a. Use green plantains or bananas.
b. Slice as thin as possible.

green plantains or bananas,   **salt to taste**
    amount desired   **oil for frying**
grated fresh ginger to taste

1. Peel each fruit and slice as thin as possible. Add ginger and salt and mix well.
2. Add oil to heated skillet (about 3 inches deep) and heat to 375 degrees. Use Suma's Onion Oil Test (p. 228) as needed.
3. Put some of the chips in oil. (Do not overcrowd.) Fry until they are light brown and crunchy. Remove from oil, drain, and set aside. Repeat until all chips are done. If possible, serve while they are still hot.

Banana Fesuewa

This dish is simple and delicious.

Helpful Hints:

a. If possible, use fresh pineapple and fresh lime juice.
b. Serve each banana in an individual serving dish.

2 ripe but firm bananas   **1 cup crushed fresh pineapple**
1 ripe mango, peeled and   **1 cup paw paw (papaya),**
    chopped   **cubed**

1 cup chunks of local berries   *shredded fresh coconut for*
juice of 1 lemon   *garnishing*
sugar to taste   *lemon wedges for garnishing*

1. Wash each banana and remove both ends. Lay bananas in serving dishes and peel off the uppermost skin portion. Slice bananas without removing them from skin.

2. Put rest of ingredients except coconut and lemon wedges in a bowl and mix. Spoon half of mixture over each banana and also between slices. Garnish with shredded coconut and lemon wedges in that order, and serve.

Banana Kula

This dish is refreshing and delicious.

Helpful Hints:

a. Use fresh lemon juice and pineapples.
b. Add bananas just before serving the dish cold.

2 ripe bananas, sliced   *juice of 1 lemon*
2 cups fresh pineapples,   *grated peel of ½ lemon*
* crushed*   *sugar to taste*
2 cups mangoes, chopped   *grated fresh ginger to taste*
honey to taste   *mint leaves for garnishing*

1. Put all ingredients except mint leaves in a mixing bowl and gently mix with a wooden spoon.

2. Put mixture in a serving bowl, garnish with mint leaves, and serve cold.

Breadfruit

BREADFRUIT—NATURE'S WONDER BREAD

Breadfruit, an African wild fruit, also grows in other warm climates around the world. This large and round wonder bread is light, airy, and fluffy like man-made bread yet without the benefit of any leavening agent.

Roasted Breadfruit

Helpful Hints:

a. The most common way breadfruit is prepared in many villages in Africa is roasting it in an open fire.
b. A large breadfruit can be larger than a soccer ball. The bigger the breadfruit, the longer the roasting time to ensure doneness.
c. Breadfruit is always served as a vegetable even though it is a fruit.
d. One can buy breadfruit in African or Asian foodstores.

1 breadfruit   *1 bucket, half full of cold water*

Note: This is how many Africans cook it. Because conditions may be different, you may not want to cook it this way because the fire can get out of hand.

1. Build a fire, using wood. Drop breadfruit into the fire and let it roast until it is as black as charcoal, all around.
2. Remove breadfruit from fire and drop it into the bucket of water. Keep it in water 20–30 minutes, pushing it down often. (Because the fruit is airy, it naturally floats.)

3. Remove fruit from water and lay it on a breadboard. Using a sharp knife, remove the dark covering, which is easy to peel off. Underneath is golden bread with a better taste than baked bread.

4. Cut in slices, away from the core, like you would serve bread or a vegetable.

Boiled Breadfruit
൭

Helpful Hint:

Like bread, this fruit is at its best when it is warm and fresh.

1 breadfruit   *salt to taste*

1. Cut fruit into quarters, lengthwise. Peel and remove the soft core.

2. Cut into equal chunks so that it is cooked at the same rate and cook over medium heat in salt water until soft. Serve like you would serve potatoes or bread.

Breadfruit Dombah
൭

Helpful Hint:

This dish must be served while it is warm.

1. To make breadfruit *dombah*, mash boiled fruit like mashed potatoes while it is still hot.

2. Add salt, butter, or oil of choice to taste, and serve hot.

Fried Breadfruit

Helpful Hint:

Serve the breadfruit while hot.

1. Peel fruit and remove the soft core. Cut into ¼-inch slices and fry in hot oil over medium heat until golden.
2. Serve while hot like you would serve fried potatoes.

Baked Breadfruit

Helpful Hint:

Serve the breadfruit while hot.

1. Peel and slice breadfruit ¼ inch thick. Add to taste sesame oil, roasted sesame seeds, and salt and mix well.
2. Put in a greased baking pan and bake at 375 degrees 30-45 minutes or until golden. Remove from oven and serve while hot.

Foo Foo—African Polenta

This is thick and stiff porridge like what Italians call polenta or soft mashed potatoes. In West Africa it is often made by cooking fermented crushed cassava. African students living abroad make *foo foo* by using food combinations such as instant mashed potatoes and corn flour, cornmeal and corn flour, cream of wheat and corn flour, and so on. Fresh lemon or lime juice to taste is then added during the cooking time to make it taste like it has been fermented.

Cornmeal Potato Foo Foo

Helpful Hints:

a. Make *foo foo* only as stiff as you want it. Adding fresh lemon juice helps to make it taste more like the real thing.
b. *Foo foo* is often served with bitter leaf meat sauce, okra fish sauce, or meat sauce of choice.

*1 cup cornmeal (white or
    yellow)*
1 cup potato flour
2 cups plus boiling water

*fresh lemon or lime juice
    to taste*
salt to taste

1. Mix together cornmeal and potato flour. Add lemon juice and salt to 1½ cups boiling water that is in a heavy cooking pot over medium heat.
2. Using a wooden spoon, slowly stir in cornmeal flour mixture. Continue to stir as you slowly add more boiling water as needed.
3. Stirring often, cook on low heat until it is done.
4. Remove from heat and serve with sauce of choice.

The Palm Oil Story

I have had the privilege to listen to what some people had to say about palm oil. I must say that most of what was said came in the negative. After I thought about their arguments, I decided to say what little I know. This is done with hopes that some new light might be shed on the subject.

Palm oil is extracted from the red outer covering of the

palm kernel. The oil palm tree naturally grows in the tropical regions of the world. The fruit, which is called *tuhweh,* is cooked and crushed underfoot, similar to the way wine grapes are mashed. After it is mixed with water and boiled, the oil is separated from the water. Palm oil has always been part of my life. I am almost sure that Mother ate it during the time she was expecting me, because it is one of the oils people from our part of the world eat. I have used it in my diet as often as it has been possible.

Fresh palm oil is simply delicious. Those who are used to the delicate flavor prefer it to any kind of oil. One day I was about to travel on an airplane with a lady who had excess baggage. She was told to leave behind some of her luggage or pay more money. She took with her all of the fresh palm oil bottles and left behind other belongings. Some people found it amusing. But I would have done what she did, had I been in a similar situation.

Ngulogboli (the red oil) is what the Mendes call this unique and colorful oil. In all of nature, it is the only known oil, animal and plant alike, that comes in bright, cranberry-red liquid form. In addition to other nutrients, it is very high in vitamin A. As we know, vitamin A, among other functions, is crucial in the prevention of night blindness and other forms of blindness, particularly in young children. It is known that children who eat a more balanced diet that includes fresh palm oil have a very low incidence of vitamin A deficient blindness, while children whose diet is poor, and also lacks the oil experience an epidemic of vitamin A deficient blindness, a diet-preventable disease.

During the time that I worked for the Evangelical United Brethren (E.U.B.) Church (now United Methodist Church) in Sierra Leone, I went from village to village and taught women sewing and good family nutrition. I also delivered their babies. One of the foods women often prepared for their babies was whole grain rice cooked with peanut butter and fresh palm oil. The ingredients were inexpensive, readily available, nutritious, and delicious. The babies and their older siblings loved it. They were healthy looking, and they also developed good eyesight.

Local UNICEF workers in developing nations have always been advocates of the use of fresh palm oil. They asked mothers to include it in their family's diet, especially in foods for young children. They also encouraged the men to plant the oil-producing palm in areas where the tree did not grow naturally but the tropical climate existed, which favored the growth of the tree.

Any oil that becomes old and rancid should no longer be used for food. In Grandmother's words, "It should only be used to make soap." To the expert, there is a world of difference between fresh and old, rancid palm oil in appearance, taste, and smell. How do I know? During my growing years, our house was very close to *johpowahun* (open market). We, the children, often ran to the market. I saw women taste and smell palm oil from one seller to the next, until they got what they wanted. When I came to buy, I tasted like the women did. I soon learned to tell which oil was fresh and which was not. Fresh palm oil is a bright red, clear liquid. It has no rancid smell, no greasy aftertaste, and it tastes delicious. Old oil, on the other hand, forms crystals that increase with age. The red color gradually becomes lighter, and the oil acquires a greasy aftertaste and then becomes rancid. Besides age, heat also can alter the oil color. When it is heated to 380 degrees and higher, or left in the sun for a long period of time, the bright red color slowly disappears.

In the past, fresh palm oil was often placed in giant-size oil drums to be exported. Quite often the people waited much too long before the ships finally arrived. The drums might be kept in the sun or in hot warehouses during the wait. It was quite some time before the drums were delivered, and perhaps more time went by before the oil was used.

I have heard some people say, "Palm oil is no good for food." I believe it would be more correct to say, "Old and rancid palm oil is no good for food." Grandmother said the same thing, and she was no scientist. I have also heard,

"Tropical oils are no good for food." That is somehow confusing to me. Africans grow on a very large scale sesame seeds and groundnuts (peanuts). Many experts tell us that oils from these foods are excellent and safe for human beings to eat. People from our part of the world have always eaten only these oils from the tropics, and some even lived to be more than a hundred years old. My conclusion is that palm oil, sesame seed oil, groundnut (peanut) oil, and all other oils should only be eaten when they are fresh because that is when they taste delicious and are good for food.

Tropical Chutneys

This thick fruit sauce is used in many parts of Africa (called by other names), but it is served most frequently in East and South African countries. Chutney consists of fruits, honey or sugar, lemon juice or vinegar, and herbs and spices, all cooked into a thick sauce. It is often served with meat, fish, or poultry to enhance flavor.

We believe you will have a great time making these tropical condiments, using different fruits. A serving costs only a few pennies to make, and a jar would make a great gift. They are easy to make, and your family and friends will enjoy eating them.

Green Mango Onion Chutney

Helpful Hint:

Mangoes must be green.

*groundnut (peanut) oil, ¼ cup
or amount desired*
1½ cups onions, chopped
*4 cups green mangoes, cut
into chunks*
⅓ cup fresh lemon juice

grated peel of 1 lemon
honey or sugar to taste
4 whole cloves
*½ cup chopped fresh hot peppers
or to taste*
salt to taste

1. Put oil and onions in a heated skillet, stir, and cook until onions are tender, 3–4 minutes.

2. Stir in rest of ingredients, cover, and continue to cook on medium to low heat.

3. Stirring often, cook until a thick sauce is formed and most of liquid or ⅔ is gone. Remove from heat, cool, and serve.

Plantain Ginger Chutney

Helpful Hint:

Use plantain that is about half ripe.

*2 cups fresh ginger, finely
chopped*
2 cups orange juice
honey or sugar to taste
*1 large plantain, peeled and
cut into chunks*

¼ cup roasted sesame seeds
1 teaspoon grated orange peel
*sesame oil, ¼ cup or amount
desired*
salt to taste

1. For about 15 minutes cook on low heat ginger, orange juice, and honey or sugar, stirring occasionally with a wooden spoon.

2. Stir in rest of ingredients and bring to a boil. Mix often and cook until a thick sauce is formed and about ⅔ is gone.

3. Remove from heat, cool, and serve.

Pineapple Coconut Chutney

Helpful Hint:

Fresh or canned pineapples may be used.

3 cups pineapples, crushed or chopped
1 cup grated coconuts
1 medium sweet pepper, chopped
¼ cup chopped hot peppers or to taste
honey or brown sugar to taste
olive oil, amount desired
1 cinnamon stick
1 cup pineapple juice
salt to taste

1. Put all ingredients in a pot and bring to a boil over medium heat.

2. Mixing often with a wooden spoon, continue to cook on medium to low heat until most—about two thirds—of liquid is gone.

3. Remove from heat, cool, and serve.

Banana Curry Chutney

Helpful Hints:

a. Use bananas that are neither too green nor too ripe.
b. To prevent them from turning brown, peel bananas just before use.

2 cups water
2 limes, use the juice and the
    grated rind
3 bananas, peeled and chopped
¼ cup corn oil or amount
    desired

curry powder to taste
sugar to taste
fresh hot peppers, chopped and
    to taste
salt to taste
1 cup corn

1. Add to skillet all of the ingredients, and bring to a boil. Cook on low.

2. Mix often and continue to cook until most of liquid is gone and a thick sauce remains.

3. Remove from heat and cool before serving.

Ripe Mango Honey Chutney

Helpful Hint:

Mangoes must be ripe but firm.

½ cup canned or frozen corn
¼ cup honey or to taste
1 cup pineapple juice
fresh ginger, chopped, 2 table-
    spoons or to taste
olive oil, ¼ cup or amount
    desired

salt to taste
4 cups mangoes, peeled and
    chopped
1 cup green onions, chopped
1 cup chopped pineapple
    (you may use crushed pine-
    apple)

1. Put all ingredients except mangoes and green onions in pot and bring to a boil.

2. Cook on low heat for about 15 minutes, mixing often.

3. Stir in mangoes and green onions. Continue to cook, stirring often, until most of liquid is gone and a thick sauce is formed. Remove from heat, cool, and serve.

Tomato-Mango-Pineapple Chutney

Helpful Hint:

May use fresh or canned pineapples.

1 large ripe tomato, chopped
1 green tomato, chopped
1 cup pineapples, chopped,
  chunks or crushed
¼ cup honey and 1 cup brown
  sugar or to taste
¼ cup fresh ginger, finely
  chopped

1 cup pineapple juice
3 whole cloves
grated peel of 1 lime
juice of same lime
2 cups medium ripe mangoes,
  chopped

   1. Put all ingredients except mangoes in pot. Bring to a boil and cook for about 15 minutes on low heat.
   2. Stir in mangoes and cook until most of liquid is gone and a thick sauce is formed. Remove from heat, cool, and serve.

Herbs, Spices, and Special Hot Peppers

I put all human beings into two major categories: The first group consists of people who eat hot and spicy foods, and the second group is made up of those who eat nonspicy, bland foods. Generally speaking, people in group one live in warm, tropical parts of the world. They eat rice, beans, corn, fish, and lots of fresh fruits and vegetables. They wear colorful cotton garments. Their music is exciting, alive, and energetic. It has a fast rhythm and interesting sounds that I call "African beats" which make you want to dance or move your feet. The hot foods help to make them perspire, re-sulting in a cooling effect. This, with color-rich cotton clothing, helps to keep them cool and comfortable all year round.

The people in the other group live in cold areas of the world. They eat meat, potatoes, and sweet desserts. Their wool garments usually come in dark and pastel colors. This helps to keep them warm and comfortable during the cold months of the year. Their music is slow and soft, and it has a soothing and relaxing effect. One can listen to it for a long period of time with great pleasure.

Ancient Egyptians were outstanding embalmers. The bodies of the dead were unusually well preserved for a very long time. The remains of the pharaohs are in excellent condition even today. Some of the ingredients they used were herbs and spices. Africans in general have always used them to treat and prepare the body for burial. The Jews also did the same. We read in John 19:39–40 that Nicodemus brought a mixture of myrrh and aloes, about a hun-dred pounds' weight. "They took the body of Jesus, and bound it in linen cloths with the spices, as is the burial custom of the Jews."

Herbs and spices have seasoned the land of Africa and its dwellers, so to speak, for thousands of years, because Africa is as much the land of herbs and spices as it is the land of great beauty, love, mystery, fantasy, and magic. Yet many of these aromatics still remain unknown to the outside world. One of the great pleasures of walking into a rain forest is to be greeted by the wonderful aro-mas of *heyweh, semengii, boohbooh,* and other herbs, for miles around.

A prominent and proud feature of an African woman's garden is the cultivation and display of herbs and spices such as *poponda,* a dozen or more varieties of hot peppers, *keyjeh* (ginger)—the list is endless. Many more are grown on the rice farm yearly. Still more are hauled home from the forest almost daily. On any given day, one is likely to see herbs and spices drying over the fire in the kitchen of an African lady; she would dry some more in the sun. In short, there is nothing insipid about African cooking.

Even today, most Africans do not have medical doctors close to home. When they become sick, they would most likely be treated by persons with no western medical background. These people are usually family members or friends. For example, someone with a cold would be given chicken or fish hot pepper soup in which would be a large dose of hot peppers. It is believed that these dishes can help clear colds and sinusitis rather quickly. Pregnant women are known to use much hot peppers and fresh ginger in the diet. They claim these spices help to diminish the frequency of early morning sickness. *Kumuhli* would frequently be given to children who harbor roundworms in the gastrointestinal tract. The same herb combined with more ingredients would be given to people with constipation. *Keyjeh*, hot peppers, and other ingredients would be added to white clay *(hojeh)* or some oil. The mixture would then be used externally for headaches, backaches, and other aches. Other herbs and spices are often used to make soap and shampoo for the treatment of ringworm and other skin disorders. Peppers and ginger are used to control the insect and snake population. For example, when ground hot pepper is sprinkled around the house, ants and other bugs stay away. There is an African saying, "The bugs dare not enter Mamanyamu's hot pepper bottle. A snake would do anything to avoid going through a ginger farm." Another saying goes, "Even the snake knows which farm belongs to Mr. Keyjeh."

Some herbs and spices have refreshing properties; others have a pleasing fragrance. They are worn as ornaments or rubbed on the body. As a little girl I very much enjoyed making herbal body rub with Grandmother. We gathered the barks of some perfume trees and dried and crushed them into powder. We put the powder, some tree sap, whole cloves, and other ingredients in a large-mouth earthen jar called *dumbu*. Grandmother then heated some lamb fat, which she put in water to remove old blood and meat particles. Then she mixed all together into the most wonderful herbal body lotion called *gbeseh*. I still remember how good I felt after I had a bath and she applied the rub on my body. Africans still do replenish the skin with homemade body rubs consisting of herbs, spices, and different kinds of plant and animal oils.

There are many ways to use herbs and spices. I most enjoy cooking with them because they awaken the flavor and goodness of food. Fresh herbs and spices have the best aromatic quality, while dry ones have longer shelf life. They should all be used with caution, especially the less familiar ones. Begin with a small amount. As they become more familiar with use, cook each herb and spice according to your taste.

Onion and Tomato Hot Pepper Sauce

Helpful Hint:

Serve with meat, fish, and poultry dishes.

groundnut (peanut) oil, amount
　desired
1 large onion, chopped

1 cup chopped fresh peppers
　or to taste
2 large tomatoes, chopped
salt to taste

1. Put oil and onion in skillet, stir, and cook until onion is tender.
2. Add rest of ingredients. Stir and cook until peppers are done.
Remove from heat and serve.

Tomato Hot Pepper Sauce

Helpful Hint:

Make only as hot as you want it.

⅔ cup fresh red hot peppers,
　washed and each top end
　removed
2 large tomatoes, cut up
¼ cup fresh green hot peppers
　(washed, seeds removed, and
　finely chopped)
juice of 2 lemons

2 green onions, chopped
1 large tomato, seeds removed
　and chopped (save seeds
　for blender)
peanut oil, olive oil, or sesame
　oil, ¼ cup or amount desired
salt to taste
sugar to taste

1. Puree the first two ingredients plus tomato seeds.
2. Stir all ingredients in a mixing bowl and serve.

Hot Pepper Ginger Sauce

Helpful Hint:

This dish can be served with any kind of meat.

*1 cup fresh ginger, thinly
    sliced
½ cup fresh hot peppers,
    chopped
½ cup green onions, chopped*

*oil of choice, ¼ cup or amount
    desired
salt to taste
½ cup fresh poponda (basil
    leaves), chopped*

1. Put all ingredients except *poponda* (basil) in a skillet.
2. Stir and cook for about 7 minutes. Stir in *poponda* (basil) and continue to cook for another 3 minutes. Remove from heat and serve.

Mboya Hot Pepper Sauce

Helpful Hints:

a. Make it only as hot as you like it.
b. Serve with meats, poultry, and fish.

*2 cups fresh red hot pepper
3 cups water
5 cloves garlic
1 onion, chopped*

*salt to taste
½ cup tomato paste
½ cup fresh lemon juice or vinegar
sugar to taste*

1. Put the first five ingredients in a pot and bring to a boil. Cook until peppers, onion, and garlic are tender.
2. Stir in rest of ingredients and bring to a boil. Remove from heat and cool to room temperature.
3. Blend all ingredients in a blender and serve.

Kehmeh's Dumbu Peppers

ରେ

African women like to keep dry hot peppers in oil because they can last a long time.

Helpful Hints:

a. Peppers must be as dry as possible.
b. Use oil of choice.

Dry hot peppers, amount desired	*clay pot (dumbu) or a large-mouth bottle*
sesame oil	*whole cloves to taste*

1. Add peppers to a heated pot. Mix with a wooden spoon until they are very dry.
2. Put peppers and cloves in clean, dry containers.
3. Cover with oil and use as needed.

Tomboya Hot Plasas

ରେ

Helpful Hint:

Serve with meat, chicken, and fish.

1 cup fresh hot peppers of choice, chopped	*⅓ cup fresh lemon juice*
1 cup green onions, chopped	*1 tablespoon sesame oil*
1 medium ripe mango, peeled and chopped	*2 tablespoons roasted sesame seeds*
1 cup fresh pineapple, chopped	*1 cup fresh parsley, chopped*
1 large tomato, chopped	*1 tablespoon honey or to taste*
½ cup fresh ginger, chopped	*sugar to taste*
	6 whole cloves
	salt to taste

1. Put all ingredients in a bowl, mix well, and put in a serving dish.
2. Serve at room temperature or chill and serve.

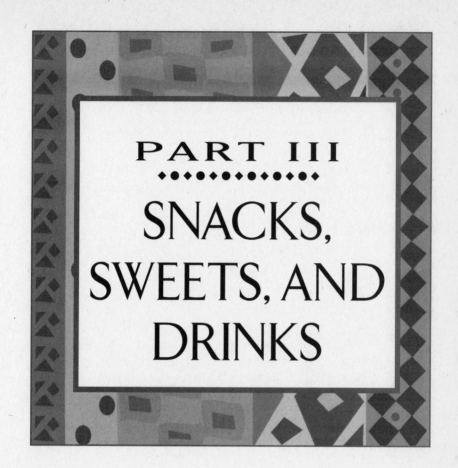

PART III

SNACKS, SWEETS, AND DRINKS

Akaras

Akaras are in the food group called *hamu hamu* (appetizers), and there are several kinds. Most of these finger foods are usually round and small. They are all easy to make and taste great. Enjoy them.

Banana Akara

One way to use overripe bananas and still come up with a delicious, nutritious, and great dish is by making banana *akara*.

Helpful Hint:

In Africa banana *akara* is made with bananas and *kpangula* rice flour. Whole wheat flour is used in this dish because it is readily available. It turns out that the result is a better quality *akara* in appearance and taste. As you know, whole wheat flour is more nutritious than rice flour, an extra bonus.

3 medium-size ripe bananas, mashed (about 1½ cups)
2 ⅔ cups or more whole wheat flour
⅓ cup white flour
2 teaspoons baking soda

1 large egg
¾ cup or more water
fresh ginger, chopped and to taste
¾ cup sugar or to taste
1 teaspoon salt or to taste
oil of choice for deep frying

1. Put all ingredients except oil in a mixing bowl. Mix well to the consistency of a creamy, pouring batter (adding a little more water or flour as needed).

2. Heat oil (about 3 inches deep) to 375 degrees in a skillet. You may also want to use Suma's Onion Oil Test (p. 228) as needed.

3. Put batter by spoonfuls in hot oil and fry until golden. (If the ratio of liquid to dry ingredients is right, each *akara* will turn itself when it is ready to turn.) Remove from hot oil, drain well, and serve hot.

Serving Ideas for Banana Akara:

a. Serve like a bread: Put in a serving basket lined with a towel and serve hot.

b. Serve like a sweet:

½ *cup confectioner's powdered sugar*	*ground cinnamon to taste* *powdered ginger to taste*

1. Add to a mixing bowl sugar, cinnamon, and ginger and mix well.

2. Dust each *akara* with mixture. Arrange in a lined basket and serve.

Papia Bean Akara

Helpful Hints:

a. Cooked black-eyed peas or cooked dry beans of various kinds may be used in this dish.

b. This dish tastes better when served hot.

c. Serve with Shrimp Mango Poponda Sauce (recipe follows).

3 cups cooked black-eyed peas (cook according to package directions and drain)
2 eggs, lightly beaten
1 tablespoon rice flour
poponda (fresh basil), finely chopped and to taste

1 tablespoon roasted sesame seeds
¼ teaspoon baking soda
fresh hot peppers, finely chopped and to taste
fresh ginger, chopped and to taste
salt to taste
oil of choice for frying

1. Put peas in a mixing bowl and mash so that about 95 percent are crushed and few whole beans are seen.

2. Stir in rest of ingredients except oil. You want the consistency of drop cookie dough.

3. Heat oil (about 3 inches deep) to 375 degrees in a skillet. Use Suma's Onion Oil Test (p. 228) as needed.

4. Put mixture by spoonfuls in hot oil and fry until golden. Remove from oil and drain; put in a serving dish to serve with Shrimp Mango Poponda Sauce (recipe follows).

Shrimp Mango Poponda Sauce

Helpful Hints:

a. This dish may also be served with boiled rice.
b. Ripe mango must be firm.

1 tomato, chopped
fresh hot peppers, chopped
  and to taste
1 onion, chopped
groundnut (peanut) oil,
  amount desired
salt to taste
1 pound large shrimp, shelled
  and deveined

1 ripe and 1 green mango, each
  peeled and cut into medium
  chunks
poponda (fresh basil), chopped
  and to taste
parsley, chopped for garnishing

1. Put in skillet all ingredients except shrimp, ripe mango, *poponda* (basil), and parsley. Cover.

2. Cook, stirring often, over medium heat or until onions are tender. Stir in rest of ingredients except parsley.

3. Cook a few more minutes or until shrimp are done the way you like them. Spoon over Papia Bean Akara and serve hot with bread of choice.

Ohleleh Bean Akara

☙☙

Helpful Hint:

Serve while it is still hot.

3 cups ohleleh beans; see How
  to Make Ohleleh Beans (p. 30)
2 tablespoons rice or wheat
  flour

¼ teaspoon baking soda
salt to taste
oil of choice for deep frying

    1. Mix all ingredients except oil in a mixing bowl. Heat oil (3 inches deep) over medium heat to 375 degrees or use Suma's Onion Oil Test (p. 228).
    2. Fry mixture by spoonfuls until golden. Remove from oil, drain, and serve hot with Shrimp Mango Poponda Sauce (p. 215).

Chick Pea Akara

☙☙

This dish is crisp and nutty with a great taste.

Helpful Hints:

a. Wash and soak dry chick peas in cold water for 4–5 hours. Drain, coarsely grind in a food processor (Africans grind it in a mortar with pestle) and use in dish.
b. Serve while it is still hot.

3 cups ground chick peas
1 tablespoon rice flour
1 egg, lightly beaten
2 green onions, finely
  chopped

¼ cup roasted sesame seeds
salt to taste
hot peppers, chopped and to taste
oil of choice for frying

1. Mix all ingredients except oil in a mixing bowl.

2. Add oil, about 2 inches deep, to a heated skillet over medium heat. Bring oil temperature to 375 degrees or use Suma's Onion Oil Test (p. 228) as needed.

3. Put mixture by spoonfuls in hot oil and fry until golden. Remove from oil, drain, and keep warm. Repeat until all of mixture is cooked. Serve hot with Lemon Pineapple Honey Sauce (recipe follows).

Lemon Pineapple Honey Sauce

This is delicious and takes very little time to make.

Helpful Hint:

For good results you must use real fresh lemon juice. No substitute will do.

2 tablespoons honey or to taste	*ground fresh ginger to taste*
juice of 3 lemons	*pinch of salt*
½ cup pineapple juice	*ground hot pepper to taste*

1. Put all ingredients in a bowl and mix well.
2. Put in a serving dish and serve at room temperature.

Lalehun Sweet Potato Akara

This dish is unique and delicious.

Helpful Hint:

Serve hot with Lemon Pineapple Honey Sauce (above).

2 cups sweet potatoes,
   cooked and mashed
1 cup sweet potatoes, grated
2 green onions, chopped
1 tablespoon rice flour
¼ cup coconut milk
sugar to taste

fresh ginger, finely chopped
   and to taste
2 eggs, lightly beaten
salt to taste
grated peel of 1 lime
oil of choice for deep frying

1. Put in a mixing bowl all ingredients except oil and mix well.

2. Add oil (3 inches deep) to skillet over medium heat and heat to 375 degrees. Use Suma's Onion Oil Test (p. 228) as needed.

3. Fry by spoonfuls in hot oil until golden. Remove from oil and drain. Serve hot with Lemon Pineapple Honey Sauce.

Sweet Potato Chicken Akara

Helpful Hints:

a. Cook Shrimp Mango Poponda Sauce (p. 215) to serve with dish.
b. Serve while *akara* is still hot.

3 cups shredded sweet
   potatoes
⅓ cup sesame seeds, roasted
   and coarsely ground
¼ cup fresh poponda (fresh
   basil), chopped
½ pound ground chicken

1 egg, lightly beaten
1 tablespoon rice flour
fresh ginger, finely chopped
   and to taste
salt to taste
peanut oil for frying
⅔ cup flour

1. Mix all ingredients except oil and flour in a mixing bowl.

2. Add oil to heated skillet (about ¼-inch deep) that is over medium heat. Use Suma's Onion Oil Test (p. 228) as needed.

3. Make flat and round spoonfuls of mixture and dust both sides with flour. Cook in oil until golden on both sides, turning over once.

4. Remove from oil, drain, and arrange in a serving platter. Spoon Shrimp Mango Poponda Sauce over *akara* and serve hot.

Curry Fish Shrimp Akara

This is a fish lover's delight. Enjoy it.

Helpful Hints:

a. Use fish steak of choice.
b. May need to use gloves when hot peppers are added. Hot peppers can irritate the skin.
c. Serve hot.

*1 ½ pounds fish, coarsely
    ground
1 cup fresh shrimp, chopped
1 small egg, lightly beaten
curry powder to taste
fresh hot peppers, chopped
    and to taste*

*3 green onions, chopped
grated peel of 1 lemon
salt to taste
1 tablespoon wheat flour
groundnut oil
½ cup rice flour or white flour*

1. Put in bowl all ingredients except oil and rice flour and mix.
2. Add oil (about ¼-inch deep) to heated skillet over medium heat.
3. Shape round and flat spoonfuls of mixture. Dust both sides with rice flour. Cook in hot oil until light golden on both sides, turning once.
4. Remove from oil and drain. Arrange on a serving platter; serve hot with Mango Nanas Tropical Plasas (recipe follows).

Mango Nanas Tropical Plasas

This dish may also be served with meat, poultry, and fish.

Helpful Hint:

If possible, use fresh pineapples in dish.

4 green onions, chopped
1 cup fresh pineapple chunks
1 cup mango chunks
1 cup avocado chunks
1 green sweet pepper, chopped
fresh hot peppers, chopped
   and to taste
fresh ginger, finely chopped
   and to taste
¼ cup orange juice
¼ cup pineapple juice
juice of 2 lemons

sesame oil to taste
2 tablespoons sesame seeds,
   roasted and coarsely ground
1 cup tomatoes, finely
   chopped
⅔ cup crushed fresh tomatoes
honey to taste
sugar to taste
salt to taste
chopped parsley for
   garnishing

1. Put all ingredients except parsley in a mixing bowl and mix well.

2. Put in a serving dish, garnish with parsley, and serve.

The Egg Story

Chicken is found in most parts of the world. This fowl has lived and thrived in Africa for a very long time. African hens lay eggs like all hens usually do, but most West African women do not eat or cook with eggs. Those who do are likely to be young and educated, having had an outside influence in school or elsewhere.

The lessons children learn from family members and people they love and respect often stay with them for life. Most African young people learn very early to be kind and respectful to the elderly, and to be mindful of what older people say to them. They also learn to be kind to animals. For example, in West Africa a grandmother would say to her granddaughter, "It is not nice for a young lady to take away eggs from a hen. The hen lays her eggs in order to have chicks. Young girls who have every right to look forward to becoming mothers, have no right to keep the hen from getting young ones." This makes a lasting impression on the young mind, because it does make sense, and it works. Most girls will not take eggs from a hen that is present or away from her eggs. In other words, girls and child-bearing women are not likely to eat eggs or cook with them. That is just the way it is.

At the time of menopause, when a mature woman would have had grown children of her own, culture would again tell her, "You may now eat eggs if you want to. You have raised your own family, done what was expected of you, and you have nothing to be afraid of." If for a long time she did not eat eggs, why would she want to start doing so now? Older and wiser, she would likely say to herself, "If I did without eggs all these years, why should I start eating them now and still be cruel to the hen? I am going to do without them for the rest of my life." That is why most West African women do not eat or cook with eggs, and they would teach and encourage their daughters and granddaughters to do the same.

Hamu Hamu—Appetizers and Snacks

The name *hamu hamu* literally means "that which starts the mouth moving." They come in small, attractive finger foods served before, during, after, and between meals. *Hamu hamu* move the mouth with joy to the point of almost dancing with pleasure. Serve them to your family and friends; serve them often to start the mouth moving with pleasure.

Shrimp Mamba with Green Mango Sesame Honey Sauce

These are juicy, delicious African shrimp you will enjoy.

Helpful Hints:

a. Do not overcook shrimp.
b. Serve with Green Mango Sesame Honey Sauce (recipe follows). Provide wooden toothpicks for your guests.

2 pounds large fresh shrimp, deveined but not shelled
fresh hot peppers, ground or finely chopped and to taste
honey to taste
grated fresh ginger to taste
sesame oil, amount desired

1 tablespoon roasted sesame seeds
2 green onions, chopped
juice of 1 lime
grated peel of same lime
salt to taste
chopped parsley for garnishing

1. Put in a heated skillet over medium heat all ingredients except parsley.

2. Using 2 wooden spoons, cook and mix until shrimp are succulent and done, about 12 minutes.

3. Arrange on a serving platter, garnish with chopped parsley, and serve with Green Mango Sesame Honey Sauce.

Green Mango Sesame Honey Sauce

This dish is made in West African countries. It is a sweet and sour sauce that is very special. Sour green mango, the sweetness of honey, and the great taste of sesame all come together in a delightful and wonderful way.

Helpful Hints:

a. Mango must be green and tart.
b. Run cooked, mashed mango through a fine strainer to remove fiber. (Mangoes are very high in fiber.)

3 large green mangos or 4 medium ones
honey to taste
¼ cup sesame seeds, roasted and ground; see How to Roast Sesame Seeds (p. 224)

ground hot pepper to taste
grated fresh ginger to taste
salt to taste

1. Peel each mango and cut meat away from seed. Steam or cook with little water until meat is soft, about 12 minutes.
2. Mash and push mango through a fine strainer to remove excess fiber.
3. Mix sauce with rest of ingredients and serve.

Note: Green Mango Sesame Honey Sauce is also served with fish, poultry, other meats, fruits, and vegetables.

Ripe Mango Sauce

This sauce is made in many African countries.

Helpful Hints:

a. Each mango must be fully ripe but somewhat firm so that it is easy to cut meat from seed.
b. Ripe mangos require no cooking.

number of ripe mangoes desired
honey and/or sugar to taste

grated fresh ginger to taste
powdered hot pepper to taste (optional)

1. Peel each mango and cut meat from seed. Put meat in a blender and puree.

2. Run puree through a fine strainer and remove excess fiber. Put sauce and rest of ingredients in a mixing bowl, mix, and serve.

How to Roast Sesame Seeds

1. Add sesame seeds to a heavy pot that is over medium heat.
2. Stir often with a wooden spoon until sesame is done.
3. Sesame that is done is easily crushed between the thumb and first finger; most of the bitter taste is removed, and it has an inviting aroma to it.

Curry Chicken Liver

This dish is from North, South, and West African countries.

Helpful Hints:

a. Do not overcook liver. Overcooking makes it dry.
b. Serve with Kobo Kobo Avocado Honey Plasas (p. 226).

2 pounds chicken liver; cut
  each in half
curry powder to taste
ground hot pepper to
  taste
grated fresh ginger to
  taste
grated peel of 1 lime
salt to taste

⅔ cup mbagbehnyeh (broken
  rice); see How to Make Mbagbehnyeh (Broken Rice)
  (p. 225) or ⅔ cup dry bread
  crumbs or flour
groundnut (peanut) oil for
  frying, ¼–½ cup or amount
  desired

1. Put in a mixing bowl liver, curry powder, pepper, ginger, lime peel, and salt; mix and set aside. Also mix together in another bowl dry bread crumbs or *mbagbehnyeh* (broken rice or flour), salt, and pepper and set aside.

2. Add oil to heated frying pan that is over medium heat.

3. Roll each piece of liver in bread crumbs or *mbagbehnyeh* (broken rice), cook in oil, turning once. Remove from oil, drain, and serve hot with sauce.

How to Make Mbagbehnyeh (Broken Rice)

Mbagbehnyeh literally means "broken rice." It is used instead of dry bread crumbs to coat meat, fish, poultry, vegetables, and fruits before frying. It is also cooked and served like *cous cous.*

Helpful Hints:

a. Any kind of rice can be broken or crushed into *mbagbehnyeh.* The rice is heated to make it easy to crush.

b. Rice can be crushed on a smooth surface with a rolling pin, or a round bottle, or it may be crushed in a nut chopper. In Africa the rice is ground between stones or in a wooden mortar *(kohdeh)* with a wooden pestle *(ngehteh).*

rice, amount and kind desired

1. Add rice to a heated skillet. Stir often with a wooden spoon until it is heated through, about 5 minutes.

2. Crush it using any of the above methods.

Kobo Kobo Avocado Honey Plasas

ை

This dish is from East, West, and South Africa. May also use other herbs and spices.

Kobo kobo is gardenegg (eggplant). The sauce is creamy and delicious, and it is easy to make.

Helpful Hints:

a. Use light and young *kobo kobo;* the seeds are few and less developed.
b. Peel avocado just before it is used to keep it from turning dark.
c. Whether you boil or steam *kobo kobo,* cool it to room temperature in a colander so that the excess liquid drains out.

1 medium kobo kobo (eggplant)	*ground hot pepper to taste*
1 large ripe avocado, peeled and cut up	*fresh ginger, grated and to taste*
	curry powder to taste
¼ cup sesame seeds, roasted and ground	*honey to taste*
	juice of 1 lime
sesame oil to taste	*salt to taste*
	chopped nuts for garnishing

1. Peel and cut *kobo kobo* into chunks. Cook in a heavy, covered pot over low heat until it is soft. (*Kobo kobo* has enough liquid for cooking.) Or steam it until it is tender and cool to room temperature. Without peeling, you can also put Kobo Kobo in an oven on 375 degrees and cook until soft and tender, 30–40 minutes. Spoon meat off skin.

2. Put cooked *kobo kobo* and the rest of ingredients except chopped nuts in a mixing bowl.

3. Crush and mix with a wooden spoon. (It does not need to be smooth unless so desired.)

4. Put sauce in a serving dish and garnish with nuts before serving.

Dabah Kii Kii Balls

ନ୍ତ

This dish is to honor Dabah.

This dish is from Central, South, and West African countries.

Helpful Hints:

a. Make in advance Green Mango Sesame Honey Sauce (p. 222) to serve with dish.

b. Serve with wooden picks.

c. May need to use gloves when hot peppers are added. Hot peppers can irritate the skin.

½ pound fish steak of choice, coarsely ground
½ pound ground lamb
½ pound crabmeat, chopped as needed
mint leaves, chopped and to taste
1 large kpohwoh (portabella mushroom), finely chopped
ground cumin to taste
1 egg, lightly beaten
fresh ginger, finely chopped and to taste

fresh hot peppers, chopped and to taste
2 cloves garlic, crushed
½ cup roasted groundnuts (peanuts), finely chopped
salt to taste
1 cup cornmeal or 1 cup mbagbehnyeh (broken rice) see How to Make Mbag-behnyeh (Broken Rice) (p. 225)
parsley, chopped for garnishing
groundnut (peanut) oil for cooking

1. Add to a bowl all ingredients except oil, parsley, and *mbagbehnyeh* (broken rice) or cornmeal.

2. Mix and shape mixture into small balls. Roll each ball in cornmeal or in *mbagbehnyeh* (broken rice) and immediately drop in hot oil.

3. Fry in 375 degrees oil (2 inches deep) until golden. Use Suma's Onion Oil Test, which follows, as needed.

4. Remove from oil and drain; arrange in a serving basket lined with banana leaves or put in a platter. Garnish with chopped parsley and serve with Green Mango Sesame Honey Sauce.

Suma's Onion Oil Test

This method of hot oil testing is dedicated to Mama Suma, who taught me how to use it.

This onion oil test is a dependable method of testing hot oil temperature. African women have used it to determine cooking oil temperature without the use of a cooking thermometer for as long as women have cooked in Africa. I often saw Mama Suma and many women use it. The method is just as useful and popular today as it was in the past. It is simple, reliable, and works so well.

When food is fried in oil that has a lower temperature than necessary, the food often absorbs more oil than it should because it cooks at a slow rate. If the same food is fried in oil that has a higher temperature than needed, the outer portion of it burns before the core is done.

African women need to know oil temperature for frying. Suma's Onion Oil Test lets the cook know whether the oil temperature is just right, too high, or not hot enough for frying. Then the cook is able to make the necessary changes.

Helpful Hints:

a. There is always the possibility of starting a fire when one leaves hot oil on the stove unattended. A child or even an adult could get hurt.
b. It is better to heat oil over medium heat, in a heavy pot, instead of over high heat.

oil, amount needed for frying 1 slice of onion

1. Heat oil in a skillet or a heavy pot over medium heat.
2. Drop a slice of onion in hot oil. If temperature is just right for frying, onion will fry golden, and a nice onion aroma will fill the kitchen.
3. If oil is too hot, the onion will burn very quickly; the cooking area will also have a bad onion smell. When this happens, remove skillet from heat and cool for about a minute, then return oil to heat, and continue with cooking.

4. If oil is not hot enough, onion will not start to fry immediately as it should. Heat it a little longer and then continue with cooking.

5. After test is done, remove onion from oil before frying is carried out.

Mamokoh Chicken Balls

These chicken balls are made in East, South, and West African countries. Other kinds of herbs and spices may also be used.

Helpful Hints:

a. Make Green Mango Sesame Honey Sauce (p. 222) in advance.
b. Hot peppers and fresh ginger can irritate the skin and mucous membranes. You may wish to use gloves when making balls.
c. Serve with wooden toothpicks.

2 pounds ground chicken
⅔ cup groundnut (peanut) butter
1 cup mushrooms, chopped
1 onion, finely chopped
fresh ginger, grated, to taste
fresh hot peppers, finely chopped, to taste
2 cloves garlic, crushed

grated peel of 1 lime
ground black pepper to taste
3 green onions, finely chopped
salt to taste
peanut or vegetable oil of choice for frying
chopped parsley for garnishing

1. Put all ingredients except oil and parsley in a bowl and thoroughly mix. Shape mixture by spoonfuls into small balls.

2. Heat oil (about 1 inch deep) to 375 degrees in skillet over medium heat. Use Suma's Onion Oil Test (p. 228) as needed. Fry chicken balls in oil until golden brown on all sides.

3. Remove balls from oil, drain, and set aside.

4. Put Green Mango Sesame Honey Sauce (amount desired) in skillet and bring to a gentle boil. Gently stir in chicken balls until they are well coated.

5. Arrange chicken balls in a serving platter, garnish with chopped parsley, and serve with wooden picks.

Variation:

Mamokoh Sesame Chicken Balls: Use ½ cup roasted and ground sesame seeds instead of groundnut (peanut) butter; make chicken balls like above.

Tii Tii Chicken Sticks

This is for Tii Tii, who enjoys eating it.

This dish is made in North, West, and South African countries.

Helpful Hint:

Do not overcook, but make sure that chicken is done to prevent salmonella infection.

*2 pounds boneless chicken
   breast, cut into thin strips*
⅓ cup sesame seeds, toasted
2 cloves garlic, crushed
powdered hot pepper to taste

ground cumin to taste
2 green onions, finely chopped
salt to taste
groundnut (peanut) or vegetable oil of choice for frying

1. Put all ingredients except oil in a mixing bowl and mix.
2. Add oil (about ½ inch deep) to a heated skillet and heat to 375 degrees. Use Suma's Onion Oil Test (p. 228) as needed.
3. Lay chicken strips in oil so that ends do not touch. Fry until golden. Remove from oil, drain, and serve with Groundnut Lime Ginger Sauce below.

Groundnut Lime Ginger Sauce

Helpful Hints:

a. Make sauce as thick or as thin as you want by using more or less liquid.
b. Use fresh lime juice in recipe.

¼ *cup fresh lime juice*
honey to taste
grated fresh ginger to taste
powdered hot pepper to taste
grated peel of 1 lime
½ *cup or more chicken broth*

1 tablespoon rice flour or
   more as desired
2 tablespoons groundnut
   (peanut) butter
salt to taste

1. Put all ingredients except honey in cooking pot and mix. Set on stove, stir, and cook over medium heat until sauce thickens. If it is too thick, add more liquid and bring it to desired thickness.

2. Add honey and green onions and bring to a gentle boil for just a moment.

3. Remove from heat and serve.

Bondoh Lendeh

These stuffed okra shells look like small African fishing boats. The name means "okra boats." There is a song in which the little boat says, "I may be thrown to the very bottom of the big river. But with a little help, I always manage to come back up again." We hope you enjoy making and eating these singing okra boats that never give up.

Helpful Hints:

a. Use large but young okra; avoid overgrown, fibrous ones.
b. Use Test for Young Okra (p. 233).
c. Make Kobo Kobo Avocado Honey Plasas (p. 226) in advance.

12 large young okra
groundnut (peanut) or veget-
    able oil for frying
Chicken Seafood Stuffing
    (recipe follows)

⅔ cup cornmeal or mbagbehnyeh
(broken rice) see How to Make
Mbagbehnyeh (Broken Rice)
(p. 225)

1. Clean each okra, remove both ends, and cut into half length-wise. With a vegetable knife remove seeds and pulp, leaving each half shell intact.

2. Stuff each shell with Chicken Seafood Stuffing and set aside.

3. Add oil (about 2 inches deep) to heated skillet over medium heat and bring the temperature to 375 degrees, or use Suma's Onion Oil Test (p. 228) as needed.

4. Roll each stuffed shell in *mbagbehnyeh* (broken rice) or corn-meal. Fry in hot oil until golden. Remove from oil, drain, and serve with Kobo Kobo Avocado Honey Plasas.

Chicken Seafood Stuffing

Helpful Hints:

a. May need to use gloves when handling hot peppers.

b. This dish is especially good when served hot.

1 pint fresh oysters, drained
    and chopped or coarsely
    ground
8 medium fresh shrimp,
cleaned and chopped finely
½ pound ground chicken
½ pound fish steak of choice,
    coarsely ground or chopped
4 mushrooms, finely chopped

⅓ cup fresh parsley, chopped
⅓ cup poponda (fresh basil),
    chopped
3 green onions, chopped
ground cumin to taste
grated fresh ginger to taste
fresh hot peppers, chopped, to
    taste
salt to taste

Mix all ingredients in a bowl and stuff shells with mixture.

Variation:

Chicken Seafood Balls: Mix stuffing and make balls by spoonfuls. Roll each in *mbagbehnyeh* (broken rice) or cornmeal. Fry in 375-degree hot oil until lightly browned. Remove from oil, drain, and serve with Lemon Pineapple Honey Sauce.

Test for Young Okra

ᏭᏬ

African women are very particular about the okra they serve their families. When it is time to harvest this vegetable (usually just before cooking it), they use a specific test to determine whether the okra in question is young and right for the table, or too old and should be left alone to go to seed. One kind of okra may be large but still young and just right, while another kind may be small yet full of hard seeds and too old to cook.

The test is so simple that most young people learn to do it in a minute.

1. Hold okra in right hand (if you are right-handed).
2. Try to break off tail end by pressing it with thumb of the same hand.
3. If okra is young, the tail will fall right off.
4. If it is too done, the tail will split into many fibers, and it will not break off. That means it is ready to go to seed and should not be used for cooking.

Jahyan Sweet Potato Fry

ᏭᏬ

This dish comes from most countries in Africa. Fried sweet potatoes are delicious and very common in the African diet.

Helpful Hints:

a. These potatoes taste best when they are served hot.
b. Make Lemon Pineapple Honey Sauce (p. 217) in advance to serve with this dish.

2 large sweet potatoes or amount desired	*¼ cup cornmeal, or ¼ cup mbagbehnyeh (broken rice), or ¼ cup toasted sesame seeds*
powdered hot pepper to taste (optional)	
salt to taste	*oil of choice for frying*

1. Peel and wash each potato; cut into equal portions lengthwise. Sprinkle with salt and pepper plus either cornmeal, *mbagbehnyeh* (broken rice), or sesame seeds. Mix and set aside.

2. Add oil (about 2 inches deep) to a heated skillet and bring temperature to 375 degrees. Or use Suma's Onion Oil Test (p. 228) as needed.

3. Fry in hot oil until potatoes are crisp and golden. Remove from oil, drain, and serve hot with sauce.

Ginger Honey Nikilii

These are great-tasting groundnuts (peanuts) made in North, South, and West African countries. We hope you'll enjoy them.

Helpful Hint:

Double recipe if so desired, because they go very fast.

3 tablespoons honey	*juice of same lime*
¼ cup sugar or more as desired	*1 tablespoon groundnut (peanut) oil*
grated fresh ginger to taste	*¼ cup water*
grated peel of 1 lime	*2 cups roasted nikilii (peanuts)*

1. Put in a skillet all ingredients except nuts. Mix and bring to a boil over medium to low heat.

2. Stirring often, continue to cook until mixture becomes syrupy and bubbly.

3. Add nuts and stir until they are well coated and sticky. Remove from heat and spread nuts on a lightly oiled oven pan. Cool and serve.

Note: Other spices that can be used are ground hot peppers or cinnamon, or the spices of your chosing. Other kinds of nuts may also be used.

Boiled Groundnuts (Peanuts)

These are so popular that they are served in all countries in Africa.

Helpful Hint:

The preferred groundnuts (peanuts) to use are unshelled, fresh, raw peanuts. Dry raw peanuts are the most readily available. They take longer to cook, but the result can also be good.

unshelled, fresh, raw peanuts,   *water*
   quantity desired   **salt to taste (optional)**

1. Put groundnuts (peanuts) in cooking pot and cover with water. With lid in place, bring to a boil over medium heat.

2. Stir in salt, cover, and cook over low heat until nuts are tender. Remove from heat, drain, and serve in a *kalabash* or a serving bowl.

Pujeh Coconatii

These are coconuts cooked with hot peppers. Herbs and spices of choice may also be used.

Helpful Hints:

a. Use only fresh coconuts.
b. Break 1 coconut; see How to Break and Remove Coconut from Shell (p. 238). Peel dark skin off, wash, and cut into thin long slices. Divide into 3 equal portions. For good results, cook only one portion at a time.
c. Make coconuts only as spicy as you can eat them.

1 batch or ⅓ portion   *salt to taste*
powdered hot pepper to taste   *sugar to taste (optional)*
grated fresh ginger to taste   *oil of choice, ¼ cup or*
powdered onion to taste   *amount desired*

1. Put in a mixing bowl all ingredients except oil and sugar. Mix well and set aside.
2. Add oil to a heated skillet that is over medium to low heat and stir in coconut. Cook and mix often with a wooden spoon until coconut is light brown on all sides.
3. Remove from skillet, drain, and put in a mixing bowl. Immediately add sugar while hot and mix.
4. Repeat until the other portions are also done. Put all in a serving dish and serve.

Variation:

Fresh Coconatii Portions: Break coconut and remove meat from shell. Peel off dark skin and wash. Cut coconut into small portions, arrange in a serving dish, and serve.

Mangala Coconatii Mango Salad

This salad is fresh and simply delicious. Please enjoy it.

Helpful Hints:

a. See How to Break and Remove Coconut from Shell (p. 238). Peel off dark skin, wash, and grate 2 cups coconut.
b. For best results use fresh coconut and fresh lime juice.

*parsley leaves to line
  serving dish
2 cups fresh coconut grated,
1 large green mango, peeled
  and shredded or finely
  chopped
1 large ripe, firm mango,
  chopped or finely chopped*

*2 tablespoons roasted sesame
  seeds
honey to taste
sugar to taste
juice of 2 limes
grated fresh ginger to taste
salt to taste
mint leaves, finely chopped
  and to taste (optional)*

1. Line serving platter with parsley leaves and set dish aside.
2. Put remaining ingredients in a mixing bowl and toss.
3. Put mixture in lined platter and serve chilled or at room temperature.

Variation:

Mangala Stuffed Kibongii Salad: Use 6 medium tomatoes or 12 large cherry tomatoes. Cut away each tomato top and scoop out seeds and pulp. Stuff each with *Mangala Coconatii Mango Salad.* Use rest of salad to make a bed on a serving platter. Arrange stuffed tomatoes on platter, garnish with finely chopped mint leaves. Serve at room temperature.

Pineapple Coconut Kabatti

This dish is from East, North, and West African countries.

Helpful Hint:

If possible, use only fresh ingredients in dish.

2 cups fresh coconut, shredded	*grated fresh ginger to taste*
2 cups fresh pineapple, chopped	*sugar to taste*
juice of 1 lime	*sliced lime for garnishing*

1. Put all ingredients except sliced lime in a mixing bowl and toss.
2. Put mixture in a serving dish, garnish with sliced lime, and serve at room temperature or chilled.

How to Break and Remove Coconut from Shell

The meat of a coconut is enclosed in a hard shell. To remove it one must break the hard shell away. In order to break a hard object, one must hit it with an equally hard or harder object.

1. Africans break a coconut by hitting it on a rock or with a rock.
2. A coconut can also be broken by holding it in one hand and hitting it with a hammer until the hard shell breaks. Use protective glasses.
3. To remove coconut meat from its shell use a strong, dull, pointed knife. (A sharp knife might cut the skin.) Gently and slowly push the pointed end of the knife between shell and the meat; then lift the meat off the shell.
4. Move to another area and repeat until the meat is completely dislodged.

How to Make Coconut Milk
୭୨

Coconut juice is the sweet liquid in the cavity of the coconut that measures from 1–2 cups.

Coconut milk is the milk-like liquid from the meat of the coconut.

To make coconut milk:
1. Remove coconut from shell; see How to Break and Remove Coconut from Shell (p. 238).
2. Grate meat or crush it in a food processor. Add 4 cups hot water to grated coconut. Mix with a wooden spoon and cool. Squeeze out milk and run liquid through a strainer.
3. Repeat as many times as desired. Each time the process is repeated, the less rich the liquid becomes. Put all of liquid together.

How to Make Coconatii Kpoteh
(Coconut Butter)
୭୨

1. To make *coconatii kpoteh* (coconut butter), boil the white coconut milk down to a creamy, sweet substance (see How to Make Coconut Milk, above).
2. At the time the butter is being formed, the oil also separates so that it is easy to pour it into another container and use it in your cooking.

Did You Know?

Did you know that coconut is a seed? It is the largest single seed in the world.

Orange Kikikanga

Helpful Hint:

Serve chilled or at room temperature.

oranges (as many as desired)   *sugar to taste*
juice of 1 lemon   *grated fresh ginger to taste*
honey to taste

1. Wash each orange. Peel with a knife deep enough to remove the thin white layer next to the meat.
2. Cut into slices, lengthwise, leaving the core of the orange intact.
3. Squeeze out juice from core and remove seeds.
4. Put orange slices and juice in a bowl. Add rest of ingredients and mix. Serve chilled or at room temperature.

Vegetables with Kobo Kobo Avocado Honey Plasas

Helpful Hints:

a. Use any local vegetables in the quantity desired.
b. Peel, wash, and dry vegetables when appropriate. Cut up and arrange them on a serving kalabash or platter.
c. Serve with Kobo Kobo Avocado Honey Plasas (p. 226).

Fruits with Green Mango Sesame Honey Sauce

Helpful Hints:

a. Use local fruits desired in the quantity desired.
b. Wash, peel, cut up, and arrange fruits on a serving platter.
c. Remember that bananas should be sliced just before serving to keep them from turning dark. Or mix bananas with lemon or lime juice before serving.
d. Serve with Green Mango Sesame Honey Sauce (p. 222).
e. Serve wooden picks along with dish.

Nime Nime Ningiliicia
(Sweets, Candies, and Desserts)

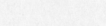

Candy Is Sweet

Candy is sweet,
Candy for a treat.
Candy is candied in sugar and honey,
Coconuts and groundnuts all for some money.
Chewy and crunchy;
Mix it and roll it;
Test it and taste it.
Be careful, don't finish it —
Save some for me.

Jebehwoh's Groundnut (Peanut) Brittle

ை

This African peanut brittle is made in Sierra Leone, West Africa. Jebehwoh, my older sister, taught me how to make it when I was about twelve years old. It is not made like regular brittle because my sister does nothing the regular way. She took out the hard work, and she replaced the not-so-good ingredients with the good stuff. You use no butter, syrup, or soda. You also have no need for testing, baking sheets, or a cooking thermometer. The only ingredients you use are roasted groundnuts (peanuts), sugar, fresh ginger, and about 15 minutes of your time. It tastes great, and it turns out right every time.

a. To make the brittle, one needs to move quickly and in an orderly fashion.
b. Hot melted sugar on the skin can cause severe burns. Children should not be in the kitchen area.
c. Fresh ginger should be finely chopped and spread on a plate for about a half hour so that some of the excess moisture evaporates before use.
d. If you plan to keep the finished dish for more than a week (this has never happened at our house), use unsalted groundnuts (peanuts). When salt is added, with time the nuts collect moisture; the moisture will make the brittle soft and crumbly. You want it dry, crispy, and crunchy—not soft.
e. Do not double the recipe because it is difficult to work with a large batch.

1⅓ cups plus 1 tablespoon roasted, chopped peanuts
½ cup cane sugar

1 tablespoon finely chopped fresh ginger or to taste

1. Heat skillet over medium heat. Add sugar to skillet and spread it out with a long-handled iron spoon. Watch closely because sugar soon starts to melt. Stir often and watch it melt into liquid.
2. Scrape unmelted sugar from spoon with a knife, add it to melted sugar, and mix it in. Continue to mix until all sugar has completely melted. At the same time, watch for smoke, an indica-

tion that the sugar is burning. If it starts to burn, remove skillet from stove for a few seconds, reduce heat, and return skillet to heat again.

3. Stir in ginger and continue stirring until most of formed air bubbles disappear.

4. Add nuts and mix until they are well coated with melted sugar and stick together in a ball.

5. Put mixture on a clean, dry breadboard. With a dry rolling pin or a round bottle, roll it out in the shape of a rectangle, about ⅕ inch in thickness. (One must work fast while sugar is still warm, soft, and easy to work with.)

6. Using a medium to large knife, cut brittle into about 1-inch strips from top to bottom; then cut across each strip into desired portions. Use knife to lift each piece off the board as quickly as possible, so that it does not get stuck to the board. Lay each piece on a dry plate and allow to cool just a few minutes before serving.

Note: Sesame seeds, cashews, and other nuts of choice can also be used instead of groundnuts (peanuts). For better results, all nuts must be roasted before use. Grated peel of lemon, lime, orange, and tangerine and ground hot pepper and cinnamon can be used instead of fresh ginger. Brittle with no spices added is also very good and popular.

BENNIE (SESAME) SEEDS

Africans have always enjoyed the nutty flavor and great aroma of sesame. Now nutritionists tell us that the tiny seeds are loaded with great nutritional value, as if we did not know that before. Bennie seeds are plentiful in Africa because the continent is the land of their origin. The paste and oil are used in many African dishes.

The seeds grow and mature in pods, and each pod may have close to a hundred seeds. Each seed comes enclosed in a very thin, grayish-white skin. If a seed that remains in the skin is exposed to high heat, it bursts open like popcorn and jumps, something African children like to watch. Sesame seeds also come in a dark color.

In my teens, when I was told to roast some bennie seeds in order to cook it with a meal, I built a big fire under the pot because I did not like doing it. Soon some seeds would jump, and some would burn. I heard a familiar voice say, "If anything is left in the pot, you will not eat it!" Grandmother always added, "It is an African belief that only people who talk too much can make sesame seeds jump that soon after they start roasting them." She knew I did not like to be told that I "talked too much" and often that made me lower the heat.

Bennie Seed Lime Lemon Drops

This dish is made in East, South, and West African countries.

Helpful Hints:

a. Use only sesame seeds that are roasted. See How to Roast Sesame Seeds (p. 224).
b. For color use ⅘ of white sesame seeds mixed with ⅕ of black sesame seeds (optional).

½ cup cane sugar
1⅓ cups roasted sesame seeds
(black and white mixed
together)

grated peel of ½ lime and
½ lemon or to taste
pinch of salt (optional)

1. Melt sugar the same way as in Jebehwoh's Groundnut (Peanut) Brittle (p. 242).

2. Stir in rest of ingredients and mix until all ingredients are well coated with melted sugar. Turn off stove but do not remove skillet from stove.

3. Drop mixture by spoonfuls on ungreased dry cookie sheet or on a dry breadboard. Cool and serve.

Ninginanga Coconatii (Rainbow Coconut)

This West African dish is delicious and so colorful, it is likely to make one think of the beautiful rainbow colors, hence the name.

Helpful Hints:

a. In Africa berry and fruit juices are concentrated, then used as food color. Use store-bought colors if so desired.
b. When using food color, remember that softer shades are more appealing than deep, dark ones. Use one drop at a time, then add more as needed.
c. The batch with no food color added should be done first to keep white as pure as possible.
d. Shredded fresh coconut is meaty, and it brings the best result. See How to Shred Coconut (p. 246). Store-bought coconut flakes can also be used as desired.
e. Always use a heavy saucepan because it helps to maintain a more even temperature.
f. Cane sugar is recommended.
g. Do not double recipe.

2 cups shredded fresh coconut   *1 cup water*
⅔ cup cane sugar   *food color of choice*

1. Put coconut, sugar, and water in a skillet. Mix and bring to a boil over medium heat. Cook, mixing occasionally, until liquid is reduced to about ½ cup.
2. Stir in food color, a drop at a time, until desired shade is reached. When more liquid is reduced, stir continuously until moisture is almost gone, but just enough is present to hold coconut shreds together. It should feel sticky when lightly touched at this time.
3. Remove skillet from stove. Drop tablespoonfuls of coconut on ungreased cookie sheet. In a few minutes the drops should be completely dry and ready to be served. Repeat, using a different color each time, or no food color at all.

Variation:

Coconatii Mongoh (Caramel Color Coconut): Use no food color. When moisture is reduced to about ¼ cup, mix continuously until sugar turns light brown or it caramelizes, and there is just enough moisture present to hold coconut shreds together. Remove skillet from stove. Drop spoonfuls of it on ungreased cookie sheet. Serve when they are completely dry.

Note: Arrange finished product so that different colors are in different locations to form *ninginanga,* or rainbow colors.

Because of the pretty colors, I have also used this candy to make flags of countries, and so can you. The candy is also used for garnishing dishes, all beautifully delicious.

For Better Understanding

Humidity can and does affect the making of this candy. The last few drops of moisture so vitally important in the making or breaking of this candy can dry too quickly and cause the shreds not to hold together like they should. There may also be too much moisture left. This will make the candy a little soft instead of dry and crispy as it should be.

How to Shred Coconut

∽

1. Break a coconut; see How to Break and Remove Coconut from Shell (p. 238). Peel off dark skin and wash meat.
2. Using a shredder, shred coconut and use in recipes.

Coconut Strips with Sesame Seeds

∽∾

In this East, West, and South African dish, thin coconut slices are cooked with sugar and dipped in or sprinkled with roasted sesame seeds. It is very special and unusually good.

Helpful Hints:

a. Break a coconut; see How to Break and Remove Coconut from Shell (p. 238). Peel off dark skin, wash, and cut coconut into thin slices lengthwise. Divide sliced coconut into 3 equal portions and use each portion as a batch.
b. Roast sesame seeds ahead of time and set aside.
c. To prepare a cookie sheet, clean and dry it. Put half of roasted sesame on sheet, spread it out, and set aside.

⅓ sliced coconut (1 batch)   *⅓ cup roasted sesame seeds*
½ cup sugar   *Food color of choice if desired*
⅔ cup water

1. Put in a skillet all ingredients except sesame seeds and food color. Bring to a boil over medium heat.
2. Cook, mixing occasionally, until liquid is greatly reduced.
3. Stir in food color, one drop at a time, until you have desired shade. Continuously mix until very little moisture is present and coconut feels sticky to touch.
4. Take skillet to prepared cookie sheet. Remove coconut from skillet and spread it on prepared sheet with a fork or a knife. Sprinkle rest of seeds over coconut and allow to dry. Repeat with other batches.

Ginger Sesame Candy

∽∾

This dish is made in East, South, and West African countries.

Helpful Hints:

a. Use large, young, and fresh ginger that has less-matured fibers.
b. If possible use cane sugar.
c. It is important that ginger is cooked for 30 minutes so that it does not sweat later.
d. This dish can also be served with meat, fish, and poultry.
e. To remove skin of ginger, you scrape skin off. You waste the bulk of ginger when you peel skin off.

1 pound fresh ginger	*grated peel of same lemon*
1⅓ cups sugar	*1 cup water*
juice of 1 lemon	*⅔ cup roasted sesame seeds*

1. Using a vegetable knife or a spoon, scrape (do not peel) skin off ginger and wash. Cut it lengthwise into slices as thin as possible.

2. Put in a heavy cooking pot all ingredients except sesame seeds. Stir and bring to a boil over medium heat.

3. Reduce to low heat and cook for 30 minutes, stirring occasionally. Increase heat to medium and stir continuously until there is only enough moisture left to allow sesame seeds to adhere to coconut.

4. At this time sugar is almost ready to crystallize; but you want it wet, and it should feel sticky when lightly touched.

5. Remove pot from heat. Using tongs and working as fast as possible, remove each piece of ginger, roll it in sesame seeds, and lay it on a non-oiled cookie sheet. Repeat until each slice is coated with sesame seeds. Cool and serve or add sesame to a dry baking sheet. Add ginger, mix with tongs. Allow to dry and serve.

Note: Ginger can also be chopped into chunks or cut into long, thin strips before cooking. Then roll in or sprinkle with sesame seeds or sugar. Allow to dry on cookie sheets. The finished product is dry and crispy. It is served as candy. It can also be used to garnish meat, fish, chicken, and fruit dishes.

Variations:

Pineapple Candy: Use fresh or canned pineapple slices instead of ginger. After cooking, sprinkle with or roll in sugar, roasted sesame seeds, or chopped nuts.

Orange Skin Candy: Cut each orange into quarters from top to bottom. Remove skin from each quarter in one piece. Cut skin into strips and use in place of ginger. If the strong orange flavor is not desired, cook skin in water for 10 minutes and drain before using in recipe.

Chin Chin

This crunchy, chewy dish is made in East, South, and West African countries.

Helpful Hints:

a. It is important to knead dough until it is soft and easy to work with.

b. Unlike candy, one can double or even triple the recipe without getting into trouble, and this is often done.

c. *Chin chin* should be made by all family members. The children will enjoy playing with the dough and may attempt to design various shapes. Be sure to keep them away from the hot oil.

d. It tastes great when served hot, but it can also be served cold.

¾ cup sugar or to taste
½ cup butter or margarine
grated fresh ginger to taste
grated peel of 1 lime
1 teaspoon vanilla
½ teaspoon nutmeg
salt to taste

2 or 3 eggs
½ cup or more milk or water
½ teaspoon baking powder
2–3 cups flour
groundnut (peanut) or vegetable
*   oil of choice for frying.*

1. Cream sugar, butter, ginger, lime peel, vanilla, nutmeg, and salt in a large mixing bowl. In another mixing bowl beat eggs one at

a time. Add milk and baking powder. Beat until eggs and milk are well mixed.

2. Add to sugar mixture about ⅓ of egg mixture and mix well. Add to same mixture about ⅓ of flour and mix well. Repeat, always adding liquid first, then flour, until a stiff dough is made.

3. Put dough on a floured board and knead until it is soft and easy to work with. Allow it to rest about 10 minutes. May chill for 1 hour (optional).

4. Divide dough in half. On floured board roll each half about ⅕-inch thick. Cut into diamond shapes, 3 inches by 1½ inches. At center of each diamond piece, cut 1-inch horizontal line. Pull one long end of diamond through cut. Also make other shapes as desired.

5. Add oil (about 3 inches deep) to a heated skillet that is over medium heat and bring it to 375 degrees. Or use Suma's Onion Oil Test (p. 228) as needed.

6. Fry in hot oil until golden. Remove from oil, drain, and serve. May sprinkle with confectioners' sugar that is mixed with powdered ginger or cinnamon to taste (optional).

TOMBOYA

In Mende the word *tomboya* means an abandoned old village site. The land, which would not be occupied or cultivated for a long period of time, would usually be covered with lush foliage including a large variety of fruit trees and vegetables, all belonging to whomever gathers them. Monkeys, chimpanzees, gorillas, birds, and other animals would periodically bring their families to this paradise to feast and enjoy themselves.

There used to be many such areas of land in Africa, especially in the western region. Today they are decreasing in number and in size at an alarming rate as the human population increases. The animal population, on the other hand, is decreasing as many *tomboyas* again become new villages for the people.

‡‡‡‡‡‡ ‡‡‡‡‡‡ ‡‡‡‡‡‡ ‡‡‡‡‡‡ ‡‡‡‡‡‡ ‡‡‡‡‡‡ ‡‡‡‡‡‡ ‡‡‡‡‡‡ ‡‡‡‡‡‡ ‡‡‡‡‡‡ ‡‡‡‡‡‡

Yayu's Encounter with Ngoloh at Tomboya

Generations have been confronted with the old question of what the connection is, if any, between man and the great apes. When apes are observed in the wild, the most renowned scientist and the rain forest *camajoh* (a professional hunter) cannot help but ask the question, "Why do apes behave so much like people?"

A six-year-old West African girl was forced to look at the same question in an unusual way. Yayu had the opportunity to closely observe *ngoloh*, the West African gorilla, in the wild. She talked and ate with him, and she took part in his family group activity, but only for a brief time. Yayu left with the impression that the great apes are intelligent, gentle, kind, and friendly. She also concluded that the leader of the group was very old. That is why she called his name Wova, or the old one. Also this child was able to see that apes did some things humans did. But she knew that apes are not humans.

One beautiful afternoon Deema said to Musu and a handful of children from Camboma Village, "Grandmother's firewood is very low. Let's go to the forest and play *keyponoh* game; then we'll bring home some wood." Every child in the village loved to play the game and worked very hard to win by collecting the most brilliant, orange-red fireball lilies in the rain forest. So they all agreed to go with her. As they were leaving, six-year-old Yayu asked, "May I come along?" Before anyone answered, she ran to join the small group that was already under the big, old breadfruit tree at the edge of the village.

"You can't go with us!" Musu, Yayu's bossy twelve-year-old sister, told her. "I cannot carry you and the firewood at the same time." The girls were now at the far end of the small village. "But I can walk!" Yayu reminded her sister, trying to sound as grown-up as possible. "I am not like Moinini," she continued. "He can't walk without falling down. I don't need your help!" A more determined Yayu followed the small group. "You can walk and make all the fuss you want, but you can't run as fast as the rest of us. Besides that," Musu told her younger sister, "we are going to play *keyponoh* game along the way. The one who runs the fastest and gathers the most fireball lilies becomes the winner. I want to be the one with the most lilies. I cannot pull you along and still gather the most flowers. You are not coming, and that is final!"

Hearing the words *"keyponoh* game" made Yayu want to be part of the group even more. She threw herself on the grass and screamed so loud that almost everyone in the small village heard her crying. Grandmother Sombo, who was babysitting Moinini, Yayu's younger brother, and other grown-ups came running to see if poor Yayu was hurt. "Please, Grandmother," Yayu cried, "tell Musu to take me with her. I will be good and will not fight with her." Grandmother tried to help her up. But she kicked, yelled, and would not stand. At this time the group had almost disappeared into the woods, trying very hard to get away before anyone was called back. "Musu!" Grandmother called out. "Come back here, all of you!" She tried one more time to help Yayu stand. Yayu quickly stood up when she saw her sister and the other girls coming back.

"This little girl gets us every time," Musu whispered to Deema. "Look at her! She does not have a tear in her eyes, even after all that yelling." Deema, the oldest in the group, reached out and held Yayu by the hand. Before Grandmother spoke, Deema said, "We will take her with us." Turning to Musu she continued, "Let's take her with us. We shall play *keyponoh* game another time." They left with Yayu, who was now all smiles, very pleased with herself and with another victory over her sister. "Hurry back before dark," Grandmother called after them as the last child disappeared into the forest.

They stopped along the way and picked some wild berries. "Don't give her so much! The rest of us want some, too," Musu objected when Deema gave Yayu more than her share of berries. Each girl ate what Deema gave her and went to gather some firewood. Yayu sat down to eat her share of berries. Most of what she had put in her small pocket got crushed and was stuck to the inside of the pocket. She pulled them out and ate what she could, and she threw away the seeds. Soon some *sokehlemasas* (birds) landed nearby and began to eat some insects. Then they came closer to her and began to eat some berry seeds she threw away. Yayu quietly picked a pebble from under her foot and threw it at the birds as she said, "Can you fly?" They flew away and landed on some branches not far away.

When she finished eating, the girls were busy collecting dry branches from under the trees and putting them all in one big pile. Yayu began to gather a few twigs into her own small pile. Soon she saw more birds eating berries in some nearby lower branches. When she went toward them, they flew away. She picked the berries, put a few in her pocket, and ate the rest. They were ripe and very sweet. She saw more birds eating berries not too far away. Again she followed them. She picked the berries, ate some, and she put a few more in her pocket. Such was the pattern of events that took Yayu, little by little, far into the forest and away from the girls. Not only was her pocket stiff and red, but her hands and lips were also red. Even her beautiful white teeth were now more pink than they were white. She had never had so much fun. That is why she did not notice how far she had left the group behind.

Suddenly Yayu was forced to stop because of unfamiliar sounds. When she did, she was totally unprepared for the scene before her. She had left one group behind, but she was now part of a large family of gorillas having a great time. Several young gorillas were jumping from branch to branch, eating or throwing pineapple chunks at one another. Many mothers sat together with their babies. One mother had a toddler sitting between her legs while he struggled to get away. Another mother had a little one hanging around her neck. Both she and the youngster played and ate pineapple, though it was clear that he wanted to play more than he wanted to eat. Two mothers breastfed while the other mothers just sat and held their babies. More of them sat under trees, in pairs, eating pineapples and grooming partners. There was a giant white-chested male gorilla not too far from the rest of the group. He sat alone on a large rock, also eating some pineapple. The large pineapple field surrounding them looked like it had just been hit by the worst tropical storm. There was not a bush left standing; pineapples were everywhere.

Yayu did not know what to make of what she was seeing. Should she yell? She was very good at doing that. But how about running away? She could run almost as fast as Musu could. But she was almost completely surrounded by the animals. How was she going to run away? When she looked again, the animals were just eating and playing. They did not look like they were going to hurt anyone. Then she thought of her pet monkey, Nunii. He never hurt anyone. These gorillas just played and ate while she stood in their midst and looked, because it was all she could do. It took some time to get used to it all. When she became a little more comfortable with her surroundings, she could not help but want to join in the fun. Everyone looked so friendly and happy. She walked a few steps, scratched her head, and hesitantly went to the giant-sized gorilla who was still sitting alone and eating.

"Wova," she said as she held out her hand. "May I, please I say, may I have some pineapple?" He seemed to understand what the little girl wanted. He looked at her with kind eyes. *Ngoloh* got hold of a nearby ripe pineapple and pulled it off the ground. He hit the large fruit just once on the rock and it split open and broke into several pieces. He gave a large piece to Yayu, took a piece for himself, and put the rest on the rock below, close to some young gorillas. She took the pineapple, said thanks, and began to sit down. She was halfway down when she stood up. She started down again, but stood up, looking uncomfortable. She looked around again and saw that nothing much had changed. Mothers were still playing with the young and caring for them. The adolescent group, the most active of all, continued to jump from low branch to low branch, threw pineapple at one another, grabbed and pushed one another, or yelled just for the joy of yelling. Most adult animals were still sitting on rocks, giving or receiving hugs, eating and enjoying themselves. Yayu hesitated for another moment. Then she sat next to Wova and began to eat.

Musu was the last to tie together her firewood. She got enough fresh palm leaves to make two head pads (fukeh). She made one head pad for herself and laid it by her bundle of wood. She tied together a few dry sticks for her sister, made her head pad, and laid it by the tiny bundle of wood. "Yayu!" she called out. "Come and get your wood." Mumbling to herself, she said, "We have to hurry home before it gets dark." She turned around, picked up Yayu's head pad, and called her the second time. Again there was no answer. "Yayu, where are you?" No answer. This time Deema's voice called, "Yayu, are you playing hide and seek again? We have to go home." But there was no answer. "Yayu!" Musu's unsteady voice came after she had searched and her sister was nowhere to be found. "Deema!" she yelled. There was one thing Musu and her sister had in common. They could really yell when they wanted to or had to. "Yayu is gone, and I don't know where she is!" Musu cried and started to shake like a leaf. They were all calling at this time. "Yayu, where are you?" came one voice. "Can you hear me?" another voice cried out. All looked under the trees, up the trees, among the branches. They searched the small stream. Deema gave a sharp cry when she thought she stepped on a baby snake. The snake turned out to be some rotten leaves. Everyone was now in tears or close to it.

Meanwhile Musu reached the village in tears and out of breath. As luck would have it, Foday, their father, and Behveh, their uncle, had just returned to the village. They had come from a hunting trip at the same time Musu arrived. "Father, Yayu is missing. We do not know where she is," Musu said between tears. Grandmother Sombo briefly explained to him and Behveh how Yayu had cried so much, that she allowed her to go with the other children to get some wood. "How I wish I had not allowed myself to be. . . ." She walked away very upset.

In a matter of minutes a search party was on the way. More people followed as the news spread. A few went toward Moa River, some through the coffee farm, and still others went by the Cambo Hills. Behveh and Foday went nowhere in particular. They looked everywhere as they rushed down the narrow path. Foday quietly began to rub both hands together. He stopped suddenly. As if pushing himself down with a great deal of effort, he roughly sat on the grass. The tropical sun was on its way out from the sky, but the air was still warm and humid. Yet Foday's skin and hands felt cold and clammy. He began to breathe fast and shallow. "My little girl!" he moaned. "Please, God, keep my girl safe." Behveh touched Foday's shoulder. He was shaking all over. "She will be all right. She has to be." He comforted Foday as he sat next to his friend.

The two men had been friends all their lives. One could almost tell what the other was thinking. They were born just two days apart. The women had lost their young husbands during a fishing trip in the rainy season. Their sons were just a few years old at the time of the accident. Foday had married Tenneh, Behveh's beautiful cousin. Tenneh and her friends had gone fishing early that morning. Grandmother Sombo, Behveh's mother, had volunteered to babysit so that the young women could go fishing now that the rice harvest was just over. It had been a very rough year. The animals and the birds had been plentiful. It had not been easy to keep them away from the farms. Everyone was now taking it easy for a change. Soon it would be time to prepare the land to plant again. That morning before she left Tenneh had said, "Yayu, help Grandmother to take care of Moinini. Do not fight with your sister, and don't forget to feed Nunii." Yayu had given her mother a hug and said, "Will you please bring me some baby crabs?" The women were going to have a good time fishing. They would be in no hurry to return to the village.

Behveh and Foday thought of Tenneh at the same time.

"Tenneh!" they called her name together. What was she going to do when she found out that her little girl, who was very much alive when she left in the morning, was now missing? They jumped up and started to run. It was at that same time that they heard a large group of gorillas close by. For no reason whatsoever, they ran toward the direction from which the noise came. Before they knew it, they were at tomboya. So was a large family of gorillas, having a great time. As professional hunters, they knew that they should and must walk around the animals without disturbing them. They had done so many times in the past. Behveh, who was leading the way, suddenly stopped. Turning to Foday with a frown, he whispered, "Did you hear that voice?" Foday asked, "What voice?" Almost immediately Foday heard the same voice. "Wova," Yayu's voice came again. "I said may I please have more pineapple?" They could not miss that voice even if they were asleep. But could it be that their ears were playing tricks on them? They were not prepared for what was coming.

When they looked, Yayu was sitting close to *ngoloh*. She was so close that she was almost leaning against the giant gorilla. The animal gave her another large piece of pineapple. She took it, said thanks, and was eating as if it was the normal thing to do. The animal also continued to eat as if it was the thing to do. A youngster threw a large piece of pineapple toward the men. It flew by Foday and landed on Behveh's head. *Ngoloh's* eyes had followed the piece of pineapple. The animal saw it as it hit his head. Then their eyes met. In a twinkling of an eye, the seemingly mild-mannered giant was transformed into the leader and protector that he was. He stood big and tall and made a single, loud sound. That was enough to bring each and every animal to full attention. Before Yayu understood what was going on, the family fled. It was like the withdrawal of an almost captured army, taking only the most essential and leaving behind its casualty.

The men ran to Yayu and held her as all three sobbed. Later she angrily said, "Wova left without saying good-bye." She thought for a moment as she added, "They were so nice. They were my friends, just like Nunii." Foday finally said, "You could have been hurt." Looking at her father, Yaju said, "Father, did you hear what I said?" Smiling for the first time,

Foday said, "I heard all you said." And he held her close again. "But I said that they were very nice, like Nunii," Yayu repeated. It was Behveh's time to speak. "You call that nice? I was hit so hard on the head, it still hurts." He put his hand over the sore area of his head. "Uncle Behveh," Yayu called, "they did not mean to hurt you. That was an accident. You got in the way." Continuing to hold his head, Behveh said, "I hope I don't get in the way ever again."

FRIED TROPICAL FRUITS AND VEGETABLES: COATINGS TO USE

Africans like to fry fruits and vegetables. It is easy to do, and the results are simply delectable. Following are recipes for batter and other coatings you may use before frying.

Helpful Hints:

a. Use local fruits and vegetables.
b. Ripe and firm fruits give better results.
c. If sugar or salt should be added to ripe fruits, add just before frying to keep the natural juices in.
d. The pieces should be uniform in size so that they cook at the same rate.
e. Use Suma's Onion Oil Test (p. 228) as needed.

Mbagbehnyeh Flour Mixture

*1 cup mbagbehnyeh; see How
to Make Mbagbehnyeh
(Broken Rice) (p. 225)
2 tablespoons rice flour or
whole wheat flour*

*grated fresh ginger to taste
sugar to taste
salt to taste*

1. Put all ingredients in a bowl and mix.
2. Use to coat fruits or vegetables before frying.
3. Do not add sugar when frying vegetables unless so desired.

Rice Flour

*1 cup African rice flour or
other rice flour
sugar to taste*

*ground semengii (cinnamon)
to taste
salt to taste*

1. Put all ingredients together in a bowl and mix.
2. Use to dust fruits and vegetables before frying.
3. Do not add sugar when frying vegetables unless so desired.

Sesame Batter

*1⅓ cups or more rice flour
1 tablespoon roasted sesame
seeds
sugar to taste
grated fresh ginger to taste
grated peel of ½ lime*

*salt to taste
1 tablespoon sesame oil
1 egg, lightly beaten
cold liquid (coconut or cow's
milk, orange juice, or water)*

1. Mix all dry ingredients, oil, and egg in a mixing bowl. Stir in some liquid a little at a time. Repeat until batter is the consistency desired. Add more flour or liquid as needed at any time.

2. Dip a piece of fruit or vegetable into batter. Remove the excess before frying in deep hot oil of choice.

3. Do not add sugar when frying vegetables unless it is so desired.

Suggested Fruits and Vegetables to Deep Fry:

green or medium-ripe mango (green mango may need some sugar added, due to its sour taste)
medium-ripe *paw paw* (papaya)
medium-ripe banana
ripe plantain
local fruits of choice
local vegetables of choice

Tomboya Fruit Bowls

Helpful Hints:

a. When bananas are used, add them just before serving.
b. Serve chilled or at room temperature.

1 cup fresh pineapple, crushed
1 large ripe mango, cut into
chunks
paw paw *(papaya) chunks*
fresh orange sections to taste
1 cup fresh orange juice
pineapple juice to taste

ripe bananas, cut up and to
taste
local berries to taste
juice of 1 lemon
grated fresh ginger to taste
sugar to taste

1. Mix all ingredients in a bowl.
2. Put in individual serving dishes and garnish with mint leaves.
3. Serve chilled or at room temperature.

Orange Sections in Taita Sauce

Helpful Hint:

This dish can be served chilled or at room temperature.

2 cups or more orange juice
juice of 1 lemon
grated peel of ½ lemon
grated fresh ginger to taste
⅓ cup sesame seeds, roasted
and ground (mixed with
¼ cup orange juice)

1 tablespoon or more corn or
cassava starch (mixed with
⅓ cup orange juice)
4 cups fresh orange sections
honey and/or sugar to taste
roasted, shredded coconut for
garnishing

1. Put in a saucepan all ingredients except orange sections, honey, and coconut. Stir and bring to a gentle boil. Cook over reduced heat, stirring often, until a light sauce is formed. Add more orange juice or starch mixed with 2 cups orange juice and the juice of a lemon to get thickness desired.

2. Stir in honey and/or sugar, remove from heat, and cool to room temperature. Fold in orange sections and put in individual serving dishes.

3. Garnish with shredded coconuts and serve chilled or at room temperature.

Variations:

Pineapple in Taita Sauce: Use fresh pineapple chunks instead of orange sections.
Mango in Taita Sauce: Use ripe mango chunks instead of orange sections.
Paw Paw in Taita Sauce: Use ripe papaya chunks instead of orange sections.

Bambara Plantain Balls

This is a West African treat. Enjoy it!

Helpful Hints:

a. Plantains must be ripe and cooked whole in the skin.
b. They mash better and taste better when they are still warm.
c. Roll some balls in roasted sesame seeds and some in chopped nuts of choice.

3 ripe plantains
1 cup roasted and ground
  sesame seeds; see How to
  Roast Sesame Seeds (p. 224)
honey and sugar to taste

grated fresh ginger to taste
⅓ cup roasted unground
  sesame seeds for coating
⅓ cup chopped roasted nuts
  of choice for coating

1. Remove both ends of each plantain, lay them in a cooking pot, and add about 2 cups water. Put lid in place and bring pot to a boil over medium heat. Cook until each is done, about 10–12 minutes.

2. Remove from water and cool only enough to be able to handle each without burning your hands. (Don't cool completely.) Peel and mash plantains like you would mash potatoes.

3. Stir in rest of ingredients except sesame seeds and chopped nuts for coating. Using mixture by spoonfuls, make some egg shapes and some balls. Roll each in sesame seeds or in nuts. Arrange them in a serving dish and serve.

Fresh Fruits with Tomboya Plasas

This dish is from Liberia, Mali, Senegal, and Sierra Leone.

Helpful Hint:

Use local fruits in season and some suggested fruits below.

mango	*banana*
paw paw (papaya)	*melons*
pineapple	

1. Wash fruits and cut and arrange them in a serving platter.
2. Spoon Tomboya Plasas over arranged fruits, or put *plasas* in a serving dish and serve as a fruit dip along with some wooden picks.

Tomboya Plasas

Helpful Hint:

Make sauce only as thick as you want it to be.

orange juice	*1 egg, lightly beaten*
¼ cup honey or to taste	*1 teaspoon or more flour*
¼ cup sugar or to taste	*⅓ cup groundnut (peanut)*
fresh juice of 1 lemon	*butter*
grated peel of same lemon	*¼ cup roasted chopped*
grated fresh ginger to taste	*groundnuts (peanuts)*
hot pepper to taste (optional)	*¼ cup fresh or toasted*
salt to taste	*shredded coconut*

1. Put in a heavy saucepan about 1 cup orange juice and all ingredients except chopped nuts and shredded coconut. Mix well and set over medium heat.

2. Continuously mix with a wooden spoon until sauce comes to a gentle boil. Continue to cook and mix for 5–7 more minutes.

3. Mixture should be the consistency of a thick sauce. If it becomes too thick, stir in more orange juice and honey.

4. Fold in nuts and coconuts. Remove from heat, cool, and serve with chunks of fresh fruit.

Hot and Cold Beverages

COFFEE

Did You Know?

Did you know that coffee is one of the main cash crops in Africa, where it also originated?

During the time I was growing up, each year I helped to harvest coffee on our farm in Sierra Leone, West Africa. After we gathered the beans and sun-dried them for many days, we peeled the shell from the seeds in large wooden mortars *(konhdeh)* with wooden pestles *(ngehteh)*. Then we separated the beans from the shells by fanning. At long last the beans were put in large bags to be sold.

My siblings and I went to boarding schools far from home. Our hometown, Kpendembu (Pendembu), had a one-room grade school building with mud walls and a thatched roof. At the end of four years, parents who could afford it sent their children to other parts of the country to go to school. Some of them lived with relatives while they attended school; others went to boarding schools. When vacation came, harvesting coffee was the one thing all of us did not like coming home to do, because it was a very difficult job. Yet it never failed, not even once. When we arrived home, the coffee was always just ready for harvest. I often wondered how the trees knew the exact time we would come home, year after year.

We usually rested and visited with family and friends for a few days, then we waited for the inevitable. I can still hear Father's kind but authoritative voice. Soon after we finished eating in the evening, he first cleared his throat, as if he had to do that to get our full attention. Then he would say, "Everyone is now well rested. As you already know, the coffee is ready for harvest. We start work two days from today." For almost three months, from early in the morning to late in the evening, our vacation time was spent on the farm, doing back-breaking work. At the end of each day, everyone had painful blisters on both hands; red eyes and stuffy noses because of so much dust; and the inevitable ant stings that came with the job. Of course, we all became experts in dodging bees and their painful stings.

Like the coffee, which never failed to show up for harvest, so also foreign companies never failed to pay the people far below the market value for all cash crops. I did not understand how the coffee trees knew when it was time for us to come home any more than I understood how the companies always reserved the right to pay African farmers only how much money they wanted to pay them—and it was never much. But when the same people brought back the finished products of the very cash crops for which so little money had been paid, they sold their merchandise for a lot of money. For example, cloth made of cotton for which so little money had been given to farmers, would now be sold for a lot of money to buyers. Parents who had children in school had no choice but to purchase the expensive cloth to make garments and uniforms for their children. That left them with little or no money for better housing, health care, books, food, shoes, and all the things African families also need.

This portion of the book is dedicated to my father, Amsumana Kallon, and other African farmers who still struggle just to survive despite their hard work.

Ginger Hot Coffee

ༀ

Coffee is used in all parts of Africa. Some people like to drink it very strong in tiny cups with as much excess sugar added to each cup as there is time spent on ritual performance. Others like to

serve it weak and use little to no sugar and less execution of ceremony. No matter how it is served, many African families and
friends drink coffee to relax and enjoy one another's company.

Helpful Hint:

Use freshly brewed coffee.

4 cups hot coffee   *sugar to taste (optional)*
grated fresh ginger to taste

　　1. Put all ingredients in a clean, heated teapot.
　　2. Stir, cover, and allow to stand a few minutes before serving. If
desired, strain and reheat before serving it hot.

Variations:

Semengii Coffee: Stir in ground cinnamon and sugar to taste.
Coffee with Cloves: Stir in ground or whole cloves and sugar to taste.
Mint Coffee: Add to a hot pot of coffee bruised mint leaves and
sugar to taste. Cover and allow to stand for about 5 minutes. Strain
and serve hot.
Coffee with Lime: Add fresh lime juice, sugar, and/or honey to taste.
Reheat and serve hot.
Coffee with Lemon: Add to hot coffee fresh lemon juice, sugar, and/
or honey to taste. Reheat and serve it hot.

Spicy Gingerbeer Coffee

This delightful African soft drink is perfect to quench any thirst.

Helpful Hints:

a. The name "gingerbeer" may be misleading because the bever-
　age contains no alcohol.
b. Add to each cup of coffee 3 cups Spicy Gingerbeer (p. 270) or
　make it to taste.

c. Use freshly brewed coffee or instant coffee, following package instructions.

d. Serve it cold with ice.

2 cups cold brewed coffee   **ice and sugar to taste**
6 cups cold Spicy Gingerbeer

1. Put all ingredients in a large pitcher.
2. Stir and serve cold.

TEA

This beverage is widely used in Africa. Many African countries also grow tea as a cash crop.

African Lemon Tea

Helpful Hint:

Use freshly brewed tea (follow directions on package).

4 cups hot tea   **1 teaspoon grated lemon peel**
juice of 1 lemon   **honey and/or sugar to taste**

1. Combine all ingredients, mix well, and run through a strainer.
2. Reheat and serve hot in a heated teapot.

Variations:

African Ginger Lemon Tea: Add 1 teaspoon grated fresh ginger to African Lemon Tea and strain. Reheat and serve hot.

Hot Pepper Tea and Lime: Use ingredients for African Lemon Tea plus ground hot pepper to taste. Strain, reheat, and serve hot.

Lemongrass Tea

ல

This beverage is made in Sierra Leone.

Helpful Hints:

a. Use fresh lemongrass leaves if possible. Cook in water until liquid turns green. (Your kitchen will be filled with the most wonderful aroma.)
b. Specialty food stores, such as African and Asian stores do carry lemongrass leaves.

> ***1 bunch lemongrass leaves***   ***fresh lime juice to taste***
> ***honey and/or sugar to taste***

1. Wash leaves and put in cooking pot. Cover with water; with lid in place bring it to a boil.
2. Cook on medium heat until liquid turns green (you will love the wonderful aroma that fills the house).
3. Remove from heat and drain. Add rest of ingredients and serve hot or cold.

For Better Understanding

Lemongrass is a grass plant that grows wild in Africa and in some warm countries around the world. Its delightful aroma greatly enhances food in taste and smell. When the fresh leaves are boiled in water, they give the liquid a fresh lime color, with lemon-lime flavor. The water is often served as hot or cold tea.

The upper root of the plant is chopped, ground, crushed, or used whole to cook with meat, fish, poultry, and vegetables. If desired, tie crushed root in a clean cheesecloth before adding it to dish, then remove it before serving the dish.

Africans also use the more matured root ends as toothbrushes. The lemongrass root keeps the teeth white and gives the mouth freshness, and the clean feeling lasts a long time.

Spice Mint Tea

Helpful Hint:

To bruise mint leaves, rub the leaves between both hands for a fraction of a minute.

4 cups fresh hot tea
12 fresh bruised mint leaves
   or to taste

whole cloves to taste
juice of 1 fresh lemon
sugar to taste

   1. In a heated teapot combine all ingredients except sugar. Cover and steep 5–7 minutes.

   2. Stir, strain, and reheat before serving hot with or without sugar.

Note: Mint tea can also be served cold with ice. When that is the case, stronger tea and more mint leaves are used. After mixing all ingredients, cool tea and run it through a strainer before adding sugar to taste.

Hibiscus Tea

The hibiscus flower is plentiful in Africa. While it is appreciated for its beautiful red, pink, and yellow colors, the people also dry the red petals to make tea. As a vegetable, the tender green leaves are often chopped and added to rice and other grains for its taste and beautiful green color.

Helpful Hint:

If possible, use sun-dried, red hibiscus petals.

dry red hibiscus petals to taste
4 cups rapidly boiling water

sugar to taste
fresh lemon juice to taste

1. Add petals and boiling water to a clean, heated teapot in that order. Cover, steep for 5–7 minutes, and stir.

2. Using a strainer, pour tea into cup and serve with sugar and lemon.

OTHER NONALCOHOLIC DRINKS

Gingerbeer

There are two kinds of this nonalcoholic, African beverage: spicy gingerbeer and fruity gingerbeer. Both kinds are made in West African countries and are delicious.

Spicy Gingerbeer

This beverage is more spicy, and it is usually boiled with lemon juice and whole cloves before it is served.

Helpful Hints:

a. Gingerbeer can be served ice cold on a hot day or boiling hot on a cold day.

b. One may double the recipe or make a fraction as desired.

¼ pound fresh ginger
  (1 large piece)
8–10 cups water
5 whole cloves

fresh juice of 2 lemons or
  to taste
sugar to taste

1. Wash ginger and cut it into smaller portions without removing skin. Crush it in a blender. Add 2 cups water

2. Put mixture in a pot and add cloves and water. Over medium heat bring to a boil, uncovered. Stir and cook over low heat for 10 minutes, making sure mixture does not boil over.

3. Stir in lemon juice and sugar and cook 3–5 more minutes. Turn off heat and allow to cool while on stove. Run mixture through a strainer that is lined with two layers of clean cheesecloth. Return cloves to liquid and serve cold or at room temperature. You may also reheat it and serve hot.

Note: Spicy gingerbeer mixed with fruit juices makes a refreshing and delightful punch. Use a 50-50 ratio.

Fruity Gingerbeer

This drink requires much less time to make and is usually not boiled. Whole cloves do not need to be added, and it tastes more fruity.

Helpful Hint:

Serve cold or at room temperature.

¼ *pound fresh ginger*	2 *cups orange juice*
(1 large piece)	2 *cups pineapple juice*
8 *cups or more water*	*sugar to taste*
juice of 2 lemons	*ice (optional)*

1. Wash ginger and cut into small portions without removing skin. Put it in a blender, add 2 cups water, and blend until ginger is crushed.

2. Put crushed ginger in a mixing bowl, stir in water, and strain through a strainer that is lined with two layers of clean cheesecloth.

3. Combine all liquids in a mixing bowl. Add sugar and mix until sugar is dissolved before serving.

Lumbehlehcia (Oranges, African Style)

ෙ

Eating oranges the African way is fun, natural, and efficient. Yet it is such a simple way to quench one's thirst that even a child can learn in a matter of minutes.

One day I talked to a group of African-American schoolchildren on a warm afternoon. We talked about African foods. I had brought enough oranges so that each child could learn to eat one the way we do in Africa. I peeled and gave one to each person. No one knew how to eat it. But after I demonstrated, everyone soon learned. We had a great time. Several of the children told me, "This is a neat way to eat oranges." In Sierra Leone, after an American missionary learned to eat oranges the way the African people do, she said, "This is a very clever way to eat oranges."

Helpful Hints:

a. Use only juicy oranges that have tough skin.
b. Use a potato peeler to peel. (In Africa we use a vegetable knife to peel.) Do not peel deeply; remove only the top skin.
c. When sucking, do not push nails into orange. By doing so one may cause it to leak.

oranges (as many as desired)   1 potato peeler

1. Using a peeler, peel each orange as one would a potato. Take care not to go too deep into the skin.
2. With a knife cut away a thin slice from the tail end of the orange. (You do not want to cut or remove the opposite end.)
3. Holding orange between both hands, gently squeeze it with the palms and fingertips (not fingernails) of both hands as you suck juice at the same time. Rotate it slightly toward left or right, and again gently squeeze while you suck. As it becomes softer, more juice is squeezed out. Repeat until most of juice is sucked out.

Did You Know?

Did you know that one can make beautiful artistic designs on an orange? By removing long, narrow strips of orange skin in one direction, then in another, rich and beautiful patterns emerge. Like any art form, this takes practice, time, and experience. It also takes a sharp knife to do a good job.

MANGO

Do you know how the name "mango" came about?

Many years ago, a brave and nice young man, Moiwa, left home in search of knowledge. He met strangers and talked with many people. They were all willing to teach him what they had learned from experience in exchange for a fee. Because he was rich, he learned much. As his knowledge increased, his money decreased, and he soon became penniless. Thinking of himself as the most knowledgeable person around, the nice young man soon became "Mr. Know-it-all." He turned into a miserable character no one cared to have around anymore.

Without money or friends, Moiwa decided to go into the forest in search of food. Tired and hungry, he saw a tree he had not seen before. The big tree was covered with hundreds of the most luscious-looking fruits he had ever seen. In and under the strange tree were monkeys everywhere. They were having a great time, eating fruit after fruit from the tree. Because he was very hungry, Moiwa wasted no time in eating one of the enticing fruits. It was so delicious that he ate many more.

He soon went to sleep on a soft bed of dry leaves. The next morning he woke up more like the nice young man he once was, before he came to know so much. After eating more of the fruit, Moiwa said, *"Gi a pialo ndolehmoh i gia."* The English translation is, "This can make a hungry *man go*." From these two words he called the fruit "mango." He put as many of the fruits in his bags as he could carry, very happy that he was going home at last. He ate mango after mango as he journeyed home. The seeds he dropped along the way grew into many mango trees.

Mango Punch Nime Nime

ᏸᏸ

This is a delicious thirst quencher.

Helpful Hints:

a. Mangos must be fully ripe.
b. The fruit has a large, hard, and flat seed at the core. Remove meat from seed by cutting away from seed. (Do not cut across fruit.)
c. The drink can be made more concentrated by adding less water and less concentrated by adding more water.

5 ripe mangos
1 medium ginger root, remove
*   skin and grate*
juice of 2 lemons

6 cups water or amount desired
sugar to taste
ice as desired

1. Peel each mango and remove meat from seed. Put in a blender the meat of mango, ginger, lemon juice, and 2 cups water. Blend until it liquifies.

2. Put the mixture into a bowl and add rest of water. Run juice through a strainer lined with a layer of clean cheesecloth.

3. Stir in sugar, put mixture in a serving pitcher, and serve with or without ice.

Did You Know?

Did you know that many African girls learn to braid hair by first learning to braid the hair-like fiber on the mango seed?

It is believed that there are close to a hundred varieties of mangoes in the African forest and around the world. The most popular variety looks like a map of Africa. (Please use your imagination here.) It is also the largest and the one most often used for the self-taught hair braiding lessons.

To prepare a seed, use a very ripe mango. Eat by gently biting into the meat instead of cutting meat away with a knife. After eating, use a spoon to remove any remaining pulp before washing seed thoroughly under running water. Dry and comb hair before braiding it. You may pull hair all you want or comb it all you like. There is never a complaint. This may be the most cooperative customer you will ever have. Learn from it.

Mrs. Lillian Treece Mango Pie

Mangoes have always been part of my life. During my growing years, mango season was a happy and busy time for me. I got up early each morning before the other children were up so that I could gather most of the fruit that fell during the night. If we had a windy night, I gathered many buckets of mangoes. Mother sold them in front of our store while I was in school. They usually sold two for a penny in the morning and four for the same amount after noon. When I got home from school, I sold them six or more for the same price. Each season my friends and I ate so many mangoes that our teeth looked their whitest all season, even if we did not brush them!

We had a mango eating contest in high school, and of course I was the champion. I had had more than enough practice for many years. Despite my experience with the fruit, I had not eaten, seen, or even heard of mangoes in a pie until a few months before my daughter was born. All I wanted to eat was a mango pie, of all things. I knew of pica, a condition whereby some pregnant women would have overwhelming desire, and would in fact eat substances such as wood, ashes, and soil—things people normally would not eat as food. One theory is that these substances may very well have some minerals deficient in the diet of the mothers-to-be. I did not think that a mango pie would be in that group.

Anyhow, I had to have a mango pie, one way or another. So I called my friend, Lillian, and said, "I have to eat mangoes that come in a pie form. Do you know how to make one?" She said, "I have heard the word *mango*, but I don't know what it looks like let alone know how to make it into a pie." I told her that I too did not have a clue, but together we should be able to come up with a recipe. Lillian is not just a kind and very special person, she is also a great cook, and I was counting on that. The pie she made was so delicious that you should make one. I hope you enjoy it as much as I did.

Helpful Hints:

a. Mangoes are juicy and as delicious as peaches. Use them as you would use fresh peaches to make a pie.
b. Use only ripe, firm mangoes.
c. Use your favorite pie crust.

1 9-inch pie pan	*¾ cup sugar or to taste*
2 9-inch pie crusts	*¼ cup all-purpose flour*
5 cups sliced mangoes	*1 teaspoon corn, rice, or*
grated fresh ginger to taste	*cassava starch*
juice of 1 lemon	*2 tablespoons butter or to*
grated peel of same lemon	*taste*

1. Prepare two 9-inch pie crusts. Heat oven to 425 degrees.
2. Add to a mixing bowl mangoes, ginger, lemon juice, and lemon peel and mix.
3. Stir together sugar and flour, add mixture to mangoes, and mix well. Line pie pan with one pie crust. Pour mixture in crust and dot with butter.
4. Cover with top crust, seal, flute, and cut slits. Cover edge with a strip of aluminum foil if so desired, which will be removed during the last 15 minutes of baking time.
5. Bake for 35–45 minutes or until crust is brown and pie bubbles through slits. Remove, cool, and serve.

African Banana Punch

This punch is the drink for very thirsty persons on a hot day. It is easy to make and very delicious.

Helpful Hints:

a. The bananas used must be completely ripe.
b. Peel just before use to keep them from turning dark.

c. For freshness, punch should be made just before serving.
d. Add more water if less concentrated drink is desired and less water if more concentrated drink is desired.

6 ripe bananas, peeled   *6 cups water*
juice of 2 fresh lemons   *sugar to taste*
1 small gingerroot, skin   *sliced lemons for garnishing*
    removed and finely chopped   *ice*

1. Put in blender bananas, lemon juice, ginger, and 2–3 cups water and blend into liquid.
2. Put mixture into a pitcher, add rest of ingredients, and stir until sugar is dissolved.
3. Pour punch into glasses and garnish with slices of lemon before serving. You may chill before serving.

PAW PAW (PAPAYA)

This luscious African fruit comes in pink, yellow, and light orange colors. The male tree bears no fruit while the female tree bears fruit all year round at irregular intervals.

I very much wanted to read and write at a young age. I believe one reason was to be able to carve my initials on my very own *paw paw* (papaya), the way I saw my older siblings claim ownership, after they got fruit from the family orchard. When I could finally write a little, I remember Father helping me carve my initials on a large but green *paw paw* I had picked with some help. I rubbed it with salt. Each day I put it out in the sun, and at night I wrapped it in a blanket the way my older brother, Allieu, did to hasten the ripening process.

I clearly remember that my *paw paw* disappeared when it was just ripe with my initials still intact. It was then that Father said, "Everything we have can be taken away at any time. Oftentimes, there is little or nothing we can do about it. I am glad that you are learning to read and write. That is one of the very few things no one will ever take away from you." He mumbled some words and then added, "My wish is that as you continue to read and write, you will put your own mark on life itself, no matter how small that may be." The trouble with Father was that he sometimes said

words I did not understand. I am still trying to figure out putting a
mark on life. How does one put one's own mark on life?

Paw Paw (Papaya) Punch
ରେ

Helpful Hint:

Paw paw must be fully ripe.

1 medium or large paw paw (papaya)	*grated fresh ginger, 1 table-spoon or to taste*
3 cups or more water	*1 lime, thinly sliced (optional)*
juice of 2 lemons	*sugar to taste*
2 cups orange juice	*ice as desired*

   1. Peel *paw paw*, remove seeds, and cut it up. Put paw paw and 2
cups of water in a blender. Also add to it rest of ingredients except
sugar, ice, and sliced lime.
   2. Crush ingredients into liquid and pour it into a pitcher.
   3. Add to pitcher rest of ingredients, stir, and serve.

Glossary of African Words

awujoh: a big celebration that includes music, dancing, and plenty of food to honor the dead

beh beh: a flounder-like African fish

bolah: a little cup

booh booh: A flat seed found in the rain forest. It is used to make sauce and is well known for its great aroma.

bondoh: okra

dambo: a dish made using chitterlings

dumbu: a clay pot with a wide mouth

ehbeh: a meat-vegetable dish

fasah: shrimp

gbeseh: an African homemade herbal rub with great fragrance

gbuhen: African asparagus

gumbondoh: a special Mende okra dish

hamu hamu: snack

heyweh: spice found in the rain forest

hojeh: clay that is naturally white

hokay: a pheasant-like African game bird

hondii: spinach

kalabash: a platter-like dish

kamajoh: a professional African hunter

keyjeh: ginger

kibongii: tomato

kobo kobo: (gardenegg) eggplant

komafaleh: a special African mushroom

kondeh keh ngeteh: mortar with a pestle

kpangula: rice most often used to make rice flour

kpee kpee: an African electric catfish

kpogii: taro

kpohwoh: African portabella mushrooms

kpokpo kplokplo: mumps

kumulii: an African herb

labonii: a halibut-like African fish

lagba lagba: tart

lanyuma: another name for appetizers and snacks

lube: baking soda

manaamu: a delicious African fish

mandeh: sesame

mbagbehnyeh: finely broken rice used instead of bread crumbs

mbah: rice

mbehbeh: a small fishing net

mbola: a trout-like African fish

moi moi: an African bean dish

ngakui: crabmeat

ngeh ngeh: a brilliant green leafy vegetable

ngeh ngeh pahnwah rice: check green rice

ngokah: (tilapia) a perch-like African fish

ngulogboli: (red oil) palm oil

ninginanga: rainbow

njolabehteh: a sweet potato leaf dish

notoh: oyster

ohleleh: a bean dish

pahnwah: rice and other cooked grains dressed in bright colors

plasas: sauce

pohveh: a clay pot

poponda: African basil

semengii: cloves

sehjeh: rabbit

tehkuh: a fish smaller than smelt

tiiwee: a package

tohluga: (porcelain) an African vegetable

tuhweh: fruit of the oil palm tree

wehganya: the most popular variety of sweet potato leaves

yameh: foods the Mendes eat while they wait to eat rice

Some Metric Equivalents
(for Quick Reference)

VOLUME

The following metric equivalents are slightly larger, but results will not be affected (just scant the measurements a bit).

1 gallon = 4 liters
1 quart = 1 liter
1 pint = 500 ml
1 cup = 250 ml

Note: "1 8-ounce can" equals 1 cup

The following metric equivalents are slightly smaller (be a bit generous with the measurements).

1 tablespoon = 15 ml
1 teaspoon = 5 ml

WEIGHT

1 pound = 450 g (approx. ½ kilo)
1 ounce = 28 g

Note: 1 tablespoon of butter equals 15 grams
1 cup of flour equals 140 grams
1 cup of sugar equals 200 grams

LENGTH

1 inch = 2.5 cm

OVEN TEMPERATURES

"Cool" = 250°–275°F =	120°–135°C	gas mark (regulo)	= ½–1
"Moderate" = 350°F =	175°C		= 4
"Hot" = 425°–450°F =	220°–230°C		= 7–8

Index

About the Author

Zainabu Kpaka Kallon can't even remember when she started cooking. She was born into a large family in Sierra Leone and into the Mende tribe. In high school she was a domestic science (home economics) major. She then studied Christian evangelism at the United Methodist Bible School. She also became a certified midwife and worked for WSWS (Women's Society of World Service), now known as the United Methodist Women. Zainabu taught the village women family nutrition, cooking, sewing, Christian living, and delivered their babies. Coming to America, she earned a bachelor of science degree in nursing and became a registered nurse. Her love of cooking made her decide to cater her own wedding banquet—for 250 guests. Zainabu relaxes by cooking, writing songs, and reading.

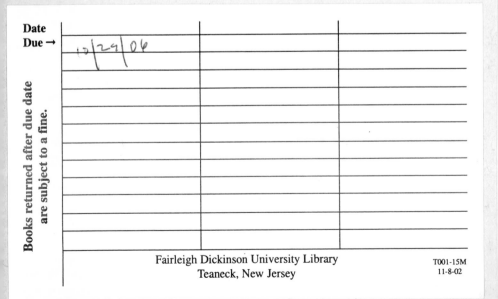